AF608228

The Right to Accuse a Marriage of Invalidity

This dissertation was approved by the Reverend John Rogg Schmidt, A.B., J.C.D., LL.B., Professor of Canon Law, as director, and by the Reverend Romaeus W. O'Brien, O.Carm., J.C.D., and the Reverend John J. McGrath, A.B., J.C.D., LL.B., as readers.

THE CATHOLIC UNIVERSITY OF AMERICA
CANON LAW STUDIES
No. 418

The Right to Accuse a Marriage of Invalidity

A DISSERTATION

Submitted to the Faculty of the School of Canon Law of The Catholic University of America in Partial Fulfillment of the Requirements for the Degree of Doctor of Canon Law

BY

THE REVEREND ARTHUR J. NACE, A.B., M.A., J.C.L.
Priest of the Archdiocese of Philadelphia

THE CATHOLIC UNIVERSITY OF AMERICA PRESS
WASHINGTON, D. C.
1961

Nihil Obstat:

JOANNES ROGG SCHMIDT, A.B., J.C.D., LL.B.
Censor Deputatus

Washingtonii, die 25 maii, 1961

Imprimatur:

JOANNES J. KROL, D.D., J.C.D.
Archiepiscopus Philadelphiensis

Philadelphiae, die 26 maii, 1961

Printed by
THE WICKERSHAM PRINTING COMPANY
Lancaster, Pennsylvania

To

My Mother and Father

FOREWORD

That no human power can sever a valid marriage bond is a truth which is taught in the present day by the living voice of Christ and His Church. Experience teaches, however, that not every marriage contract entered into by a man and a woman is a valid contract. Precluding a valid marriage between unbaptized persons is the existence of an impediment of the natural law. Forbidding a valid marriage between persons one of whom, at least, is baptized is the existence of an invalidating impediment of the natural or of the ecclesiastical law. In the latter instance, the determination of the existence of an alleged invalidating impediment rests with the public authority of the Church through the judgment of a competent ecclesiastical tribunal, or by the Ordinary himself in cases in which the law permits exceptional procedure. The following study represents an attempt to assay the fundamental juridic principles which establish and specify the right of persons who are permitted by the law of the Church to stand in judgment before a competent tribunal or before the Ordinary himself to accuse a marriage of invalidity.

This dissertation is divided into two parts. The first part provides a brief outline of the general and particular legislation of the Church affecting the right to accuse a marriage of invalidity before the promulgation of the Code of Canon Law in 1917. The second part embraces a commentary on the prescription of Canon 1971 in the light of the authentic interpretations of the Code Commission, the norms of the Instruction, *Provida Mater,* of the Sacred Congregation for the Discipline of the Sacraments, responses of the Congregation of the Holy Office and of the Congregation of the Sacraments, decisions of the Sacred Roman Rota, and commentaries of canonists. Particular attention is devoted to disputed questions pertaining to the nature of an accusation, the response of the Code Commission of January 4, 1946, the interpretation of the clause, *"nisi ipsi fuerint impedimenti causa,"* and the articles of the Instruction, *Provida Mater,* affecting the public accusation of a marriage by the promoter of justice.

Not all will agree with the conclusions drawn from this study. It is hoped, however, that from the presentation that follows, the controversies that attend this topic will be more clearly understood, and that a basis for further study will be more readily available to students of procedural law.

In prayerful gratitude, the writer recalls the memory of His Eminence John Cardinal O'Hara, late Archbishop of Philadelphia, under whose patronage his graduate studies in Canon Law were begun. The writer is most grateful to the Faculty of Saint Charles Seminary, Overbrook, Pennsylvania, and to the Dean and Faculty of the School of Canon Law of the Catholic University of America, in particular, to the Reverend John Rogg Schmidt, for their gracious assistance, judicious advice, and scholarly guidance; and to all those who, through prayer, encouragement and assistance of every kind, contributed to the completion of this study.

TABLE OF CONTENTS

PAGE

CHAPTER V

CHAPTER VI

PART ONE

HISTORICAL SYNOPSIS

CHAPTER I

MARRIAGE AND DIVORCE IN ROMAN LAW

INTRODUCTION

Marriage, according to the jurisprudence of the Romans, was considered as a *coniunctio maris et feminae et consortium omnis vitae, divini et humani iuris communicatio.*[1] The nature of this union must be understood in order to gain some appreciation of the manner in which marriages were "accused" in the Roman Empire. The essence of a marital union among the Romans consisted in an *affectio maritalis* which amounted to little more than a sustained habit of mind to live together as husband and wife.[2] Thus, a Roman marriage was devoid of the contractual character of the consent necessary in Canon Law. The latter must be present at the time when the contract is made, and once exchanged, the marriage remains, independent of any future change of consent by the contracting parties. In Roman Law, however, the mutual consent of the parties consisted in the willingness of a man and a woman to effect a marital union, and if, at any time, one or both of the parties retracted their willingness to live as husband and wife, their marriage ceased to exist.[3]

[1] *Corpus Iuris Civilis,* 3 vols., Vol. I, *Institutiones,* quae recognovit P. Krueger; *Digesta,* quae recognovit T. Mommsen et retractavit P. Krueger, ed. stereotypa 15.; Vol. II, *Codex Justianianus,* quem recognovit et retractavit P. Krueger, ed. stereotypa 10.; Vol. III, *Novellae Constitutiones,* ed. stereotypa 5., a R. Schoell; opus Schoelli morte interceptum absolvit G. Kroll; (Berolini: apud Weidmannos, 1928-1929), I. *Digesta* (23.1) 1 (hereafter the *Digesta* will be cited as D.: the *Codex* as C., and the *Novellae Constitutiones* as Nov.).

[2] D. (24.1); C. (5.17) 11; Nov. (18.4) 1, (22.3).

[3] ". . . nuptias enim non concubitus, sed consensus facit."—D. (35.1) 15, (50.17) 30, (25.7) 4; ". . . quicumque mulierem . . . sua voluntate maritali affectu in matrimonium acceperit etiamsi dotalia instrumenta non intercesserint nec dos data fuerit, tamquam si cum instrumentis dotalibus tale matrimonium processisset, firmum coniugium eorum habeatur; non enim dotibus sed affectu matrimonia contrahuntur."—C. (5.17) 11.

Accordingly, Ulpian († A.D. 228),[4] whose works were excerpted to a great extent by the compilers of the *Digesta* of the Emperor Justinian (527-565), asserted that nothing was so natural that an obligation should cease to exist in the same way in which it was contracted. He concluded that a verbal obligation is abrogated by words, and an obligation based upon the mere consent of the parties is annulled by a contrary consent.[5] Thus, just as marriage was freely entered, it was just as freely terminated, for the permanence of the union depended on the *affectio maritalis* and not on a contractual promise.

Section I. Period of the Early Republican Law

Article 1. Marriage with Manus

During the period of the early Republic (500-250 B.C.), Roman marriages were contracted with *manus.* Through *manus,* the acquisitions of the wife were placed under the control of her husband, and the wife herself was now *filiae loco,* that is, by a fiction of law she was made, as it were, the sister of her own children and had the same right of succession as her daughter.[6] *Manus* was acquired in three ways, namely, through *confarreatio, coemptio,* and *usus.*

A. *Confarreatio*

Confarreatio was a religious ceremony at the altar of Jupiter, before the *Pontifex Maximus* and the *Flamen Dialis* and ten witnesses, in which there was a sacrifice and the consumption of a cake known as *far.*[7] A confarreate marriage was broken by

[4] Ulpian was a Roman jurist whose works comprise about one-third of the *Digesta.* Berger, "Encyclopedic Dictionary of Roman Law," *Transactions of the American Philosophical Society,* New Series, n. XLIII (Philadelphia: The American Philosophical Society, 1953), 750 (hereafter cited as Berger).

[5] "Nihil tam naturale est quam eo genere quidquid dissolvere, quo colligatum est; ideo verborum obligatio verbis tollitur: nudi consensus obligatio contrario consenus dissolvitur."—D. (50.17) 35; cf. Nov. (22.4), (22.18).

[6] Gaius, *Institutiones* (7. ed. by P. Krueger, Berolini: apud Weidmannos, 1923), II, 96, 139.

[7] Gaius, *Institutiones,* I, 112; cf. Buckland, *A Textbook of Roman Law*

disfarreatio or a reversal of the union through the media of religious observances corresponding to those performed in *confarreatio*.[8]

B. *Coemptio*

Coemptio was a modified form of bride buying in which the wife "sold" herself to the husband with the consent of her father or tutor. It was a fictitious sale to the extent that it was expressly understood that she was not in *mancipio* but in *manu*.[9] A marriage effected by *coemptio* was severed by what was substantially the process of emancipation.[10]

C. *Usus*

Finally, a marriage with *manus* was perfected through *usus* or through the cohabitation of the parties for the period of a year.[11] Here, it should be noted, that the mere *usus* for a year did not of itself give rise to the marital union, but rather that it constituted the basis for the presumption that a marriage did exist.[12] The prescribed time of a year was interrupted if the wife absented herself from her husband's house for three nights with this purpose in mind.[13]

---

from Augustus to Justinian (2. ed., Cambridge: University Press, 1932), p. 118 (hereafter cited as Buckland, *Roman Law*).

[8] Buckland, *Roman Law*, p. 121; Muirhead, *Historical Introduction to the Private Law of Rome* (3. ed., London: Black, 1916), p. 105 (hereafter cited as Muirhead, *Private Law of Rome*). It has been questioned whether confarreate marriages were susceptible to any kind of dissolution in the early era of the Roman Empire. Cf. Jolowicz, *Historical Introduction to the Study of Roman Law* (2. ed., Cambridge: University Press, 1952), p. 117 (hereafter cited as Jolowicz, *Study of Roman Law*); Corbett, *The Roman Law of Marriage* (Oxford: Clarendon Press, 1930), pp. 220-222.

[9] "Coemptione vero in manum conveniunt per mancipationem, id est per quandam imaginariam venditionem . . ."—Gaius, *Institutiones*, I, 113.

[10] Gaius, *Institutiones*, I, 114, 137; cf. Buckland, *Roman Law*, p. 121; Muirhead, *Private Law of Rome*, p. 107.

[11] Gaius, *Institutiones*, I, 111.

[12] " . . . nuptias enim non concubitus, sed consensus facit."—D. (35.1) 15; "Concubinam ex sola animi destinatione aestimari oportet."—D. (25.7) 4.

[13] Gaius, *Institutiones*, I, 111.

Article 2. The Dissolution of Marriage in Relation to the Termination of Manus

A distinction should be made here between the termination of *manus* and the dissolution of the marriage itself. The marriage, it will be remembered, was a *de facto* relationship consisting in a mere factual willingness of the parties to live as husband and wife. The severing of this union came about by a recalling of this *affectio* between the husband and the wife which was followed by a separation with the intention of not returning. But so long as *manus* existed, such a parting was not possible except at the instance of the husband, since the *manus* gave him control over his wife in such a way that, even though they were no longer married, the woman could not leave the man until he formally dismissed her.[14]

Section II. Period of the Late Republican and Early Classical Law

Article 1. Marriage without Manus

A. *The Concept of* Liberum Matrimonium

In the late Republican and early Classical Law (200 B.C.-A.D. 200), the concept of *liberum matrimonium* was prevalent in the Empire and with it came the right to end a marriage at any time in a transaction that was practically formless. If the marriage was terminated by the mutual consent of the parties, it was called a *divortium.* If the marriage was dissolved at the instance of only one of the parties, a *repudium* was involved.[15]

[14] Jolowicz, *Study of Roman Law,* p. 117. It is generally held that during the first five centuries of the Roman Empire, divorce was a rare occurrence. From the beginning, the law denounced careless and causeless separations. Custom is said to have required that the husband, before dismissing his wife, should summon a family council in which the wife's relatives were represented and show a reasonable cause for his action. Among the justifying causes for divorce were adultery and witchcraft. Cf. Muirhead, *Private Law of Rome,* pp. 107, 223; Jolowicz, *Study of Roman Law,* p. 117; Corbett, *The Roman Law of Marriage,* p. 128.

[15] D. (24.1, 2); cf. Buckland, *Roman Law,* p. 117; Corbett, *The Roman Law of Marriage,* p. 68; Sherman, *Roman Law in the Modern World* (2. ed., 3 vols., New York: Baker Voorhis, 1924), II, n. 485.

B. *The Juridic Causes for Divorce*

Among the causes that were allowed by law to effect a dissolution of the marriage bond were sterility, old age, illness, and the husband's departure for military service or for the priesthood.[16] Marriage could also be dissolved if the party was discovered to be a slave, or if either became a victim of captivity or any other kind of servitude.[17] Moreover, a husband was permitted to attack his marriage if his wife had become insane. And though the insane wife was forbidden to initiate a separation on her own account, the law permitted that her father could institute divorce proceedings in her behalf.[18] It is of interest to note that the concept of the reservation of an accusation for certain causes to the husband alone may be found in Roman Law,[19] a notion which in its rudimentary form was to be developed in the earliest stages of canonical jurisprudence.

C. *Lex Julia de Adulteriis*

Sometime between 18 B.C. and 16 B.C., the *Lex Julia de Adulteriis* was enacted under the Emperor Augustus († A.D. 14) [20] in a fruitless effort to purge the morass of moral corruption into which Roman society had sunk as a result of the doctrine of "free marriage" and the concomitant collapse of centralized family government. According to *Lex Julia,* no divorce could be ratified unless it took place in the presence of seven adult Roman citizens and a freedman of him who instituted the proceedings.[21] Thus, the husband's right to dismiss his wife was conditioned on the calling of the necessary witnesses or the presenting of a written declaration to them relating to the dismissal. It may well be that the written

[16] D. (24.1) 60, 61.

[17] D. (24.2) 9.

[18] D. (24.2) 4; cf. (24.3) 22, 7.

[19] "Quare si accusare eam adulterii coeperit vel alio crimine postulare, quod uxori nemo obicit, magis est ut diremptum sit matrimonium . . ."—D. (24.2) 11, 2.

[20] D. (48.5) 1.

[21] "Nullum divortium ratum est nisi septem civibus Romanis puberibus adhibitis praeter libertum eius qui divortium faciet."—D. (24.2) 9.

or oral declaration of the dismissal was merely an indispensable element of publicity affording the actual separation its legal significance. In other words, the witnesses were not the efficient cause of the divorce but merely provided public proof that the divorce had actually taken place.[22]

Also among the prescriptions of *Lex Julia de Adulteriis* were those which tightened the procedural norms for accusing a woman of adultery. It was decreed that before a husband could accuse his wife of adultery, a separation witnessed by the prescribed seven adult Roman citizens was first necessary.[23] During sixty *dies utiles* subsequent to the separation, the husband and the father of the alleged *adultera* had the exclusive right of accusation, the former being preferred in case of conflict.[24] For four *menses utiles* following, accusations were permitted to *extranei*. But no one was permitted to accuse a woman of adultery beyond six *menses utiles* counted from the day of separation, or after five *anni continui* computed from the time of the crime itself.[25]

According to Modestinus († A.D. 237),[26] a woman accused of adultery could not remarry during the lifetime of her husband even though she had not been juridically convicted of the crime.[27] *Lex Julia* prescribed that unless the accuser had, before the remarriage of the suspected woman, informed her of his intention to accuse, it was necessary that he secure the conviction of the *adulter*. If the accuser neglected to issue this denunciation, or if he failed to prove his case against the *adulter*, no one could place an action against the woman as long as the marriage, into which she had entered, perdured.[28]

[22] Corbett, *The Roman Law of Marriage*, p. 234.

[23] D. (48.5) 11, 10.

[24] D. (48.5) 2, 8.

[25] D. (48.5) 4, 1; cf. Corbett, *The Roman Law of Marriage*, p. 144.

[26] Herrenius Modestinus was one of the last representatives of Classical Roman jurisprudence and a pupil of Ulpian. Cf. Berger, *Dictionary of Roman Law*, p. 585.

[27] D. (23.2) 26.

[28] D. (48.5) 2, pr.; 17, 1.

Article 2. Later Limitations of the Juridic Causes for Divorce

In A.D. 331, Constantine restricted, to some extent, the area of the causes of separation. Thus, he decreed that a wife could not dismiss her husband for drunkenness, gambling, or flirting with other women. And a husband could not dismiss his wife except for homicide, preparing poisons, or violating cemeteries. Adultery remained as the chief reason for divorce.[29] Finally, before the middle of the sixth century, the Emperor Justinian († 565) forbade all divorces *communi consensus* unless the parties wished to complete their married life in the observance of perfect chastity.[30]

Article 3. Summary

From the foregoing outline of the concepts of marriage and divorce in the Roman Empire, it should be apparent that the juridical notion of the right of a party to accuse a marriage in a court competent to entertain such an accusation can scarcely be said to have its origin in Roman Law. And even if a Roman marriage can be looked upon as being accused by either one of the parties, it must be admitted that Roman jurisprudence did not consider matrimony as a matter for court action, but treated it as an essentially private transaction.[31] Only in the later eleventh and twelfth centuries of the Christian era did the norms governing a person's right to question judicially the validity of a marriage begin to crystallize.

[29] *Codex Theodosianus* (ed. P. Krueger, Berolini: apud Weidmannos, 1926), (3.16) 1.

[30] "Quia vero et ex consensu aliqui usque ad praesens alterna matrimonia solvebant, hoc de cetero fieri nullo sinimus modo nisi forte quidam castitatis concupiscentia hoc fecerint."—Nov. (117.10).

[31] D. (50.17) 35; Nov. (22.3, 4). Cf. Buckland, *Roman Law*, p. 117; Joyce, *Christian Marriage* (London: Sheed and Ward, 1933), pp. 216, 309; Sherman, *Roman Law in the Modern World*, II, n. 485; Corbett, *The Roman Law of Marriage*, pp. 226-229.

CHAPTER II

THE RIGHT TO ACCUSE A MARRIAGE OF INVALIDITY FROM THE DECREE OF GRATIAN (ca. 1140) TO THE COUNCIL OF TRENT (1545-1563)

SECTION I. THE *Decree* OF GRATIAN

Before the middle of the twelfth century, probably in 1140, Gratian († ante 1159), a Camaldolese monk of the monastery of Saint Felix and Saint Nabor in Bologna, introduced to the medieval world the first handbook of the laws of the Catholic Church and, in so doing, inaugurated the development of the science of Canon Law. This work comprises an analytical and synthetical presentation of the immense and divergent store of ancient and contemporary ecclesiastical prescriptions that had been previously spread throughout independent and uncorrelated collections in the eastern and western parts of the then-known world of Christianity. Thus, it was entitled the *Concordia Discordantium Canonum,* and later, the *Decretum.*[1]

The *Decree* of Gratian, while it superseded all previous collections of Church law, was never accorded the official approval of the Church as an authentic and exclusive code of law. Nevertheless, it was recognized universally as the most complete and efficient compilation of existing ecclesiastical legislation. The juridical significance of the documents which it contained was founded in the authority of the ecclesiastical source from which they were derived. Hence, many of the canons found in the *Decretum* had the force of universal law.[2]

[1] Cf. Van Hove, *Commentarium Lovaniense in Codicem Iuris Canonici,* 2. ed., Vol. I, tom. 1, *Prolegomena* (Mechliniae, Romae: Dessain, 1945), pp. 339-348; Kurtscheid-Wilches, *Historia Iuris Canonici,* Tom. I, *Historia Fontium et Scientiae Iuris Canonici* (Romae: Officium Libri Catholici, 1943), pp. 168-172, 234-235; Cicognani, *Canon Law* (2. ed. authorized English version by Joseph M. O'Hara and Francis J. Brennan, Westminster, Maryland: Newman, 1934), pp. 273-288; Kuttner, "The Father of the Science of Canon Law," *The Jurist* (Washington, D. C., 1941-), I (1941), 2.

[2] Van Hove, *Prolegomena,* pp. 345-346.

A careful study of the papal decrees and conciliar enactments and patristic writings contained in the *Decree* of Gratian reveals little evidence of appreciable development in the rules regulating the right to impugn a marriage. The marriage bond itself is, indeed, treated with a surprising degree of clarity and detail. The institution of marriage by Almighty God, the elevation of the contract of marriage to the dignity of a sacrament, the qualities of a valid marriage, such as the *consensus, pactio coniugalis,* and *idoneitas personarum,* and the impediments to marriage all find a place in the Church's legislation collated in Gratian's *Decree.* Even the procedure and causes for canonical separation are elaborated upon at length in Part Two of the *Decree,* beginning with *Causa* XXX and extending to *Causa* XXXIV.[3] But explicit legislation delineating the substance of the law governing the right of accusation or denunciation of marriage is not to be found.

Article 1. The Right to Accuse a Marriage Because of an Error of the Status of the Spouse

There is, however, a specific reference in the *Decree* to a case in which one of the parties to a marriage erred in regard to the status of the spouse. Such a case was considered by the Council of Verberie, France, in 756.[4] The Council decreed that a free man, who unknowingly took a slave woman as his wife and only after the marriage discovered that she was not free, could leave this woman and take another as his wife. Similarly, a free

[3] The canonical causes and procedure for separation cases (canons 1128, 1129, 1130, 1131, 1132) will not be embraced within the scope of this work. For a noteworthy treatise on this subject the reader is to be referred to James Patrick King, *The Canonical Procedure in Separation Cases,* The Catholic University of America Canon Law Studies, n. 325 (Washington, D. C.: The Catholic University of America Press, 1952).

[4] *Corpus Iuris Canonici,* editio Lipsiensis secunda, post Aemilii Ludovici Richteri curas ad librorum manu scriptorum et editionis Romanae fidem recognovit et adnotatione critica instruxit Aemelius Friedberg, 2 vols., Vol. I, *Decretum Magistri Gratiani,* Vol. II, *Decretalium Collectiones Gregorii* IX (Lipsiae: Tauchnitz, 1928), c. 4, C. XXIX, q. 2. Cf. *Monumenta Germaniae Historica,* 188 vols., incomplete, Legum Sectio III: *Concilia,* Tom. II, pars prior (Hannoverae, 1904), p. 55, n. 9.

woman was permitted to accuse a marriage if unknowingly she took to herself a husband who was a slave.[5] The right given to the parties in this case was not a matter of precept but of counsel.[6]

Article 2. The Right to Accuse a Marriage Because of the Existence of an Impediment of Consanguinity

In a spurious letter attributed to Pope Fabian (236-250), there can be found a decree directing that a marriage that is alleged to be invalid because of an impediment of consanguinity existing between the spouses can be accused only by the father, mother, sister, brother, uncle, aunt and maternal aunt of one of the parties.[7] If none of these was living, or if they could not be reached, or if they did not wish to testify, then the more distant relatives of the spouses or the elders in the town in which the parties were residing could be subjected to a canonical inquisition of the bishop, and if the impediment was thereby

[5] Commenting on this case, the glossator asks the question, what would happen if the woman wanted to retain the slave as her husband and the slave refused? He answered that neither the free woman nor the slave could be forced to remain with each other since no bond of matrimony existed between them. But he noted that the slave's refusal would be meaningless because a true marriage existed as far as the woman [the free party] was concerned: "Dicunt quidam hoc matrimonium esse ex una parte et non ex altera. . . ." This observation will be noted again in a discussion of the influence of *dolus* on the right to accuse marriage under c. 1, X, *de eo qui duxit in matrimonium quam polluit per adulterium*, IV, 7. Cf. *Decretum Gratiani*, emendatum et notationibus illustratum una cum glossis, 2 vols. (Romae, 1582), Vol. II, *Glossa Ordinaria* ad c. 4, C. XXIX, q. 2, s. v. *faciat* (hereafter cited as *Glossa Ordinaria*); Guido a Baiiso, *Rosarium, seu in Decretorum Volumen Commentaria* (Venetiis, 1577), ad c. 4, C. XXIX, q. 2, s. v. *si quis*, fol. 344, col. 2 (hereafter cited as Guido a Baiiso, *Commentaria*).

[6] Rufinus, *Die Summa Decretorum,* herausgegeben von Dr. H. Singer (Paderborn: Schoningh, 1902), ad c. 4, C. XXIX, q. 2, s. v. *Si quis igenuus.*

[7] C. 1, C. XXXV, q. 6; Jaffé, *Regesta Pontificum Romanorum ab condita ecclesia ad annum post Christum natum* MCXCVII (2. ed. by F. Kaltenbrunner, to 590; by P. Ewald, 590-882; and by S. Lowenfeld, 882-1198, Lipsiae, 1885-1888, hereafter cited as JK, JE, JL), JK, n. 100; cf. Esmein, *Le Mariage en Droit Canonique* (2 vols., Paris: L. Larose et Forsel, 1891), I, 408, 410.

discovered, the parties were to be separated.[8] Moreover, it was required that the accusers be two or three in number and that the allegations of the accusers be made under oath. The accusers were to be "... *bonae famae et veracis testimonii* ..., *remoto amore, timore, precio et omni malo studio* ..."[9] If the accusers were unable or unwilling to accuse under oath, then no consideration of a declaration of nullity was to be given to the case. But if they proved the existence of the impediment under oath, "... *sine omni mora coniugia dissolvantur.*"[10]

Article 3. "Matrimonium dicitur impropie accusari"

It is of interest to note that in his commentary on this decretal Guido a Baiiso objected to the term *accusatio* when applied to marriage. The term *accusatio* was seemingly reserved only for criminal and civil cases. And since ordinarily, there was no civil crime committed in a marriage that was contracted invalidly, not only Guido a Baiiso but also the generality of medieval canonists repeated what practically amounted to an adage, namely, "*matrimonium dicitur improprie accusari.*"[11] He added, however, that the accusation of a marriage in which the impediment of consanguinity was involved could possibly be considered as an *actio quasi civilis* if the crime of incest was present.[12]

Article 4. Accusations in Criminal and Civil Cases

Other than these references to the accusation of marriage because of an error of the status of a party and because of the

[8] C. 1, C. XXXV, q. 6.

[9] C. 3, C. XXXV, q. 6. This canon represents a fragment of a letter written by Pope Urban II (1088-1099) to the Bishop of Geneva sometime between 1090 and 1095. It is cited only in the first edition of Jaffé, n. 4143. It was included by Raymond of Pennafort († 1275) in the Decretals of Gregory IX (1227-1241) and will be studied more closely in the following chapter.

[10] C. 3, C. XXXV, q. 5; cf. Rolandus, *Summa* (ed. by Friedrich Thaner, Innsbruck, 1874), pp. 229-231. Rolandus Bandinelli wrote his *Summa* before 1150, the year of his appointment as Cardinal. He was raised to the Papacy in 1159 and assumed the name of Alexander III; cf. Van Hove, *Prolegomena*, pp. 427, 349; Cicognani, *Canon Law*, pp. 275, 283, 328.

[11] *Commentaria*, ad c. 3, C. XXXV, q. 6, s. v. *Consanguineos*, fol. 383-384, col. 1-2.

[12] Cf. Esmein, *Le Mariage en Droit Canonique*, I, 405.

existence of the impediment of consanguinity between the spouses, the *Decretum* is chiefly concerned with those who were admitted or who were forbidden to accuse in criminal and civil cases. While no direct application is made to the accusers of marriage, an indication of what the law was in this matter may possibly be ascertained. For example, no one was permitted to accuse in criminal or civil procedure unless he did so personally, and unless the person accused was present at the time when the accusation was made.[13] In criminal proceedings, the accusation was to be made in writing for validity.[14] In civil actions, a vocal presentation of the accusation sufficed.[15]

In general, anyone whose testimony was suspect was not permitted to act as an accuser. Thus, those who were enemies of the accused or who had reason to inflict harm on him were forbidden to accuse.[16] Those who were known to be calumniators, those who were of evil reputation, or who possessed impious characters, those who were easily prone to initiate cases of litigation, and those whose past life indicated that they simply could not be trusted were not to be admitted as accusers.[17] Elsewhere it was stated that those who themselves were accusable, those who were apostates, and those "... *qui non sunt bonae conversa-*

[13] C. 1, C. II, q. 8. This canon was taken from a spurious fragment of a letter attributed to Pope Callistus (217-222) and allegedly addressed to the Bishops of Gaul.

[14] Rufinus, *Summa*, ad c. 1, C. II, q. 8, s. v. *De accusatione vero . . .*; cf. D. (48.2) 1, (48.16) 1; C. (9.2) 16.

[15] Rolandus, *Summa*, p. 19.

[16] C. 2, C. III, q. 5. This canon was taken from a letter addressed to ". . . omnibus episcopis ac reliquis Christi sacerdotibus . . ." and spuriously attributed to Pope Anacletus (76?-88?); JK, n. 4; cf. Rufinus, ad C. III, q. 5, s. v. *Quod vero testes.*

[17] C. 10, C. III, q. 5. This decree was taken from the VI Council of Carthage held in 419. It is apparent that it was adopted by the Council from the *Digesta* of Justinian, (48.2) 4, which reads that the right of accusation was taken from those who had been rendered infamous, or who had vile reputations, or who had been convicted of calumny, or who were intent on merely inflicting injury on the defendant. Cf. Mansi, *Sacrorum Conciliorum Nova et Amplissima Collectio*, 53 vols. in 59 (Parisiis: 1901-1907), IV, 438-439 (hereafter cited as Mansi).

tionis . . ." were similarly to be rejected.[18] Also forbidden to accuse were those characterized as infamous because of some personal fault. In this category were included those who failed to live according to Christian morality, those who held ecclesiastical statutes in contempt, those who were sacrilegious or guilty of capital crimes, those guilty of incest, adultery, abduction, perjury, calumny; in short, anyone whose mind was filled with evil intentions or whose life was marred by wicked deeds.[19]

In a spurious letter attributed to Pope Fabian (236-250) to the Bishops of the Orient, it is stated that no one could presume to be an accuser and at the same time be a judge or a witness, since in every judicial procedure at least four persons were necessary, namely, the properly appointed judge, the qualified accuser, the defendant, and the lawful witness.[20] To be noted here is the observation made in the gloss on this letter. This glossator states that while it is true that in civil procedure the accuser cannot at the same time be a witness, the converse is to be held in regard to matrimonial cases. Thus he cites as an example a marriage that is accused on the grounds that the impediment of consanguinity is present. In this case, the same person could be both the accuser and the witness at the same time.[21]

Article 5. Summary

In summary, the rules governing the accusation of marriage are scarcely considered in the legislation of the Church up to

[18] C. 4, C. III, q. 5. This canon, spuriously attributed to Pope Pontianus (230-235) may have originated with the VII Council of Carthage held in 421; JK, n. 88; Mansi, IV, 449-450.

[19] C. 17, C. VI, q. 1. This canon was taken from a spurious letter attributed to Pope Stephen I (254?-257); JK, n. 130; Mansi, I, 885; cf. cc. 1-17, C. III, q. 4; c. 3, C. IV, q. 2; c. 1, C. IV, q. 1; c. 4, C. VI, q. 1; Rolandus, *Summa*, p. 20.

[20] C. i, C. IV, q. 4; JK, n. 93; cf. Rufinus, Summa, ad c. 1, C. IV, q. 4, s.v. *Nullus umquam quatturo personas.* The functions of each participant are delineated in this letter with classical conciseness. "Iudices autem debent uti equitate, testes veritate, accusatores ad amplificandum causam, defensores extentuatione ad minuendam causam."

[21] *Glossa Ordinaria,* ad c. 1, C. IV, q. 4, s. v. *accusator;* cf. Guido a Baiiso, *Commentaria,* ad c. 1, C. IV, q. 4, s. v. *nullus,* fol. 174, col. 2.

and including the time of Gratian's *Decree* in the middle of the twelfth century. Even the prescriptions and restrictions pertaining to the accusation of marriage in which the impediment of consanguinity existed seem to be based more on purely natural conclusions than on any juridic considerations. During the next seventy-five years, however, and primarily through the contributions of Pope Alexander III (1159-1181) and Pope Innocent III (1198-1216) and their commentators, some of the basic components of the law made their appearance.

Section II. The Decretals of Gregory IX (1227-1241)

The Decretals of Gregory IX represented the first, complete, authentic collection of Canon Law. The actual labor involved in gathering into one volume the numerous constitutions and decretal letters which compose this work was begun by Saint Raymond of Pennaforte († 1275) in 1230. It was officially promulgated by Pope Gregory IX on September 5, 1234 as a universal and authoritative code of law. Before pursuing a study of the principles and norms that constituted the laws of the Church as revealed in Gregory's Decretals relative to the accusation of marriage, a presentation should first be made of certain basic concepts that form the foundation of this discussion.[22]

Article 1. The Concepts of Accusation and Denunciation

The first title of the fifth book of the Decretals devoted attention to the solution of cases in which accusations, inquisitions, and denunciations were made by laymen, clerics, and their ecclesiastical superiors.[23] It is true that the twenty-seven *Capitula* under this title reveal little or no information concerning the accusation or denunciation of marriage. Nevertheless, they do assist in an attempt to arrive at an understanding of the concept of *accusatio* and *denunciatio* as they were described and understood by the canonists of the thirteenth century.

[22] Cf. Van Hove, *Prolegomena*, pp. 357-361; Kurtscheid-Wilches, *Historia Iuris Canonici*, I, 180-184; Cicognani, *Canon Law*, pp. 298-305.

[23] Cc. 1-27, X, *de accusationibus, inquisitionibus, et denunciationibus*, V, 1.

The meaning of the term *accusatio* in the Decretals of Gregory IX was crystallized by Hostiensis († 1271) [24] as "... *quidem criminis alicujus hominis apud iudicem competentem inscriptione interveniente legitima facta delatio.*" [25] Hence, he concludes that "... *accusare nihil aliud est quam reum criminis aliquem per libellum deferre, vel facere ad vindictam.*" [26] It should be noted that the juridic motive for making an accusation, then, was one that was purely vindictive in nature; that is, it was solely concerned with the punishment of a person who was guilty of a crime.

Denunciatio, on the other hand, was described by Hostiensis as: "*Criminis alicujus apud iudicem sine inscriptione legitime facta delatio ad poenitentiam peragendam vel aliam poenam legitimam imponendam vel etiam utrumque.*" [27] To be observed here is the emendatory purpose essential to a denunciation as compared to the juridic vindictive intention characteristic of an accusation. Pope Innocent III (1198-1216) called attention to this distinction between the two terms in a decretal letter, in which he undertook to explain the reason why accusations were to be executed in writing though denunciations could be made viva voce. Thus, he asserts: "*Quando crimen in modum denunci-*

[24] Henricus de Segusia (Henry of Susa), later Cardinal-Bishop of Ostia, hence, "Hostiensis," studied at Bologna and taught at Paris and probably also at Bologna. After the time of Pope Innocent IV (1243-1254), Hostiensis is the most worthy of all decretalists. He is frequently referred to as the "Monarch" and the "King of Both Laws." Between the years 1250 and 1253, Hostiensis composed his *Summa* of the Decretals of Gregory IX, which consisted of an orderly and systematized presentation of the decretal law according to the title arrangement found in the Decretals themselves. So famous did this work become that it merited the title, *Summa Aurea*. Cf. Van Hove, *Prolegomena*, p. 476; Cicognani, *Canon Law*, p. 333.

[25] *Summa Aurea* (Lugduni, 1568), Lib. V, *de accusationibus*, fol. 334, n. 1; cf. c. 16, X, *de accusationibus, inquisitionibus, et denunciationibus*, V, 1; Potthast, *Regesta Pontificum Romanorum, inde ab anno post Christum natum* MCXCVIII ad annum MCCCIV (2 vols., Berolini, 1274-1275), I, n. 1824 (hereafter cited as Potthast).

[26] *Summa Aurea*, Lib. V, *de accusationibus*, fol. 334, n. 1.

[27] *Summa Aurea*, Lib. V, *de denunciationibus*, fol. 338 n. 1; cf. cc. 2, 3, 16, 20, X, V, 1; cf. Esmein, *Le Mariage en Droit Canonique*, I, 411-413.

ationis opponitur, non est inscriptio necessaria; sed, quum in modum accusationis obiicitur, oportet inscribi, quoniam ad depositionem instituitur accusatio, sed ad correctionem est denunciatio facienda." [28]

Unfortunately, though the distinction between these terms seems sufficiently evident when employed in the context of criminal and civil causes, caution must be exercised when attempting to discover their signification in the specific sphere of marriage. Thus, it will be seen that, at this time, *accusatio* and *denunciatio* were used rather loosely and sometimes interchangeably when employed in reference to the bond of marriage. Pope Innocent IV (1243-1254) [29] called attention to the misuse of the expression *accusatio* as employed in a decretal letter written by Pope Innocent III to the Prior of the Monastery of Saint Mary in Albario, Italy: [30] *"Matrimonium enim non proprie dicitur accusari nisi ab uxore; nam cum non sit publicum crimen non admittitur nisi quorum interest sed denunciari dicitur crimen in quo manet."* [31] Panormitanus (Nicholaus de Tudeschis, † 1453) was even more specific in observing that "*. . . potius tamen est quaedam denunciatio quam accusatio cuius finis tendit ad vindictam sed finis hujus causae tendit ad separationem matrimonii, ne stent coniuncti simul in peccato. . . .*" [32]

[28] C. 16, X, *de accusationibus, inquisitionibus, et denunciationibus*, V, 1; Potthast, n. 1824.

[29] Pope Innocent IV (Sinibaldo de Fieschi), an outstanding jurisconsult, wrote a commentary as a private doctor on the Decretals of Gregory IX after his election to the Papacy in 1243. Hence, he is the first instance of a papal canonical commentator; cf. Van Hove, *Prolegomena*, p. 480; Cicognani, *Canon Law*, p. 332.

[30] C. 5, X, *qui matrimonium accusare possunt vel contra illud testari*, IV, 18 (hereafter cited as *qui matrimonium accusare possunt*); Potthast, n. 2241.

[31] *Commentaria in V Libros Decretalium* (Venetiis, 1570), ad c. 5, X, *qui matrimonium accusare possunt*, IV, 18, s. v. *ab accusatione.* Pope Innocent IV also cited the misuse of the word *accusatio* in c. 2, X, *qui matrimonium accusare possunt*, IV, 18: ". . . prius dicitur denunciatio, quam accusatio; quia ad hoc intentio dirigi debet accusantis, ut a peccato cessent nec aliter interest. . . ."

[32] *Commentaria in Quinque Libros Decretalium* (5 vols. in 7, Venetiis,

Under the eighteenth title of the fourth book of the Decretals, there can be found the substance of decretal law relative to the accusation of marriage. From an analysis of this title and from the contemporary commentaries concerning them, there can be deduced the answers to the following questions. Who was permitted to accuse a marriage according to decretal law? Who was admitted to denounce a marriage? Who was forbidden to accuse a marriage. Who was forbidden to denounce a marriage?

Article 2. Persons Permitted to Accuse a Marriage

Before an action could be placed against the bond of marriage in order that it be officially declared null, it was necessary that there be present some question concerning the existence of a perpetual invalidating impediment in one of the parties to the contract.[33] Now this impediment was either the occasion of a sinful union or it was not. If, in a given case, the impediment was not necessarily the occasion of a sinful union, the right to place an action against such a union was restricted to the parties themselves.[34] Thus, the example is cited of a marriage in which *frigidita* was verified in the wife, and yet both spouses continued to live a chaste and continent life.[35] According to Hostiensis, no one could attack such a union except the parties themselves. No one but the spouses could accuse because accusation implied the vindication of a right. No one at all could denounce the union because denunciation inferred the purgation and emendation of sin. Moreover, only the spouses were admitted to accuse a marriage *ad separationem thori.*[36] This re-

1588), ad c. 5, X, *qui matrimonium accusare possunt*, IV, 18, n. 2 (hereafter cited as *Commentaria*).

[33] Hostiensis, *Summa Aurea*, Lib. IV, *quis admittatur ad accusationem matrimonii*, fol. 321, n. 1.

[34] C. 7, X, *de cognatione spirituali*, IV, 11; Potthast, n. 1683; cf. Durandus, *Speculum Iuris* (Venetiis, 1577), Lib. IV, partic. 4, fol. 468, § 4, n. 2; Hostiensis, *Summa Aurea*, Lib. IV, *quis admittatur ad accusationem matrimonii*, fol. 321, n. 1.

[35] C. 4, X, *de frigidis et maleficiatis, et impotentia coeundi*, IV, 15; JE, n. 14125; cf. Hostiensia, *Summa Aurea, ibid.*, n. 1.

[36] C. 1, X, *de divortiis*, IV, 19; Panormitanus, *Commentaria*, ad 1, X, *qui matrimonium accusare possunt*, IV, 18, ad *rub.*, fol. 75; Hostiensis, *Summa*

striction to the parties themselves was based on the sound principle "... *alterius non interest*"; that is, no one else's right was prejudiced or impaired.[37]

In this regard, Boich († 1350) approached, in a somewhat different manner, the question of who was permitted to accuse a marriage. He held that before answering this question one must distinguish between a marriage that was accused *ad totalem separationem*, and a marriage that was accused *ad separationem thori propter adulterium*.[38] In the first case, if the impediment in question arose *ex defectu*, then only the spouses could accuse the marriage.[39] Moreover, if the impediment was founded on an error concerning the status of one of the parties, the accusation was also restricted to the spouses.[40] But if the impediment "... *provenit ex peccato, seu inducit peccatum* ...," then anyone could be admitted to attack the marriage by way of denunciation.[41] Hostiensis would extend this right even to minors in these cases because of what he considered to be the baseness of such unions, and because of the danger that they could be incestuous in nature, particularly if the impediment of consanguinity was present. On the other hand, if the marriage was accused *ad thori separationem propter adulterium*, then only the spouses could be given a hearing.[42]

Aurea, ibid., fol. 321, n. 1; Boich, *In Quinque Libros Commentaria* (Venetiis, 1576), Lib. IV, *qui matrimonium accusare possunt*, fol. 69, col. 1, n. 1.

[37] Panormitanus, *Commentaria*, ad c. 1, X, *qui matrimonium accusare possunt*, IV, 18, ad *rub.*, fol. 75 (hereafter cited as *Commentaria*).

[38] Boich, *Commentaria*, Lib. IV, *qui matrimonium accusare possunt*, fol. 69, col. 1, n. 1; cf. Durandus, *Speculum Iuris*, Lib. IV, partic. 4, fol. 468, § 4, n. 2; Raymond of Pennaforte, *Summa* (Verona, 1744), Lib. IV, *de divortio* . . . *propter perpetuum impedimentum*, 20, fol. 524, col. 2.

[39] C. 4, X, *de frigidis et maleficiatis, et impotentia coeundi*, IV, 15; Boich *Commentaria*, Lib. IV, fol. 69, col. 1.

[40] C. 2, X, *de coniugio servorum*, IV, 9; JE, n. 14021; Hostiensis, *Summa Aurea, ibid.*, fol. 321, n. 1; Boich, *Commentaria*, fol. 69, col. 1, n. 1; Durandus, *Speculum Iuris, ibid.*, fol. 468, § 4, n. 2.

[41] Cf. *infra*, p. 21.

[42] *Summa Aurea, ibid.*, fol. 321, n. 1. A typical *libellus accusationis* is presented by Hostiensis: "Ego Petrus consanguineus Gulielmi in tali

Article 3. Persons Permitted to Denounce a Marriage

The cases in which the Decretals were more concerned, however, were those in which "*. . . legitimi accusatores et testes appareant omni exceptione maiores . . .*" for the purpose of denouncing a sinful union.[43] Perhaps, such cases Boich had in mind when he stated "*. . . impedimentum provenit ex peccato seu inducit peccatum ut puta impedimentum consanguinitatis vel affinitatis et tunc quilibet admittitur. . . .*"[44] Note should be made of the particular attention given by the decretal law to cases involving the canonical impediments of spiritual relationship and consanguinity.

The first case in which the denunciation of marriage is cited in the Decretals can be found in a letter of Pope Alexander III (1159-1181) addressed to the Bishop of Paris.[45] Here there is revealed the problem of a couple who had contracted marriage and had subsequntly lived together for some time. Of a sudden, the husband, having committed a murder, left his wife and fled to another city. Following the separation of the spouses it was discovered "*. . . quod pater praedictae puellae ad Christianitatem iuvenem tenuit, et . . . eum de sacro fonte levavit. . . .*" Now by virtue of this baptism, the husband, according to the prevailing law, had contracted the impediment of spiritual relationship with the father's daughter "*. . . unde est matrimonium*

gradu accuso matrimonium provoco ad divortium quantenus de facto consistit inter ipsum Gulielmum et Margaritam uxorem suam et puto pronuntiari matrimonium inter ipsos nullum fuisse et utrique dari licentiam cum alio contrahendi, hoc illa ratione: quia praedicti G & M attinent sibi in quarto gradu consanguinitatis et hoc offero me legitime probaturum et comprobatur."—*Summa Aurea*, Lib. IV, *Libellus accusationis*, fol. 322, n. 1. Again, it may be noted that, as stated on p. 18, the terms *accuso* and *denuntio* were used interchangeably.

[43] C. 1, X, *qui matrimonium accusare possunt*, IV, 18; JE, n. 14052.

[44] Boich, *Commentaria*, Lib. IV, *qui matrimonium accusare possunt*, fol. 69, col. 1, n. 1; Hostiensis, *Summa Aurea, ibid.*, fol. 321, n. 1.

[45] C. 1, X, *qui matrimonium accusare possunt*, IV, 18. Both the glossator and Friedburg cite the possibility that this letter was directed to the Bishop of Parma, Italy, and not to the Bishop of Paris. In either case, the authenticity of the letter is unquestioned.

separandum. . . ." [46] Thus, the Supreme Pontiff ruled that "*. . . si manifestum est quod asseritur, aut legitimi accusatores et testes appareant omni exceptione maiores, postquam iuvenis fuerit cum omni diligentia requisitus, etiamsi nequiverit inveniri, testes recipere poteris, et fine canonico iudicium terminare.*" [47] Neither the glossator nor Hostiensis made any appreciable attempt to elaborate on the meaning of "*legitimi accusatores.*" They simply noted that these were to be understood "*. . . secundum quod traditur.*" Perhaps the significance of this rather terse observation can be deduced from the contents of a letter probably written by Pope Celestine II (1143-1144) to the Bishop of Florence in a response to a question involving an accusation *in causa matrimoniali super consanguinitate.*[48] The Pope stated that a mother and father, sister and brother, and other blood relatives of either sex could be admitted to testify on behalf of or against the matrimonial bond. Moreover, in the absence of

[46] C. 1, X, *qui matrimonium accusare possunt,* IV, 18; cf. cc. 1-8, X, *de cognatione spirituali,* IV, 11; Hostiensis, *Commentaria in Quinque Decretalium Libros* (6 vols. in 4, Venetiis, 1581), ad c. 1, X, IV, 18 (hereafter cited as Hostiensis, *Commentaria*).

[47] C. 1, X, *qui matrimonium accusare possunt,* IV, 18. The glossator noted here that the acceptance of *legitimos testes et accusatores* was conditioned on the absence of fault on the part of the wife and the contumacious refusal to appear on the part of her husband. The influence of *dolus* on the right to accuse a marriage will be treated below. *Decretales Gregorii Papae IX suae integritati una cum glossis restitutae* (Romae, 1582), *Glossa Ordinaria,* ad c. 1, X, IV, 18, s. v. *testes* (hereafter cited as *Glossa Ordinaria*).

Attention is to be called to the use of the term *accusatores* in the Pope's response. Hostiensis indicates that it is not an *accusatio* that should be made here but rather a *denunciatio,* since the prevention of a sinful union is intended and not the vindication of a right: ". . . unde est matrimonium separandum . . . et denunciatione facta in ecclesia . . ."—*Commentaria,* ad c. 1, X, IV, 18, s. v. *levavit.*

[48] C. 3, X, *qui matrimonium accusare possunt,* IV, 18; JK, n. 191. The Roman Edition of 1582 attributed this letter to Pope Clement III (1187-1191). The Editors noted, however, that in some manuscripts Pope Celestine I (422-432) was the author, but that the majority of manuscripts favored Pope Celestine III (1191-1198). Friedburg endorses the latter opinion; Jaffé attributes it to Pope Celestine I. Kehr is probably correct in assigning it to Pope Celestine II. Cf. c. 3, C. XXXV, q. 6 and Kehr, *Regesta Pontificum Romanorum* (3 vols., Berolini: Apud Weidmannos, 1906-1908), III, 10, n. 15.

those mentioned, other relatives familiar with the genealogy of the couple whose marriage was questioned on the grounds of the impediment of consanguinity could also be admitted. Such a procedure was, according to Pope Celestine ". . . *tam antiqua consuetudine quam legibus approbatur, et tam divinis quam humanis legibus similiter approbatur.*" [49] The glossarist noted here that the laws to which the Pope referred could be found in the *Decree* of Gratian and specifically in *Pars Secunda, Causa* XXXV, *questio* 6.[50] Thus it would seem that the clause *secundum quod traditur* as it is related to the *legitimi accusatores* refers to the prescriptions of Gratian regarding admissibility of an accuser. Moreover, the fact that these laws were rooted in ancient custom could be easily explained with practical reasons. Panormitanus suggested ". . . *quia unus quisque suam consanguinitatem scire laborat testibus et chartis et recitatione maiorum et illi melius recipi debent qui melius sciunt et quorum interest.*" [51] Hostiensis added: ". . . *et qui melius sciunt veritate illam dicere praesumuntur. . . .*" [52] Hostiensis visualized, as a last resort, the possibility of the judge admitting an *extraneus* who knew the facts and was willing to tell the truth.[53] In any event, discretion was left to the judge in determining the actual fitness of a parent or a relative or anyone else to accuse the marriage.[54]

A question was asked of Pope Innocent III, whether a person could be admitted to denounce a marriage if that same person failed to do so during the time prescribed for such a purpose. Concerning this question the Pope ruled that if a *justa causa* impeded the denouncer, he could be heard at a later time. How-

[49] C. 3, X, IV, 18.

[50] Cf. *supra*, p. 12.

[51] *Commentaria,* ad c. 3, X, IV, 18, fol. 76, n. 1; cf. Boich, *Commentaria,* Lib. IV, *ibid.*, fol. 69, col. 2, n. 1; Hostiensis, *Commentaria,* ad c. 3, X, IV, 18, s. v. *videtur.*

[52] Commentaria, ad c. 3, X, IV, 18, s. v. *videtur;* cf. Panormitanus, Commentaria, ad c. 3, X, IV, 18, fol. 76, n. 1.

[53] *Summa Aurea,* Lib. IV, *quis admittatur ad accusationem matrimonii,* fol. 321, n. 1.

[54] Hostiensis, *Commentaria,* ad c. 3, X, IV, 18, s. v. *videtur;* Panormitanus, *Commentaria,* ad c. 3, X, IV, 18, fol. 76, n. 5.

ever, since it was reasonably presumed that the customary public announcements of the marriage were known by all, the denunciation by such a person should be repelled as suspect if there was any doubt concerning it.[55]

Again, relative to a case involving the impediment of spiritual relationship, Pope Innocent III ruled that anyone who knew of a marriage in which this impediment existed not only could but should denounce such a union to the Church.[56] In his comment on this statement by the Holy Father, the glossator explained that the right to denounce a marriage illicitly contracted was not only reserved to the prelates of the Church but extended to anyone. He further noted that if anyone other than the spouses themselves attacked such a marriage they were not to be considered as accusing the marriage but as denouncing it.[57] Furthermore, in a letter to the Bishop of Amiens, Pope Alexander III declared that the right to denounce a marriage could be exercised by anyone, particularly in those cases in which the impediment to the marriage was manifestly known to all. And in the event that someone appeared to denounce such a marriage, the Bishop *ex officio* was empowered to declare the marriage null according to the rules of judicial procedure.[58]

Article 4. Persons Forbidden to Accuse a Marriage

It is not an oversimplification of the truth to state that the decretal law was far more specific in its delineation of the disqualifying factors relating to the accusation and denunciation

[55] C. 6, X, *qui matrimonium accusare possunt*, IV, 18; Potthast, n. 4614; cf. *Glossa Ordinaria*, ad c. 6, X, IV, 18, s. v. *excluderet;* Panormitanus, *Commentaria*, ad c. 6, X, IV, 18, fol. 77, n. 1; Boich, *Commentaria, ibid.*, fol. 70, n. 2-3.

[56] C. 7, X, *de cognatione spirituali*, IV, 11; Potthast, n. 1638.

[57] *Glossa Ordinaria*, ad c. 7, X, IV, 11, s. v. *nunciare*.

[58] C. 3, X, *de divortiis*, IV, 19; JE, n. 11866. "Evidentia patrati sceleris non indiget clamore accusatoris."—c. 9. X, *de accusationibus, inquisitionibus, et denunciationibus*, V, 1; ". . . quod in notoriis ordo iuris servandus est."—*Glossa Ordinaria*, ad *casus*, c. 3, X, IV, 19. Cf. Hostiensis, *Summa Aurea*, Lib. V, *De Inquisitionibus*, fol. 339, nn. 1-2; Lib. IV, *Libellus accusationis*, fol. 322, n. 2; *Commentaria*, ad c. 3, X, IV, 19, nn. 1-4; Raymond of Pennafort, *Summa*, Lib. IV, *de divortio propter . . . perpetuum impedimentum*, 20, fol. 524, col. 2.

of marriage than it was in describing the positive qualifying requirements. Unfortunately, however, because the term *accusatio* was so often employed to signify the notion of *denunciatio*, it is sometimes difficult to draw an accurate distinction between those who were forbidden to accuse and those who were forbidden to denounce a marriage. The commentators were agreed, nevertheless, that one who himself could be accused of *turpitudo propria* could not bring accusation against another.[59] This rule is most clearly taught by Pope Alexander III in his solution to a case of a woman dismissed by her husband on his own authority because of adultery. The woman, in turn, sought to return to him, insisting that her dismissal was unjust, since the husband had been the occasion of her sin. The Pope replied that if the alleged adultery was notorious, the husband should not be compelled to take her back, "*. . . nisi constaret, ipsum cum alia adulterium commisisse.*"[60] Moreover, it would seem that it was also determined in decretal law that the party who was the *causa dolosa* of an impediment to a marriage was not to be admitted to accuse that marriage. Evidence for this assertion can be found in a decretal letter of Pope Alexander III to the Abbot of the Monastery of Saint Alban, Italy, in which he discussed a case in which a validly married man took to himself a second wife who was unaware that this man was already bound by the impediment of *ligamen*. In the course of time, the first and real wife of the man died, and the man intent on leaving his second consort, sued for a separation from her. The Pope declared that such a petition was to be rejected. The Pontiff gave as his reason that because the innocent woman had attempted marriage with the man unaware of the existence of the impediment, it was not fitting that this man who knowingly contravened the law of the Church should thereby profit from his own guilt. Hence, unless the woman herself sought the separation, the petition of the man was not to be heard. Again, the Pope repeated his reason, namely, that the man would be benefitting by his own crime.[61]

[59] Hostiensis, *Summa Aurea, de denunciationibus*, fol. 338, n. 1.

[60] C. 4, X, *de divortiis*, IV, 19; JE, n. 14107; cf. c. 5, X, IV, 19.

[61] The letter reads: "Propositum est nobis, quod vir quidam O. uxorem habens sibi aliam, huiusmodi rei insciam, copulavit, de qua plures filios

To be noted is the fact that it was because of her innocence that the woman was permitted to separate from the man, and that it was because of his guilt in precipitating such a union that the man was deprived of this right. In his preliminary discussion of this case, the glossator made two observations. First, that the man in question "*. . . non potest . . . contrahere cum ea, cum qua adulteratus est.*" And second, "*. . . de dolo suo non debet quis commodum habere.*" It is apparent that even after the impediment of *ligamen* no longer existed, the attempted marriage between the man and his second wife was understood to have remained null and not to have been ratified by subsequent consent.[62] And it is equally clear that the man, because he was the guilty cause, was forced to remain with his second wife.[63] But just what the status of the man and his second wife was understood to be as long as the wife did not sue for a separation is not clear. The principle governing such a union was that "*. . . quod contractus pro parte tenet, et pro parte non tenet.*"[64] But this principle alone does not reveal whether the man was obliged to renew matrimonial consent, or whether he was simply to remain with the woman in a union similar to that of a brother and sister. The glossator seems to favor the former opinion in his observation, "*. . . tamen si mulier vult compellitur ipsam ducere propter dolum, et fraudem illius, ut in fine dicitur.*"[65]

---

habuit; sed prima mortua nititur discedere a secunda asserens, quod uxore sua vivente eam non licuit sibi copulare. Licet autem in canonibus habeatur, ut nullus copulet in matrimonio quam prius polluerat adulterio, et illam maxime, cui fidem dederat uxore sua vivente, vel quae machinata est in mortem uxoris; quia tamen praefata mulier erat inscia, quod ille aliam haberet uxorem viventem, nec dignum est, ut praedictus vir, qui scienter contra canones venerat, lucrum de suo dolo reportet: consulationi tuae taliter respondemus, quod, nisi praedicta mulier divortium petat, ad petitionem viri non sunt aliquatenus separandi, quum ex suo delicto videretur commodum reportare."—c. 1, X, *de eo, qui duxit in matrimonium quam polluit per adulterium*, IV, 7; JE, n. 12636.

[62] Hostiensis, *Commentaria*, ad c. 1, X, *de eo, qui duxit . . .*, IV, 7, s. v. *nisi mulier*.

[63] "Et ita compellitur vir manere cum ea si voluerit propter culpam et dolum ipsius viri, sed non econverso . . ."—*Glossa Ordinaria*, ad c. 1, X, IV, 7, s. v. *nisi mulier*.

[64] *Glossa Ordinaria*, ad c. 1, X, IV, 7, ad *casus;* cf. s. v. *nisi mulier*.

[65] *Glossa Ordinaria*, ad c. 1, X, IV, 7, s. v. *insciam*. "Sed si vir, qui

On the other hand, this assertion is tempered in the commentary concerning the exclusive right of the woman to accuse the marriage: "... *ita compellitur vir remanere cum ea si ipsa voluerit.* ..." The writer is in agreement with Marquardt,[66] who insists that the decretal letter of Pope Alexander prescinds from any consideration of whether the man could be forced to contract a valid marriage with his second wife following the death of his real wife and the consequent cessation of the impediment of *ligamen.* And, therefore, the clause "*ut in fine dicitur,*" which obviously refers to the closing lines of the Pope's decretal, seems to be without foundation. Probably the safer opinion regarding this matter is that of Hostiensis who, repeating the principle, "*ne de dolo suo commodum reportet,*" held that the man was compelled merely to remain with the innocent partner unless the latter "*divortium petat.*"[67] In any case, the point to be made here is that it seems quite clear that the principle by which Pope Alexander III decided this case was not one that was based on any consideration of whether or not the guilty party could accuse the marriage in the light of a possible valid bond existing between the man and his second "wife" subsequent to the death of his first wife. Nor was it the principal concern of the Pope to define the moral obligation of the man to contract a valid marriage with his second partner once the impediment of *ligamen* no longer existed. Rather, the principle was clearly based on the juridic consideration that "... *nec dignum est, ut praedictus vir, qui scienter contra canones venerat, lucrum de dolo suo reportet.* ..." Thus, the man could not separate from the woman unless she herself sought the separation.

Article 5. Persons Forbidden to Denounce a Marriage

When approaching the topic of those who were forbidden by decretal law to denounce a marriage, caution must be exercised. The reason is that the glossators and commentators often spoke

sciebat impedimentum, nunc, cum potest, nollet matrimonialiter consentire in eam, cogi debet de novo contrahere."—Innocent IV, *Commentaria*, ad c. 1, X, IV, 7.

66 *The Loss of Right to Accuse a Marriage* (Rome: Catholic Book Agency, 1951), pp. 17-18.

67 Hostiensis, *Commentaria*, ad c. 1, X, IV, 7.

of those who were forbidden to "accuse" a marriage, though juridically they clearly referred to persons who were forbidden to denounce. In any event, exceptions could be raised against the following: those whose testimony was suspect; [68] those who were strangers, especially if the defendant was one of sound reputation; [69] those who were under the censure of excommunication, or who were notoriously guilty of sacrilege, fornication, or usury; [70] those whose attack was motivated *propter turpem quaestum;* [71] those who refused to take an oath, or who were enemies, or who were motivated by ill-will toward the defendant; [72] those who knew of the impediment at the time when the marriage was contracted, and who knowingly and willfully remained silent; [73] those who deliberately refused to denounce the marriage within the time assigned for the proclamation of banns; [74] and, those whose previously invalid marriage was later validated by mutual consent subsequent to the removal of the impediment.[75]

A question entertained by the commentators was whether one who himself was guilty of a crime should be rejected from denouncing the sinful union of another. On the one hand, it was held that anyone could be admitted to denounce a marriage, as long as he did so motivated by the spirit of evangelical correc-

[68] C. 5, X, *qui matrimonium accusare possunt*, IV, 18; cf. Innocent IV, *Commentaria*, ad c. 5, X, IV, 18, s. v. *ab accusatione*; Esmein, *Le Mariage en Droit Canonique*, I, 408.

[69] Hostiensis, *Summa Aurea*, Lib. IV, *quae exceptiones competant contra accusatorem matrimonii*, fol. 322, nn. 1, 2.

[70] C. 20, X, *de accusationibus, inquisitionibus et denunciationibus*, V, 1.

[71] C. 5, X, *qui matrimonium accusare possunt*, IV, 18.

[72] Cc. 5, 6, X, IV, 18; cc. 13, 20, X, V, 1; ". . . malitiis hominum non est indulgendum . . . auditur ille qui tantum vult nocere."—*Glossa Ordinaria*, ad c. 5, X, IV, 18, ad *casus*.

[73] C. 6, X, *qui matrimonium accusare possunt*, IV, 18; "Scienti et consentienti non fit inuria neque dolus."—R. I. XXVII in VI°; cf. Hostiensis, *Summa Aurea*, Lib. IV, *quae exceptiones competant contra accusatorem matrimonii*, fol. 322, n. 1.

[74] C. 6, X, IV, 18; cf. *Glossa Ordinaria*, ad c. 6, X, IV, 18, ad *casus;* Hostiensis, *Commentaria*, ad c. 6, X, IV, 18, s. v. *culpabilis*.

[75] C. 4, X, IV, 18.

tion. But one who himself was immersed in sin was never presumed to be so motivated, and therefore his testimony would necessarily be suspect.[76] However, Hostiensis believed that anyone, even a "*particeps criminis et vilis persona,*" could denounce a marriage, provided that the denunciation was made in good faith and for the purposes of correction. Thus, he concluded that one who was repelled from accusing was not necessarily excluded from denunciation.[77] Moreover, he held that even an occult sin could be denounced by one who was personally affected by it or by any Christian, provided always that the purpose of such a denunciation was directed toward the excitation of repentance on the part of the sinner. In short, Hostiensis felt that sin on the part of the denouncer played no part in cases in which a soul might be saved. He added that if the purpose of the denunciation was merely vindictive in nature, and not for the purpose of assisting a soul from sin, then the denouncer was to be repelled.[78]

This discussion and, indeed, this section may be concluded with a comment of Panormitanus on the relation between the accusation and denunciation of marriage; namely; that one is scarcely in a position to effect a reconciliation with God of a person living in a sinful union unless the marriage is declared null by proving the existence of the impediment. Hence, to this extent, he would consider both accusation and denunciation as ultimately having the same effect.[79]

Article 6. Summary

To summarize, it is apparent that the decretal law distinguished between the right to accuse and the right to denounce a marriage. The right to accuse a marriage was founded on the

[76] Hostiensis, *Summa Aurea, de denunciationibus,* fol. 338, n. 2.

[77] Hostiensis, *Summa Aurea, de denunciationibus,* fol. 338, n. 2; *Commentaria,* ad c. 5, X, *qui matrimonium accusare possunt,* IV, 18, s. v. *ab accusatione;* cf. c. 7, X, *de cognatione spirituali,* IV, 11.

[78] Hostiensis, *Summa Aurea, de denunciationibus,* fol. 338, n. 2; cf. Innocent IV, *Commentaria,* ad c. 6, X, *qui matrimonium accusare possunt,* IV, 18.

[79] Panormitanus, *Commentaria,* ad c. 6, X, *qui matrimonium accusare possunt,* IV, 18, fol. 77, n. 8.

spouse's duty to contract a valid marriage. The right to denounce a marriage was based on the duty, rooted in the virtue of charity, to condemn sin and to prevent others from living in sin. Specifically, in whom and to what extent did these rights exist? Perhaps the most succinct answer to this question can be found in an observation made by Pope Innocent IV in alluding to a decision of Pope Innocent III to repel a mother who, after the marriage of her daughter to a young man, attempted to denounce their marriage in an effort to extort money from her son-in-law.[80] Thus, Innocent IV remarked: *"Matrimonium non proprie dicitur accusari nisi ab uxore: nam cum non sit publicum crimen non admittitur nisi quorum interest sed denunciari dicitur crimen in quo manet."* [81] From the cases that have been discussed above, and from this statement of Pope Innocent IV, it can be concluded that the right to accuse marriage, unless otherwise prohibited by law, was reserved to the parties themselves if the accusation was concerned merely with the vindication of a right, or with an impediment that arose *ex defectu,* for example, the impediment of impotence, or with an impediment that was founded on an error concerning the servile condition of one of the parties. Moreover, a plea for separation because of adultery could be made only by the spouses themselves. On the other hand, if the impediment was known to be the occasion of sin for one or both of the parties, then anyone could denounce such a marriage. And finally, if the impediment was notoriously public, and no denouncers appeared to attack the marriage, the Bishop *ex officio* could proceed *motu proprio* and according to the rules of judicial procedure declare such a marriage null. Among the most notable of those who were prohibited by law to accuse a marriage was a person who was the *causa dolosa* of the impediment. Chief among those who were forbidden to denounce a marriage were excommunicates and those whose testimony, for one reason or another, was considered suspect.

[80] C. 5, X, *qui matrimonium accusare possunt,* IV, 18; Potthast, n. 2241.

[81] Commentaria, ad c. 5, X, IV, 18, s. v. *ab accusatione.*

CHAPTER III

THE RIGHT TO ACCUSE A MARRIAGE OF INVALIDITY FROM THE COUNCIL OF TRENT (1545-1563) TO THE CODE OF CANON LAW (1918)

SECTION I. THE COUNCIL OF TRENT

In the twenty-fourth session of the Council of Trent, held on November 11, 1563, twelve doctrinal canons were enacted that related to the Sacrament of Matrimony. Since the primary purpose of the Council was to combat the erroneous teachings of the Protestant revolt, its legislation was geared more toward the broad principles of general reform than toward isolated norms of judicial procedure. The only reference made by these canons to the litigation of a matrimonial cause can be found in the twelfth and final canon in which the Council decreed that matrimonial causes were reserved to the exclusive examination and sole jurisdiction of ecclesiastical judges.[1] The Decree relating to the reform of matrimony included legislation on the form of marriage, the dispensation from banns, the impediments, and the marriages of *vagi,* temporal leaders, and magistrates. No mention is made nor any question raised concerning the rights of a person to introduce a matrimonial cause into an ecclesiastical tribunal.[2]

SECTION II. THE SEVENTEENTH AND EIGHTEENTH CENTURIES

Introduction

The jurisprudence of the early seventeenth century relating to the accusation of marriage reveals very little development in scope or in detail other than that which had already been determined by decretal legislation, and which had been explained by the earlier decretalists. Not until the late seventeenth and

[1] "Si quis dixerit causas matrimoniales non spectare ad judices ecclesiasticos anathema sit."—Conc. Trident., sess. XXIV, *de matrim.,* c. 12.

[2] Conc. Trident., sess. XXIV, *de ref. matrim.*

early eighteenth centuries did the canonical commentary on the decretal law of the right to accuse marriage attain its highest stage of clarity and refinement. This result was accomplished principally through the efforts of the canonists, Anacletus Reiffenstuel († 1703) and Franciscus Schmalzgrueber († 1735), assisted by the writings of Ludovicus Engle († 1674), Emmanuel Gonzalez-Tellez († 1649), and Enricus Pirhing († 1679).

The ecclesiastical law, at this time, had repeatedly insisted that no Catholic, on his own authority, was capable of establishing the nullity of a marriage invalidly contracted.[3] Every cause of nullity was to be proposed to the proper ecclesiastical judge and was to be decided by his sentence. To this end, an accusation accompanied by the depositions of witnesses was regularly required.[4]

Article 1. The Right to Accuse a Marriage Determined by the Nature of the Marriage Impediment

The right to accuse a marriage was explicitly related to and qualified by the nature of the impediment which constituted the material cause of the accusation. A distinction was made between those impediments which the spouses themselves were capable of removing and those which the spouses could not remove.[5] Gonzalez-Tellez and Pirhing chose to identify the former as temporary impediments and the latter as permanent impediments.[6] If the impediment was temporary, that is, if the impedi-

[3] "Ad quem judicem pertineat causarum matrimonialium cognito? Certum est apud omnes catholicos, eam ad judicem ecclesiasticum pertinere . . ."—Schmalzgrueber, *Jus Ecclesiasticum Universum* (5 vols. in 12, Romae, 1843-1845), Lib. IV, tit. 18, n. 2 (hereafter cited as Schmalzgrueber).

[4] "Causa nullitatis proponenda est judici, et hujus judicio terminanda, quod ut legitime fiat, regulariter praerequiritur accusatio matrimonii, et receptio testium contra id deponentium."—Schmalzgrueber, Lib. IV, tit. 18, n. 1.

[5] Reiffenstuel, *Jus Canonicum Universum* (5 vols. in 6, Romae, 1831-1834), Lib IV, tit. 18, nn. 3-4 (hereafter cited as Reiffenstuel); Schmalzgrueber, Lib. IV, tit. 18, nn. 14-15.

[6] Gonzalez-Tellez, *Commentaria Perpetua in singulos textus quinque Librorum Decretalium Gregorii* IX (5 vols., Lugduni, 1673), Lib. IV, tit. 18, n. 3 (hereafter cited as Gonzalez-Tellez); Pirhing, *Ius Canonicum*

ment was one that the spouses themselves were capable of removing, the accusation of the marriage was reserved exclusively to the spouses. In such cases, an accusation by a third party would not be heard, because there existed the possibility that the parties would remove the impediment and reconcile themselves in a valid union.[7] As an example of a temporary impediment, Pirhing suggested an error regarding the status of the spouse which was tantamount to an error of person. He also included the impediment of impotence, not, however, because it was temporary, but because it was of such a private and intimate character.[8] Gonzalez-Tellez included the impediments of force and fear as examples of impediments that the spouses themselves could remove. To these Reiffenstuel added the impediment of an invalidating condition and all other obstacles affecting consent and removable by the renewal of consent. Reiffenstuel also mentioned the impediment of impotence, because the parties could conceivably yield their right to accuse their marriage and live together as brother and sister. In this case, no third party could attack such a union.[9] In general, then, the rule was that only the parties could accuse a marriage that was estopped by an impediment which they themselves were capable of removing. An exception to this rule was present if after accusing their marriage, the parties consummated the union. In this case, neither the parties nor anyone else could impugn the marriage, because consent was presumed to have been expressly renewed through the placing of the conjugal act.[10]

On the other hand, if the impediment was permanent, that is, if the impediment was such that it was not able to be removed by a renewal of the consent of the spouses, then anyone, particularly anyone affected by the union, could accuse the mar-

(5 vols., Dilingae, 1674-1678), Lib. IV, tit. 18, n. 1 (hereafter cited as Pirhing).

[7] Gonzalez-Tellez, Lib. IV, tit, 18, n. 3.

[8] Pirhing, Lib. IV, tit. 18, n. 1.

[9] Reiffenstuel, Lib. IV, tit. 18, nn. 3-4; Schmalzgrueber, Lib. IV, tit. 18, nn. 14-15.

[10] Reiffenstuel, Lib. IV, tit. 18, nn. 5, 12; Schmalzgrueber, Lib. IV, tit. 18, n. 20.

riage, provided that he or she was trustworthy and had knowledge of the impediment.[11] The reason for the complete release of restriction of the right to accuse a marriage in these cases was that sin was a matter of public interest, and since an invalid union which the parties themselves could not rectify was presumed to be a sinful union, *"quilibet de populo"* could accuse the marriage.[12]

If the marriage was invalid because of the impediment of consanguinity, or affinity arising from consummation, or public decency, then anyone was permitted to accuse, provided that he had knowledge of the impediment, preference being given first to the parents of the spouses, then to the brothers and sisters, and finally to other blood relatives. In the absence of these, *"extranei, antiquiores et veraciores, praesertim e vicinia"* were also admitted. [13]

Article 2. The Right to Accuse a Marriage in Cases Affecting the Public Good

In cases in which there were no accusers, and in which the public good demanded it, the Bishop, with the advice of his Chapter, could intervene and issue a declaration on the validity or invalidity of a marriage, even though the spouses were unwilling. According to Gonzalez-Tellez, this action of the Bishop could be justified under the head of three different titles. Thus, the Bishop could settle a matrimonial cause by virtue of the demands of the public good, by virtue of his authority as judge, and by virtue of the necessity to rid the community of sin. Gonzalez-Tellez concluded that if the ecclesiastical judge could declare a marriage null even though the parties were unwilling, so the Bishop, whose pastoral office demanded that he purge sin

[11] Reiffenstuel, Lib. IV, tit. 18, n. 7; Schmalzgrueber, Lib. IV, tit. 18, nn. 17-18; Gonzalez-Tellez, Lib. IV, tit. 18, n. 3.

[12] "Si vero propter aliquod impedimentum perpetuum, et cui coniuges ipsi renunciare non possunt, matrimonium nullum fit, aeque ad accusandum omnes admittuntur, quia ita publice interest propter peccatum simili matrimonio implicitum . . ."—Gonzalez-Tellez, Lib. IV, tit. 18, n. 3.

[13] C. 1. C. XXXV, q. 6; c. 3, X, *qui matrimonium accusare possunt,* IV, 18; Reiffenstuel, Lib. IV, tit. 18, n. 6; Schmalzgrueber, Lib. IV, tit. 18, n. 16.

and crime from his diocese, could, *ex officio,* rule on the invalidity of a marriage.[14]

The ecclesiastical judge had the power and the obligation to "dissolve" a marriage the nullity of which was certain and notorious.[15] Moreover, even though the impediment lacked the quality of notoriety, if it was commonly known through hearsay, the judge, *ex officio,* could inquire into the truth of the question and compel anyone to give testimony concerning it.[16]

Article 3. The Juridic Withdrawal of the Right to Accuse a Marriage

Pirhing was the first canonist to use the term *innocens* in reference to a spouse's right to accuse a marriage. The right to accuse a marriage, according to Pirhing, was the sole prerogative of the innocent party if there was present in the matrimonial cause any question of fraud or deceit.[17] Pirhing called attention to two instances in which the party could not be considered as innocent. The party could not be regarded as innocent if he attacked the marriage moved by some base advantage which he would attain from the accusation, or if he knew of the existence of the impediment at the time when the marriage was contracted and failed to reveal it.[18] Outside of these cases, Pirhing cited no other restrictions of the right to accuse marriage provided that the accuser was beyond suspicion.

[14] Gonzalez-Tellez, Lib. IV, tit. 19, n. 2; cf. c. 3, X, *de divortiis*, IV, 19.

[15] Reiffenstuel, Lib. IV, tit. 19, n. 19; Lib. II, tit. 28, n. 299; Lib. III, tit. 2, n. 17.

[16] Reiffenstuel, Lib. IV, tit. 19, n. 20; ". . . sed si fama spargatur, quosdam conjugatos aliquo impedimento Canonico laborare, Judex de veritate ex officio inquirere debeat . . ."—Engel, *Collegium Universi Juris Canonici* (editio nona, a Gaspare Barthel, Beneventi, 1760), Lib. IV, tit. 18, n. 2 (hereafter cited as Engel).

[17] "Si accusetur matrimonium . . . tunc admittitur ad accusandum solum conjux innocens, quia hujus tantum interest, non autem alterius." —Pirhing, Lib. IV, tit. 18, n. 1.

[18] "Hinc patet, quod repellitur accusator matrimonii, propter turpem quaestum. . . . Praeterea repellitur ab accusatione matrimonii contracti, qui tempore praemissae denunciationis, sciens, impedimentum dirimens tacuit, et illud non manifestavit . . ."—Pirhing, Lib. IV, tit. 18, n. 2; cf. cc. 5, 6, X, *qui matrimonium accusare possunt*, IV, 18.

Sanchez, though he wrote voluminously on the Sacrament of Matrimony, directed no formal address to the question of the right to accuse marriage. But he did speak of the loss of this right by a person who was aware of his own impotence at the time when he contracted marriage. To this case, Sanchez applied the principle of Pope Alexander III found in c. 1, X, *de eo, qui duxit in matrimonium . . .*, IV, 7, namely, *de dolo suo non debet quis commodum habere*. Thus, because of his deceitfulness in not revealing the impediment, the court would give no hearing to his accusation on the grounds that no one should profit by his own delinquency.[19]

Also repelled from accusing marriage were those who refused to accuse personally, and those who by a renewal of consent were capable of removing an impediment to their marriage and after accusing their marriage ratified their consent by a conjugal act.[20] Pagans, heretics, Jews, and excommunicates were not permitted to accuse a Christian in criminal cases, but nothing was mentioned by the authors at this time regarding their right to impugn a marriage.[21] It would seem, however, that if those mentioned were denied the right to accuse a Christian of a crime, *a fortiori* or at least *a pari*, they would similarly be denied the right to attack a Christian marriage allegedly invalid as an existing wrong against the public interest and well-being.

Article 4. Summary

The basic laws governing the right to accuse marriage experienced no alteration from the time when they were promulgated in the Decretals of Gregory IX to the eighteenth century. The

[19] ". . . ut liceat vero proclamare suam impotentiam, quando illius ignarus fuit tempore matrimonii. Cum enim dolus nemini patrocinari debeat, minime audietur, si illam tunc norit. Argumento ex c. 1, *de eo qui duxit*."—Sanchez, *De Sancto Matrimonii Sacramento Disputationum* (Venetiis: Apud Nicolaum Pezzana, 1726), Lib. VII, d. 114, n. 4; cf. c. 6, X, *qui matrimonium accusare possunt*, IV, 18; Pirhing, Lib. IV, tit. 18, n. 2; Schmalzgrueber, Lib. IV, tit. 15, n. 71.

[20] Cc. 2, 4, X, *qui matrimonium accusare possunt*, IV, 18; Reiffenstuel, Lib. IV, tit. 18, n. 13; Schmalzgrueber, Lib. IV, tit. 18, n. 15.

[21] C. 24, C. II, q. 7; cc. 1, 2, C. IV, q. 1; c. 7, C. III, q. 4; c. 20, X, *de accusationibus, inquisitionibus et denunciationibus*, V, 1; Reiffenstuel, Lib. IV, tit. 1, nn. 24, 28.

most notable contribution to the jurisprudence related to these laws during the intervening years was the clarification of the norm that determined the cases in which the right to accuse a marriage was reserved exclusively to the spouses, and the cases in which this right was shared by others. If a marriage was invalid because of the impediment of occult impotence or because of a defect of consent which could be remedied by the spouses themselves, they alone could impugn the marriage. If the marriage was estopped because of an impediment over which the parties had no control, anyone who was trustworthy, and who had knowledge of the impediment could attack the marriage. If the impediment was a matter of public knowledge and detrimental to the public good, the Bishop or the ecclesiastical judge, *ex officio,* could accuse the marriage.

The right to accuse a marriage was forfeited if the accuser was guilty of fraud, collusion, or deceit; or, if the accuser refused to make his accusation in person, or, if after an accusation of defect of consent was made, the accused parties consummated the marriage. In all likelihood, non-Catholics and excommunicates were also deprived of the right to accuse marriage.

Section III. The Nineteenth Century to the Code of Canon Law

On November 3, 1741, Pope Benedict XIV (1740-1758) promulgated to the universal Church his celebrated Constitution *Dei Miseratione* which clarified and stabilized many basic norms of judicial procedure which were to be observed in matrimonial causes until the enactment of the Code of Canon Law, almost two centuries later.[22] Though this Constitution was quite specific in its prescriptions concerning the rights and duties of the ecclesiastical judge and of the defender of the bond, it did not consider the question of the right of the parties to impugn a marriage.[23]

[22] *Codicis Iuris Canonici Fontes,* cura Emi. Petri Card. Gasparri editi, 9 vols., Romae (postea Civitate Vaticana): Typis Polyglottis Vaticanis, 1923-1939 (Vols. VII-IX, ed. cura et studio Emi. Iustianiani Card. Seredi) I, n. 318 (hereafter cited as *Fontes*).

[23] Bouix, *Tractatus de Judiciis Ecclesiasticus* (2 vols. in 1, Parisiis, 1855) II, 434 (hereafter cited as *De Judiciis*); Gasparri, *Tractatus*

The first enactment of the nineteenth century pertinent to judicial procedure was the Instruction *Cum Moneat Glossa* of the Sacred Congregation of the Council issued on August 22, 1840.[24] This Instruction was intended to explain and to develop the rules prescribed in *Dei Miseratione,* and to remind ecclesiastical tribunals of their serious obligation to fulfill these norms in order to preclude the possibility of malice or collusion by the parties whose marriage had been accused. Though *Cum Moneat Glossa* was a complement to the Constitution of Pope Benedict XIV, no mention was made in this Instruction of the right to accuse.

On June 20, 1883, the Sacred Congregation of the Holy Office issued the Instruction *Quemadmodum Matrimonii Foedus* to the Bishops of the Oriental Rites, in which explicit reference was made to those who had the right to accuse marriage.[25] With the exception of the introductory paragraphs and with certain additions relating to the rules determining the competence of a tribunal, this Instruction was directed specifically to the Bishops of the United States by the Sacred Congregation for the Propagation of the Faith within six months after its issuance by the Holy Office.[26] It may well be that these Instructions of 1883 emanating from the Holy See were a result of or were, at least, occasioned by an earlier directive issued on May 4, 1855 by Joseph Cardinal Rauscher (†1875), Archbishop of Vienna, and approved by Pope Pius IX (1846-1878) as a norm *"pro judiciis ecclesiasticis quoad causas matrimoniales"* for the Austrian-Hungarian Empire. This Instruction, most notable for its clarity and precision, is most frequently referred to as the *Instructio Austriaca.*[27] Note should be made here that the Instruction of

Canonicus de Matrimonio (2 vols., Paris, 1891), n. 1162 (hereafter cited as *De Matrimonio*).

[24] *Fontes,* VI, n. 4069.

[25] *Collectanea S. Congregationis de Propaganda Fide,* Romae: Typographia Polyglotta, 1893, n. 1572; *Fontes,* IV, n. 1076.

[26] *Fontes,* VII, n. 4901; cf. S.C.S. Off. (Colonien.), 23 jun. 1903,—*Fontes,* n. 1266.

[27] *Instructio Austriaca* Josephi Cardinalis Rauscher, 4 maii, 1855—*Acta et Decreta Sacrorum Conciliorum Recentiorum, Collectio Lacensis* (7 vols., Friburgi Brisgoviae: Herder, 1870-1890), V, coll. 1286-1316 (here-

the Sacred Congregation of the Propagation of the Faith of 1883 was incorporated into the Acts of the III Plenary Council of Baltimore in 1884 in respect to marriage cases. The Fathers of the Council also called the attention of the American Bishops to the procedural norms of the Austrian Instruction of 1855.[28]

Article 1. The Austrian Instruction

Though the Austrian Instruction represented authentic legislation only for the particular territory of the Austrian-Hungarian Empire, it would be difficult to exaggerate the significance of this contribution made by Joseph Cardinal Rauscher to the rules governing the judicial procedure according to which matrimonial causes were to be accepted, heard, and decided by ecclesiastical tribunals.[29] However, it should be observed that the

---

after cited as *Instr. Austr.*); *Anacleta Iuris Pontificii* (28 vols., Romae, 1855-1869; Parisiis, 1872-1891, II, coll. 2515-2562.

[28] "In agendis hisce causis pro rei gravitate exacte servetur tum Constitutio Benedict XIV, *Dei Miseratione*, 3 nov. 1741, tum Instructio a Cong. de Prop. Fide Nobis communicata quae incipit *Causae Matrimoniales*. . . . Utiliter etiam consuli poterit Instructio pro judiciis ecclesiasticis Imperii Austriaci in causis matrimonialibus, a. 1855 a gravibus theologis et canonistis Romanis, licet solo privato suo judicio, commendata."—*Acta et Decreta Concilii Plenarii Baltimorensis Tertii*, A.D. MDCCCLXXXIV (Baltimore: John Murphy and Co., 1886), n. 304.

[29] The occasion of the Austrian Instruction was the signing of a Concordat between Pope Pius IX (1846-1878) and the Austrian Emperor Franz Joseph († 1916) which was ratified on September 25, 1856. In general, the effect of the Concordat was the termination of unjust interference of the Austrian Empire in the jurisdiction of the Church. Article X of the agreement stated that all ecclesiastical causes, especially those which concerned the faith, the sacraments, and sacred functions "ad Ecclesiae forum unice pertineant, easdem cognoscet judex ecclesiasticus, qui perinde de causis quoque matrimonialibus juxta sacros Canones et Tridentina cumprimis decreta judicium feret. . . ." The Instruction of Cardinal Rauscher was written as an adjunct to Article X in order to define and to clarify for the ecclesiastical judge in what manner he was to proceed in applying the decretal laws and Tridentine decrees to matrimonial causes. Within twelve years, the Concordat was abrogated by subsequent civil legislation, but the Instruction retained its binding force on the ecclesiastical tribunals. Cf. Aichner, *Compendium Juris Ecclesiastici* (6. ed., Brixinae, 1887), Appendix I, *Concordatum Austriacum*; see also pp. 538-540.

value of this document does not derive principally from its content, because the basic laws contained in the Austrian Instruction were rooted in the Decretals of Gregory IX. Neither does its significance lie chiefly in the synthetical presentation of the laws, because this result had been accomplished with a notable degree of success in the commentaries on the Decretals by Reiffenstuel and Schmalzgrueber. It is submitted that the importance of the paragraphs of the Austrian Instruction pertaining to the right to accuse marriage consists principally in the precision and conciseness with which the laws were formulated. Thus, the Instruction represents the first successful codification of the laws on the right to accuse marriage, in a manner that can be described as truly "canonical." Since the Austrian Instruction was expressly recommended by the III Plenary Council of Baltimore for use by the ecclesiastical tribunals of the Bishops of the United States, and since it was cited so frequently by the pre-Code authors who wrote after its publication, it would be well to examine the paragraphs of the Instruction that relate to the right to accuse marriage.

In the one hundred and fifteenth paragraph, the first of eight paragraphs which treat of the *jus accusandi matrimonium,* there is set down the general principle that the right to accuse marriage belongs to any Catholic, except to one who was suspected of making the accusation for his own benefit, or who, when he knew that the marriage was to be contracted and after the banns were duly announced, failed to reveal any impediment to the marriage without a legitimate reason. However, this right was possessed by every Catholic only insofar as it was not expressly restricted to the spouses.[30]

The six paragraphs that follow indicated the cases in which the *"jus accusandi conjugibus aut uni ipsorum . . . privative competit. . . ."* [31]

[30] "Matrimonium impugnandi jus, in quantum haud expresse ad conjuges restringitur, competit catholico, exceptis iis, qui sua hac in re commoda quaerere suspecti sunt, vel quamvis matrimonium contrahendum esse sciverint ac proclamationes debito modo institutae fuerint, impedimentum tamen absque legitima excusatione reticuerunt."—*Instr. Austr.,* § 115.

[31] Cf. *Instr. Austr.,* § 122.

The first of these cases which was of reserved right, or in which the right to accuse was restricted to the spouses, was one in which the marriage was contracted because of an invalidating error or unjust force. Only the party who was in error or who was the victim of the unjust force had a right to accuse the marriage. This right was lost, however, if after he recognized his error, or if after his fear had ceased, the accuser knowingly and freely rendered the conjugal debt, or continued to live voluntarily with the consort for six months.[32]

In cases in which it was permitted to contract marriage *"sub conditione,"* the marriage was able to be accused only by the parties themselves on the grounds that the condition was not fulfilled. However, the right to accuse was lost by a party if he was guilty of lying about a fact he had placed in the condition, or if he maliciously failed to admit the non-existence of the object of the condition, or if, because of his own fault, he impeded the fulfillment of the condition.[33]

In cases in which the marriage was not capable of being consummated because of the impediment of impotence, only the spouses could accuse the marriage unless the fact of the impotence was notorious.[34]

In cases in which the marriage was invalid because of the lack of puberty, after the arrival of puberty, only the party who had not attained puberty was permitted to accuse the marriage.[35]

[32] "Propter errorem et coactionem injustam ea tantum pars, quae in errore versata aut cui consensus coactione injusta extortus est, matrimonium accusare potest. Juro suo excidit, quando, postquam errorem agnovit aut metus, qualis ad matrimonium irritandum sufficit, cessavit, debitum conjugale voluntarie ac scienter praestiterit vel etiam, quin circumstantia ista probari possit, conjugale vitae consortium per sex menses voluntarie continuaverit."—*Instr. Austr.*, § 116.

[33] "Quando nuptus sub conditione jungi per exceptionem conceditur, matrimonium propter conditionem non impletam ab eo tantum conjuge accusari potest, qui neque in conditionem positum adesse falso asseveraverit, aut id non adesse dolo reticuerit, neque sua culpa impedierit, quominus conditio impleretur."—*Instr. Austr.*, § 117.

[34] "Propter impotentiam matrimonium consummandi, nisi notoria sit, conjuges tantum matrimonium accusare possunt."—*Instr. Austr.*, § 118.

[35] "In valorem matrimonii, cui impedimentum impubertatis obstat, pubertate impleta inquirendum non est, hisi id exigat conjux, qui matri-

In cases in which the marriage was invalid because of the impediment of abduction, the abductor could not accuse the marriage. The woman who consented to the abduction had the right to accuse, provided that she used this right at the first moment of her regained liberty; otherwise, she was not able to be heard.[36]

And last among the cases which the Instruction listed as being of reserved right was that which involved a marriage which was first estopped by the impediment of *ligamen* that later ceased to exist because of the death of the first spouse. The party who had been inculpably ignorant of the impediment could accuse the marriage. The party who was aware of the impediment did not possess this right.[37]

Having established the right of Catholics in general and the right of the spouses in particular to accuse a marriage, Cardinal Rauscher then cited the right possessed by the ecclesiastical tribunal to impugn a marriage. Thus, he stated that the ecclesiastical tribunal, *ex officio,* should proceed, as soon as possible, in all cases and for all impediments concerning which the right to accuse was not restricted either to both or to one of the spouses. This right of the tribunal could be exercised when the fact of the impediment was notorious, or when denunciations had been made against the marriage or when, in some other way, a sufficient reason was afforded for the tribunal to act.[38]

---

monii contracti tempore pubertatem nondum attigerat."—*Instr. Austr.*, § 119.

[36] "Propter impedimentum raptus raptor adversus matrimonium reclamare nequit. Rapta, quae raptui consensit, suo matrimonium accusandi jure in exordio libertatis plene recuperatae utatur; alias non amplius audiatur."—*Instr. Austr.*, § 120.

[37] "Impedimento ligaminis mutatione facti sublato, quando una pars, dum invalidas celebraret nuptias, impedimenti existentiam absque sua culpa ignoraverit, altera, quae impedimenti conscia fuerat, matrimonium accusandi iure haud potitur."—*Instr. Austr.*, § 121.

[38] "Omnibus casibus et propter omnia impedimenta, quorum respectu *jus accusandi* conjugibus aut uni ipsorum haud privative competit, tribunal matrimoniale ex officio procedere debet, quamprimum aut notorietate facti aut denuntiationibus allatis aliove modo sufficiens rei ratio subministrata fuerit."—*Instr. Austr.*, § 122.

Some general observations can be made here concerning the relationship between the teachings of the seventeenth and eighteenth century authors and the nineteenth century directive of Cardinal Rauscher. The Austrian Instruction retained the basic principle that the right to accuse marriage was qualified by the nature of the impediment invalidating the marriage. Moreover, the right to accuse a marriage, invalidated by the impediments of error, force, fear, condition, or impotence mentioned in the Instruction as being restricted to the spouses, was a direct carryover from the commentaries of the earlier authors.[39] On the other hand, far more explicit attention was paid by the Instruction than by the earlier authors to the loss of right to accuse by a person who was the culpable cause of the impediment.

Relative to the individual paragraphs of the Instruction, some noteworthy studies have been made. Thus, in commenting on paragraph 115, Gasparri pointed to some of the typical cases in which the right to accuse was enjoyed by every Catholic. He included those marriages that were null *"ob impedimentum consanguinitatis, affinitatis, criminis, etc., aut ob defectum Tridentinae formae. . . ."*[40] Referring to those Catholics who were forbidden to accuse according to paragraph 115, Lega noted that while no formal accusation could be made by persons who were suspect, this situation did not prevent the admission of the case by way of denunciation if necessity demanded an investigation into the truth of the matter.[41]

In paragraph 116, the Instruction asserted that in cases of error or unjust force, the right to accuse was possessed only by the injured party. In reference to this paragraph, Lega observed that the possibility that a marriage contracted because of error or unjust force could be convalidated by a simple renewal of consent applied only in those cases in which the impediment was secret, or in which the impediment was public, provided the

[39] Gonzalez-Tellez, Lib. IV, tit. 18, nn. 1-3; Pirhing, Lib. IV, tit. 18, n. 1; Reiffenstuel, Lib. IV, tit. 18, nn. 3, 4.

[40] *De Matrimonio* (ed. 1891), n. 1183.

[41] Lega, *De Judiciis Ecclesiasticis* (4 vols., Romae: Typis Vaticanis, 1896-1901), IV, n. 456 (hereafter cited as *De Judiciis*). Compare paragraph 115 of the Austrian Instruction with Pirhing, Lib. IV, tit. 18, n. 2.

marriage was contracted in a place where the *Tametsi* was not promulgated. For in places where the Tridentine Law was in effect, if the fear was public, the marriage was not able to be revalidated without a dispensation from the Holy See or without a renewal of consent according to the form prescribed by the Council of Trent. Again, if the impediment was public and the party who suffered the fear mentioned it frequently *in tempore non suspecto,* but later was prevented from accusing, then *"certe etiam alter coniux, vel quisque de populo vel iudex ex officio accusationem instaurare valent."* [42]

The same rule that Lega applied to paragraph 116 would affect also paragraph 117. In other words, in marriages that were permitted to be entered *"sub conditione,"* the right to accuse such a union was restricted to the spouse who was aggrieved *propter conditionem non impletam* when the case was either not publicly known or if the Tridentine form was not in force in the place in which the marriage was contracted. Otherwise, any Catholic would be permitted to accuse the marriage.[43]

Paragraph 118, which related to the exclusive right of the spouses to accuse *propter impotentiam matrimonium consummandi* unless the case was notorious, is notable for the absence of any reference to the party who knew of the existence of the impediment at the time when the marriage was contracted. It will be recalled, that in the commentaries of the earlier canonists, a person who had such knowledge would be forbidden to accuse on the principle that no one should benefit by his own fraud or deceit, a principle that was employed by Pope Alexander III in c. 1, X, *de eo, qui duxit in matrimonium . . . ,* IV, 7.[44] Neither Gasparri nor Lega raised any question of the right of a person to accuse his marriage who knew that the impediment of impotence existed at the time when the marriage was contracted. Wernz, however, did consider the case. He denied that the principle, *de dolo suo non debet quis commodum habere,* employed in c. 1, X, *de eo, qui duxit in matrimonium . . . ,* IV, 7,

[42] Lega, *De Judiciis,* IV, n. 453; Gasparri, *De Matrimonio,* (ed. 1891), n. 1182.

[43] Lega, *De Judiciis,* IV, n. 453.

[44] Cf. *supra,* p. 25; c. 4, X, *de frigidis et maleficiatis,* IV, 15.

should be employed in this instance, because of the lack of parity existing between the case of a person who had knowledge of a prior bond and the case of a person who knew of his own impotence or that of another. In the first case, the man was free to convalidate his second marriage after the death of his first wife. In the second case, the person was unable to contract any marriage at all. Moreover, Wernz argued that no couple could be obligated to live as brother and sister if one or both parties were impotent. Therefore, he concluded that a person who was unaware of the impediment of impotency at the time when he contracted the marriage could, at least, approach the ecclesiastical judge so that the judge, *ex officio,* could institute proceeding against the marriage and hand down both a sentence of nullity and a prohibition of further cohabitation. But regarding the question whether or not the *pars dolosa* had a *jus accusandi* properly so-called, Wernz did not commit himself.[45] Finally, in his comment on the *nisi notoria sit* clause of paragraph 118, Lega noted that if the circumstances were such as to constitute a scandal to Christian people, "*tunc curia sive ex officio, sive ad accusationem aut denuntiationem de rerum veritate inquisitionem instituere potest etiam iudicialem.*"[46]

Concerning the impediment of age treated in paragraph 119, the party who had attained puberty at the time of marriage was apparently to blame for having married a person who had not yet reached pubescence. Clearly, if the *pubes* erred concerning the other party, paragraph 116 would control the case. And if the Tridentine form was necessary for validity, "*tunc et alter coniux et omnes accusare matrimonium valent.*"[47]

The presumption of paragraph 120, that an abducted woman gave tacit consent to her marriage if she did not accuse it at the first opportunity, could be dispelled, according to Gasparri, even

[45] "Si unus ex coniugibus conscius impotentiae suae vel alterius coniugis matrimonium mala fide contraxit . . . certe etiam pars dolosa saltem iudicem ecclesiasticum adire potest, ut is ex officio contra tale matrimonium procedat feratque sententiam nullitatis atque ulteriorem cohabitationem prohibeat."—Wernz, *Jus Decretalium* (4 vols., Romae: Ex Typographia Polyglotta, 1899-1905), IV, n. 349.

[46] *De Judiciis,* IV, n. 452.

[47] *Loc. cit.*

if her silence perdured for a long time, provided that the woman could give reason for her silence. If she delayed her accusation for a short time even without a reasonable cause, she would still be permitted to accuse.[48] And if the renewal of consent was demanded according to the Tridentine form, then anyone could accuse the marriage.[49]

Paragraph 121 was a restatement of c. 1, X, *de eo, qui duxit in matrimonium* . . . , IV, 7, which denied the right to accuse to a person who entered marriage already bound by a prior bond even though the first marriage was dissolved by death. It should be noted that Cardinal Rauscher inserted an additional restriction of the right to accuse not found in the decretal nor in the commentaries of the earlier authors. The restriction consisted in this, that the ignorance of the bond on the part of one party must be *"absque sua culpa."* Thus, if the single party was at fault for not coming to recognize the marital status of the other, neither party would have the right to accuse. In practice, the solution to this case would be effected by a denunciation of the marriage by the parties, or by the accusation of a third party, or by an *ex officio* intervention of the ecclesiastical tribunal, especially if the renewal of consent was demanded according to the form prescribed by *Tametsi*.[50]

It has been previously noted that paragraph 122, which gave to the ecclesiastical tribunal the broad power and obligation to proceed, *ex officio,* in matrimonial causes in which the impediment was notorious or in which *"aliove mode sufficiens rei ratio subministrata fuerit,"* included a restriction of this power, namely, that it was not to be exercised in cases in which the impediment was of reserved right. It follows that the ecclesiastical tribunal, *ex officio,* did possess the right to accuse any marriage that was invalid by an impediment of public right. The significance of this distinction will unfold in later discussions

48 Gasparri, *De Matrimonio* (ed. 1891), n. 1182, p. 353, footnote n. 1; Lega, *De Judiciis,* IV, n. 452.

49 Lega, *loc. cit.*

50 Cf. *Instr. Austr.*, § 122; Lega, *De Judiciis,* IV, n. 453; Gasparri, *De Matrimonio* (ed. 1891), n. 1184.

of the post-Code *publica natura sua* impediments mentioned in Canon 1971 and in the article that follows.

Article 2. The Impediments of Public Right and Private Right

Henricus Feije († 1894), a canonist from Batavia, Holland and a professor of the University of Louvain, was one of the first commentators to call specific attention to the distinction between public impediments and private impediments.[5] It is most important to understand that this division of impediments into public and private is not to be equated or confused with the distinction between public and occult impediments.[52] The distinction between public and occult impediments was made *ratione notitiae.* The distinction between public and private impediments was made *ratione praesertim iuris accusandi vinculum matrimoniale.*

Ratione notitiae, those impediments were designated public which either *natura sua* were considered public because they were based on a *facto de se publico,* or which, because of the circumstances, were truly notorious, or which, at least, were known by many people, so that there was probable danger of divulgation and possible proof in the external forum.[53] The impediments which, under this aspect, were understood to be *publica natura sua* were *consanguinitas, affinitas ex copula licita, cognatio spiritualis et legalis, disparitas cultus, ordo sacer, votum solemne, honestas publica saltem ex matrimonio rato in facie Ecclesiae contracto aut ex sponsalibus publicis.*[54] In the event

[51] Feije, *De Impedimentis et Dispensationibus Matrimonialibus* (3. ed., New York, Benziger, 1885), nn. 85, 584 (hereafter cited as *De Impedimentis*).

[52] Feije, *loc. cit.;* Gasparri, *De Matrimonio* (ed. 1891), n. 251; Wernz, *Jus Decretalium,* IV, n. 216.

[53] "Ratione notitiae. . . . Publica dicuntur, quae aut sua natura pro publicis habentur, quia nituntur facto de se publico, aut propter circumstantias sunt vere notoria vel famosa, aut saltem a tot personis cognoscuntur, ut probabile sit periculum divulgationis atque possibilis probatio in foro externo."—Wernz, *Jus Decretalium,* IV, n. 216; cf. Gasparri, *De Matrimonio* (ed. 1891), n. 251.

[54] Wernz, *Jus Decretalium,* IV, n. 216, footnote n. 9.

that these impediments were, as a matter of fact, unknown, they were to be considered as *natura publica et de facto occulta,* but were still to be treated as public impediments.[55] Occult impediments, on the other hand, were those which were known by no one or by just a few persons, or which were easily able to be concealed and could not be proved in the external forum.[56]

Ratione juris accusandi, those impediments were *juris publici* which had as their end the sanctity of the Sacrament of Matrimony, the purity of Christian marriage, and the preservation of the common good. Among the impediments of public right were *impubertas, defectus aptitudinis ad consentiendum, disparitas cultus, ligamen, ordo sacer, et votum solemne, crimen, raptus, cognatio naturalis et spiritualis et legalis, consanguinitas, affinitas, et publica honestas.*[57] Because such impediments related directly to the good of the Church and to society as well, the right of accusing a marriage invalid by force of such a public impediment was in no way reserved to the spouses but extended to the ecclesiastical judge or to the *promotor fiscalis,*[58] *ex officio,* and

[55] ". . . notandum nonnulla impedimenta esse natura publica, quae scilicet resultant ex facto de se publico, idest impedimentum consanguinitatis, affinitatis ex copula licita, cognationis legalis et spiritualis, disparitatis cultus, Ordinis Sacri, voti solemnis, honestatis publicae *saltem* ex matrimonio in facie Ecclesiae inito et ex sponsalibus publicis. Igitur si haec impedimenta de facto ignota sunt, erunt natura publica, et de facto occulta, sed habentur uti publica."—Gasparri, *De Matrimonio* (ed. 1891), n. 252.

[56] Aichner, *Compendium Juris Ecclesiastici,* p. 569; Feije, *De Impedimentis,* n. 584.

[57] Aichner, *Compendium Juris Ecclesiastici,* pp. 570-578. Feije identified the impediments of public right as all those which were not of private right.—*De Impedimentis,* n. 85.

[58] In compliance with the decree *Cum Magnopere* of the Congregation for the Propagation of the Faith in 1883, the III Plenary Council of Baltimore established and defined the office of the Promotor Fiscalis, as it was to be practised in the curias of the United States. The Council thus stated: "Procurator Fiscalis (qui etiam Promotor et Advocatus Fiscalis nominatur) ab Episcopo constituatur, 'ut justitiae et legi satisfiat' (a. III). Generale igitur ejus officium est, justitiam et legem tueri, ne violentur; si vero violatae sint, vindicare. Itaque quando earum violationem quoque modo compererit, apud Episcopum instabit, ut inquisitio

to any Catholic who was capable of accusing marriage. Those impediments were *juris privati* which were principally but not exclusively constituted *ob privatum utilitatem*. Marriages that were contracted invalidly because of the existence of such an impediment could be accused, as a rule, only at the instance of the contracting parties themselves and could not be attacked by the *promotor fiscalis, ex officio.* Of private right were the *impedimenta erroris substantialis personae vel conditionis servilis, vis et metus, defectus conditionis appositae, et impotentiae occultae.*[59]

This distinction between *impedimenta publica et impedimenta privata ratione juris accusandi,* which Feije described as originating "*ab aliquibus, praesertim recentioribus in Germania,*" was rejected as unsound by Feije.[60] The principal objection of Feije was directed toward the concept of impediments of private right. No impediment, he argued, was constituted solely for the good of the individual. Moreover, rights possessed by an individual for his own good were capable of being renounced. But a renunciation of a right to accuse an invalid marriage in order to continue fulfilling the duties of conjugal life was inconceivable. Renunciation of a private right would extend only insofar as the party did not seek a declaration of nullity, or was willing to live as brother and sister or convalidated the marriage by his own will and consent. And even such renunciation could not be done at times. Hence, Feije concluded, the foundation was not that which was assigned to it. He did admit, however, that impediments were "private" to this extent, that in some cases, persons other than the spouses were not able to accuse a marriage because they were not in a position to know of the impediment or, at least, they were not able to know whether the parties,

---

instituatur, et si opus fuerit, judicialiter in inquisitum procedatur."—*Acta et Decreta Concilii Plenarii Baltimorensis Tertii,* A.D. MDCCCLXXXIV, n. 301; cf. *Fontes,* VII, n. 4900.

[59] Wernz, *Jus Decretalium,* IV, n. 216; Feije, *De Impedimentis,* n. 85; Aichner, *Compendium Juris Ecclesiastici,* p. 569.

[60] Feije, *De Impedimentis,* n. 85. "Quae divisio a compluribus recentioribus adoptata sane etiam sensum sinistrum admittit, qui utique non est probandus."—Wernz, *Jus Decretalium,* n. 216, footnote n. 12.

who entered the nuptial union invalidly, had validated it by a renewal of consent.[61]

It is submitted here that this distinction between impediments of public and private right, allegedly introduced by German canonists in the nineteenth century, was not an entirely new concept, but rather a new manner of expressing a division of impediments *ratione iuris accusandi* made by the seventeenth and eighteenth century authors. It will be recalled that the impediments of occult impotence,[62] force, fear, error, and condition, which were characterized as of "private right" in the ninteenth century, were the same as those which in the seventeenth century were regarded as "temporary" in nature. Regardless of the terms employed to describe the classification, the effect was the same, namely, the right to accuse marriage was restricted to the spouses if the impediments of occult impotence, force, fear, error, or condition were involved.

Thus, it is of interest to note that the observation of Feije regarding the proper understanding of the term "private" contains the same reasoning employed by the earlier canonists for restricting the right of accusation to the spouses. Gonzalez-Tellez and Reiffenstuel, for example, made no mention of distinction between impediments that were directed toward the private good of individuals and those which were intended to protect the public good. But these authors did point to the private right of the spouses to accuse a marriage invalid by impediments which the spouses themselves were capable of removing. In this sense, the impediments of impotence,[63] force, fear, error, and condition

[61] "Sed res tota sita est in eo, quod alii ne possint quidem accusare matrimonium, quia aut scire impedimentum nequeunt, aut saltem scire non possunt an is qui sic nuptias inivit, sua voluntate eas non validaverit." —Feije, *De Impedimentis*, n. 85.

[62] In the seventeenth and eighteenth centuries, the right to accuse a marriage invalid because of the impediment of occult impotence was restricted to the spouses not because it was temporary in character or because the impediment was capable of removal by the spouses themselves, but rather because of its intimate and private nature and the fact that the parties could conceivably yield their right to accuse their marriage and live together as brother and sister. Cf. *supra*, p. 19.

[63] Cf. *supra*, p. 19.

were "private," that is, the right to accuse a marriage because of the existence of such impediments was reserved to the spouses. All other impediments were "public," that is, the right to accuse a marriage because of such impediments could be exercised by the public at large.

The distinction between impediments of public right and private right did, however, indirectly introduce a new element into the law of the right to accuse marriage, the significance of which can be seen in paragraph 122 of the Austrian Instruction. It should be remembered that neither the Decretals of Gregory IX nor the writings of the decretalists up to the eighteenth century placed any restriction on the right of the Bishop or the ecclesiastical judge, *ex officio,* to attack a marriage invalidly contracted with an impediment that was publicly known. In decretal law and especially in the writings of Reiffenstuel, the consideration of the right of the ecclesiastical judge, *ex officio,* to attack a marriage was distinct from that of the right of the spouses and of the right of the public in general. In other words, the distinction between the private right of the spouses and the right of anyone else other than the spouses was based on whether or not the spouses themselves were capable of removing the impediment by a mere renewal of consent.[64] On the other hand, the right of the Bishop or ecclesiastical judge, *ex officio,* to accuse a marriage was governed by an entirely separate norm, namely, the notoriety of the impediment involved.[65] However, paragraph 122 of the Austrian Instruction represented a departure from the decretal law and jurisprudence insofar as it restricted the right of the ecclesiastical tribunal to proceed *ex officio* to cases which were not of private right. And in cases which were of public right, the element of notoriety was not a controlling factor, for paragraph 122 prescribed that the tribunal *ex officio* was to intervene also in cases in which denunciations were made or when any other sufficient reason was afforded to the tribunal to act. Wernz, it may be noted, quoted paragraph 122 *verbatim*

[64] Cf. *supra,* pp. 32-33.

[65] Only in the writings of Gonzalez-Tellez does one find that the demands of the common good also provided the occasion for the matrimonial tribunal to intervene *ex officio.* Cf. Lib. IV, tit. 19, n. 2, *supra,* p. 34.

in his outline of the common law of the right to accuse marriage just prior to the promulgation of the Code.

Article 3. The Instruction of the Sacred Congregation for the Propagation of the Faith in 1883

The Instruction *Causae Matrimoniales* of the Sacred Congregation for the Propagation of the Faith, issued in 1883, encompassed the Constitution *Dei Miseratione* of Pope Benedict XIV of 1741 and the Instruction *Cum Moneat Glossa* of the Sacred Congregation of the Council in 1840, and therefore constituted a résumé of the general law of the Church on matrimonial causes in the mid-nineteenth century. Two of the forty-seven paragraphs that comprised this Instruction were devoted to the right to accuse marriage. These paragraphs represented the first pieces of general legislation on the accusation of marriage since the promulgation of the Decretals of Gregory IX in 1234.

The Instruction first undertook to establish that before a matrimonial cause could be accepted by an ecclesiastical tribunal, there must precede a regular and juridic accusation by a person or persons who were considered capable of accusing according to the rules of common law.[66] The Instruction then intimated that the capacity of a person to accuse a marriage was related to the nature of the impediment which invalidated the marriage.[67] For in some impediments, only the spouses themselves were admitted as accusers. In others, they were admitted who were related to the parties by blood. At times, "*quilibet de populo*" would also be admitted to accuse.[68] Finally, an *ex officio* investigation could be made, and at times, should be made, especially when a simple denunciation had been made against the validity of the matrimonial bond, or when a public report,

[66] "Ut in tribunali ecclesiastico causa aliqua matrimonialis tractanda suscipiatur, necesse est ut contra matrimonium regularis et iuridica accusatio praecesserit; quae numquam erit admittenda, nisi proficiscatur a persona vel personis, quae communi iure habiles ad accusandum habeantur."—*Fontes,* VII, n. 4901, § 3.

[67] *Supra,* p. 32.

[68] "Etenim in quibusdam impedimentis ipsi coniuges tantum uti accusatores admittuntur; in aliis, qui sunt iisdem sanguine propinqui, vel etiam quilibet de populo . . ."—*Fontes, loc. cit.*

which contained a foundation of truth, had revealed the existence of some impediment.[69]

Having cited the rules which were to govern the procedure of adjudicating matrimonial causes in general, the Instruction then presented the particular norms that applied to individual cases, depending upon the nature of the impediment involved. Mention was made of the right to accuse marriage in relation to three impediments only, namely, the impediments of force, fear, and impotence. Thus, the Instruction asserted that only the party who suffered the force or fear was permitted to accuse. And only the spouses could accuse a marriage on the grounds of impotence because the fact of impotence was known by them alone and because the spouses alone had the duty to do something about it.[70]

It is apparent that the directives given by the Instruction of 1883 were rather generic in character. Thus, no attempt was made to specify the impediments in which the right of the spouses to accuse could be exercised as opposed to those in which anyone possessed this right. Only when the impediments of impotence, force, and fear were treated by the Instruction was an incidental mention made of the exclusive right of the spouses. Moreover, the loss of right of the guilty party was noted only in relation to the impediment of force and fear. Hence, it may be stated that it was not the purpose of this Instruction to delineate an exhaustive and definitive digest of rules governing the right to accuse marriage.

Article 4. Summary

Since no further canonical contribution of any notable significance was made to the concept of the right to impugn a mar-

69 ". . . ac tandem ex officio etiam inquisitio fieri potest, et quandoque debet, quando praesertim contra alicuius matrimonii validitatem simplex denunciatio facta fuerit, aut fama fundamentum veritatis praeseferens de alicuius impedimenti existentia divulgata sit."—*Fontes, loc. cit.*

70 ". . . . neminem a iure admitti ad matrimonium ex hoc capite impugnandum nisi qui violentiam et coactionem passus dicitur. . . . Ad impugnandum ex capite impotentiae matrimonium solummodo coniuges admittuntur, quia ipsis solummodo hoc factum cognitum esse potest et ipsi tantummodo de hac re solliciti esse debent."—*Fontes,* n. 4901, §§ 36, 46.

riage other than the observations of those authors who wrote subsequent to the Austrian Instruction of 1855, and who have been cited above, a final summary can be made of the entire development of the *jus accusandi matrimonium* prior to the Code of Canon Law promulgated in 1917, as explained in the previous pages.

The right to accuse a marriage was possessed by every Catholic, except in those cases in which the impediment was that of occult impotence, or in which the impediment was such that the parties themselves were capable of removing the impediment and renewing consent, or in which it could not be determined whether the parties themselves had convalidated the marriage by a renewal of consent, that is, if such consent was permitted without the Tridentine form. In these excepted cases, the right of accusation was restricted to the spouses. In cases in which the spouses themselves enjoyed the exclusive right of accusation, only the innocent spouse was permitted to accuse. In all cases and for all impediments concerning which the right to accuse was not restricted to the spouses, the ecclesiastical tribunal *ex officio* impugned the marriage when the fact of the impediment was notorious, or when simple denunciations had been made, or when, in some other way, a sufficient reason was afforded to the tribunal to act.

PART TWO

CANONICAL COMMENTARY

CHAPTER IV

THE ACCUSATION OF A MARRIAGE

SECTION I. THE CONCEPT OF AN ACCUSATION OF A MARRIAGE

Article 1. The Definition of an Accusation

Before undertaking a study of the right to accuse a marriage as null, it will be necessary first to determine what is meant by the term "accusation." Regatillo and Bartoccetti define an accusation of nullity as a petition, made according to law, for a declaration of nullity.[1] DeSmet, Vlaming and Sipos hold that to accuse a marriage is to set forth to a judge a cause to be acted upon and to vindicate a right.[2] Cappello states that to accuse a marriage is to institute a judicial action or to exercise the right of acting before a competent tribunal in order to obtain a declaration of nullity or to secure a separation.[3] Marquardt defines an accusation as that act by which a person proposes to a competent tribunal facts pointing to the nullity of a marriage

[1] Regatillo, *Institutiones Iuris Canonici* (2 vols., Santander: Sal Terrae, 1941-1942), II, n. 750; Lega, *Commentarius in Iudicia Ecclesiastica iuxta Codicem Iuris Canonici* (2. ed., 3 vols., ed. V. Bartoccetti, Romae: Azienda Libraria Cattolica Italiana, 1950), III, 73* (hereafter cited Lega [ed. Bart.] *Iudicia Ecclesiastica*).

[2] DeSmet, *De Sponsalibus et Matrimonio* (4. ed., Brugis: Carolus Beyaert, 1927), n. 203; Vlaming, *Praelectiones Iuris Matrimonii* (4. ed., Bussum, Holland: Paulus Brand, 1950), p. 544; Sipos, *Enchiridion Iuris Canonici* (6. ed., Romae: Herder, 1954), p. 785; cf. Noval, *Commentarium Codicis Iuris Canonici*, Liber IV, *De Processibus*, Pars, I, *De Judiciis* (Augustae Taurinorum-Romae: Marietti, 1920), n. 294 (hereafter cited Noval, *De Judiciis*).

[3] Cappello, *Summa Iuris Canonici* (3 vols., Romae: Apud Aedes Universitatis Gregorianae, 1940), II, n. 342; Coronata, *Institutiones Iuris Canonici* (4 vols., Vols. I-III, 4. ed., Vol. IV, 3. ed., Romae: Marietti, 1950-1956), III, n. 1485; Vermeersch-Creusen, *Epitome Iuris Canonici* (3 vols., Vol. I, 7. ed., 1949; Vol. II, 6. ed., 1940; Vol. III, 6. ed., 1946, Mechlinae-Romae: H. Dessain), III, n. 286; Roberti, "De Iure Denuntiandi Nullitatem Matrimonii," *Apollinaris*, III (1930), 249.

and invokes the ministry of that tribunal to declare the nullity. According to Marquardt, an accusation of marriage is an extrajudicial, not a judicial act, because at the time when the accusation is made, the tribunal is not yet completely constituted and the trial has not yet begun.[4]

The definition as represented by Cappello seems to be essentially correct. Certainly, it must be held that an accusation is a judicial, procedural act, at least to the extent that the tribunal, after the presentation of the *libellus* in which the accusation is framed, is bound to proceed further and either admit or reject the plaintiff and the *libellus*.[5] The nature of an act is determined by its inherent purpose. The purpose of an accusation is to place before a tribunal an action to be exercised in the prosecution of a right. According to the clear language of Canon 1706, such an act is one of judicial procedure. Canon 1706 states that to institute an action, the plaintiff must present to the competent judge a bill of complaint in which the object of the controversy is exposed, and the service of the judge is invoked for the obtaining of the rights which he claims. In other words, even though it is true that at the time when the accusation is made, the tribunal is not yet constituted, and that the trial has not yet begun, the accusation should not be viewed merely as an extrajudicial or administrative act by the petitioner. For at the very moment when the accusation is presented to the collegiate tribunal, a judicial relationship arises, initiated by the act of accusation, which is clearly governed by laws of judicial, not of administrative procedure. These laws are carefully outlined in Canons 1609, § 2, 1646, 1706-1710, 1892, 2°, and 1970.[6]

Article 2. The Distinction between an Accusation and an Action

To grasp more clearly the concept of an accusation, it would be well to understand the relationship that exists between an

[4] Marquardt, *The Loss of Right to Accuse a Marriage*, pp. 53-54.

[5] Canons 1609, § 2, 1709, § 1; cf. S. C. de Sacramentis, *Instructio servanda a tribunalibus dioecesanis in pertractandis causis de nullitate matrimoniorum*, 15 aug., 1936.—AAS, XXVIII (1936), 313-361 at Art. 34 (hereafter cited Instr. *Provida*).

[6] Cf. Instr. *Provida*, Art. 13, 34, 55-67, 207; cf. *infra*, pp. 64-67; 72-74.

accusation and an action. In its technical, juridical sense, action was defined by the Emperor Justinian (527-565) as the right of pursuing in trial that which is one's due. This definition was derived from that of the Roman jurist, Celsus[7] who had asserted: *"Nihil aliud est actio, quam jus quod sibi debeatur, iudicio persequendi."*[8] The definition presented by Justinian has been adopted by canonists today. The common definition of action offered by canonists is the right of pursuing in trial that which is ours or that which is due to us.[9] Perhaps the notion of action is best understood if viewed as a judicial prosecution recognized by positive law of a substantive right which is controverted, violated, or in danger of being violated. Rights are certain to be abused or even doomed to extinction if they are without juridical protection. The faculty of invoking such protection in favor of a controverted substantive right is rooted in the principles of the natural law. In the ordinary course of human events, the private vindication of rights by force is not permitted, except for cases of legitimate self-defense or emergency. Hence, it is necessary that public authority assure the exercise of the rights of individuals by affording to them a judicial remedy whereby the object of the substantive right may be secured.[10] As a rule, all rights are protected by positive law.[11] But rights can and do exist without actions, especially if the law does not protect them juridically. Canon 1017 states that even though a promise of marriage is valid and even though there is no just reason to excuse the non-fulfillment of the promise, neither party has the right of action to force the other to contract the marriage. Conversely, not every action has a cor-

[7] Celsus was a prominent jurist during the first decades of the second century after Christ.

[8] D. (44.7) 51.

[9] Regatillo, *Institutiones Iuris Canonici*, II, n. 452; Coronata, *Institutiones Iuris Canonici*, 4. ed., III, n. 1192; Noval, *De Judiciis*, n. 294.

[10] Wernz-Vidal, *Ius Canonicum* (7 vols. in 8, Vol. I, 2. ed., 1951; Vol. II, 3. ed. a P. Aguirre recognita, 1943; Vol. III, 1933; Vol. IV, pars 1, 1934, pars 2, 1935; Vol. V., 3. ed. a P. Aguirre recognita, 1946; Vol. VI, 2. ed. a F. Cappello, 1949; Vol. VII, 2. ed. 1951, Romae: Apud Aedes Universitatis Gregorianae), VI, n. 244.

[11] Canon 1667.

responding objective substantive right. For one who truly doubts the validity of his marriage because of defect of consent has an action which does not correspond to an objective right if the consent was actually present.[12]

It will be found that some authors identify the term action with both the right to seek in trial that which is one's due and the actual exercise of this right.[13] The first is termed *in actu primo;* the latter, *in actu secundo.* Marquardt feels that the actual exercise of the action is better designated as the "instance" of the case, which begins with the joining of the issue and concludes with the passing of the judicial sentence.[14] It would seem that this opinion is not in accord with the prescription of Canon 1725, 2°, namely, that when the defendant has been legitimately summoned, or when the parties, of their own accord, have appeared in court, the case has become proper to the judge before whom the action has begun. Clearly, the Code itself implies here that the exercise of the action does not begin with the joining of issues, but at the moment when the regular accusation or legitimately framed petition is presented to the judge. Hence, the relationship between the action and the accusation should now be apparent. The accusation is the medium through which the action is instituted.[15] It is the first act of the exercise of the right of action.

Canon 1667 states that every right can be enforced by an ac-

[12] Whether there is a real distinction between action and the controverted right is disputed by authors. The more common and more sound opinion affirms a real distinction. Action differs from the controverted right in the same manner as a defender differs from that which he defends. Cf. Coronata, *Institutiones Iuris Canonici*, 4. ed., III, n. 1192; Regatillo, *Institutiones Iuris Canonici*, III, n. 456; Vermeersch-Creusen, *Epitome Iuris Canonici*, 6. ed., III, n. 86; Roberti, *De Processibus* (4. ed., Romae: Apud Custodiam Librariam Pontificii Instistuti Utriusque Iuris, 1956), nn. 28-29.

[13] Vermeersch-Creusen, *Epitome Iuris Canonici*, 6. ed., III, n. 87; Cappello, *Summa Iuris Canonici*, III, n. 342.

[14] Canon 1732. Cf. Marquardt, *The Loss of Right to Accuse a Marriage*, p. 54.

[15] Torre, *Processus Matrimonialis* (3. ed., Neapoli: M. D'Auria, Pontificus Editor, 1956), p. 75; cf. Instr. *Provida*, Art. 55, §§ 1, 2.

tion in court, unless the law expressly provides otherwise. It must be remembered, however, that it is only through the medium of a legitimate accusation that judicial action can be exercised. Thus, Canon 1970 states that the collegiate tribunal cannot try or decide any marriage case, unless a regular accusation or legitimately made petition has preceded.[16]

Article 3. The Distinction between a Regular Accusation and a Legal Petition

Much has been written on the meaning of the expressions *regularis accusatio* and *iure facta petitio.*[17] Generally speaking, four different opinions are presented by the authors. The majority of commentators hold that the term "regular accusation" refers to the presentation of a cause to a judge in order to vindicate a right. On the other hand, the term "legal petition" refers to the seeking of a favor, specifically, the dissolution of a ratified, non-consummated marriage.[18] For the most part, the authors make no effort to substantiate this opinion. Cappello holds that this opinion is demanded by the wording of Canon 1970 which distinguishes between accusation and petition not by reason of form but by reason of object.[19] Beste and Wernz-Vidal state that an accusation obtains when one party attacks the validity of a marriage against the consent of the other party. But if a declaration of nullity is sought by both parties, there is present a legal petition. Neither author gives a reason for the

[16] Canon 1970.—Tribunal collegiale nullam causam matrimonialem cognoscere vel definiri potest, nisi regularis accusatio vel iure facta petitio praecesserit.

[17] Canon 1970.

[18] DeSmet, *De Sponsalibus et Matrimonio*, 4. ed., n. 703; Noval, *De Judiciis*, n. 849; Cappello, *Tractatus Canonico-Moralis de Sacramentis* (5 vols., Vol. V, *De Matrimonio*, 5. ed., Romae: Marietti, 1947), n. 878 (hereafter cited *De Matrimonio*); Vlaming, *Praelectiones Iuris Matrimonii*, 4. ed., p. 544; Sipos, *Enchiridion Iuris Canonici*, 6. ed., p. 785; Doheny, *Canonical Procedure in Matrimonial Cases* (2 vols., Vol. I, *Formal Judicial Procedure*, 2. ed., 1948; Vol. II, *Informal Procedure*, 2. printing, 1948; Milwaukee: Bruce Publ. Co.), I, p. 105 (hereafter cited *Canonical Procedure*).

[19] Cappello, *De Matrimonio*, 5. ed., n. 878.

support of this opinion.[20] Marquardt thinks that the term, legal petition, is used in appositive or complementary sense, and is simply an explanation of the expression, regular accusation. For Marquardt, a legal petition is simply a more generic term than that of a regular accusation. He holds that the term, petition, is used in Article 57, 2° and 3°, and in Article 87 of the Instruction *Provida,* as a synonym for the term accusation.[21] Torre affirms that for an accusation to be regular, it is necessary that the petition be made according to law.[22] For Torre, a regular accusation is one that is made in writing, according to Canon 1706. Moreover, Canon 1707 provides that if the plaintiff does not know how to write or is legitimately impeded from presenting a written complaint, he may make an *oretenus petitionem* in court. Torre submits that Canon 1970 should be interpreted in the light of Canons 1706 and 1707. Canon 1970 deals with the introduction of matrimonial causes. Canon 1706 and 1707 treat the introduction of causes in general. A regular accusation is one executed according to Canon 1706. A petition made according to law is one provided for by Canon 1707.[23] The writer submits that none of these opinions appears to be totally satisfactory.

The first suggestion, namely, that "regular accusation" refers to a vindication of a right and "legal petition" refers to the seeking of the dissolution of a ratified, non-consummated marriage can be called into question. Canon 1970 speaks in terms of a collegiate tribunal, whereas Canon 1966 states that only one judge is to take the evidence for a dispensation from a ratified, non-consummated marriage. Again, it would seem that since the Instruction *Provida Mater* deals only with causes of the nullity of marriage, the Sacred Congregation for the Discipline of the Sacraments would have deleted "*iure facta petitio*" found

[20] Beste, *Introductio in Codicem* (4. ed., Collegeville, Minnesota: St. John's Abbey Press, 1956), p. 922; Wernz-Vidal, *Ius Canonicum*, V, 3. ed., 1946, n. 698.

[21] Marquardt, *The Loss of Right to Accuse a Marriage*, p. 58.

[22] Torre, *Processus Matrimonialis*, 3. ed., p. 73.

[23] Torre, *loc. cit.*

in Article 34 if this expression referred to a cause of non-consummation.[24]

The opinion that the distinction between accusation and petition is based on whether or not the consent of both parties is present does not appear to be justified, because an accusation is directed against the bond, not against the opposing spouse. Moreover, Canon 1971, § 1, 1° and Article 35 of the *Provida* state explicitly that: "*Habiles ad accusandum* (*sic*) *coniuges. . . .*"[25]

The view that "legal petition" is simply used in apposition to "regular accusation" has merit, but is not in accord with the normal economy of words used by the Code. Moreover, from the clear language of the words themselves, there is indicated a difference between their formal objects.

The opinion of Torre is not to be dismissed too hastily. Yet, Articles 57, §§ 2, 3 and Article 87 of the Instruction *Provida* which use the term "petitio" make no suggestion whatsoever that an oral accusation has been made.[26]

The writer submits that Canon 1970 should be interpreted in the light of Canon 1552, § 2, 1° which treats of the subject matter of canonical trials. Here it is stated that the subject matter of a canonical trial consists in the prosecution or vindication of the rights of physical or moral persons, or the declaration of the juridic facts concerning such persons. Thus, the "regular accusation" has for its object the prosecution or vindication of a right. A "legal petition" has for its object the declaration of a juridic fact by the tribunal. One accuses his marriage of nullity in order to vindicate a right that one has to a valid marriage. One petitions the tribunal in order that a juridic fact (e.g., baptism, freedom to marry) be declared by the Church. This

[24] Article 34 of the Instruction *Provida* repeats word for word the prescription of Canon 1970.

[25] Cf. Instr. *Provida*, Art. 113, §§ 1, 2.

[26] ". . . indicetur petitio; nempe ut matrimonium declaretur nullum . . ."; ". . . sufficit ut appareat haud temere fuisse petitionem exhibitam . . ."; ". . . litis contestatione, seu formali conventi contradictione petitioni actoris, facta animo litigandi coram iudice."

opinion is in harmony with the observation of Cappello that the distinction between the terms accusation and petition is made by reason of object, not of form. This opinion explains the use of the term, collegiate tribunal, in Canon 1970. This opinion clarifies the inclusion of the term, *iure facta petitio,* in Article 34 of the *Provida.* And finally, this opinion is not out of harmony with Article 57, 2° and 3°, and Article 87 of the *Provida.*

SECTION II. THE CONCEPT OF THE RIGHT TO ACCUSE A MARRIAGE

Article 1. The Definition of the Right to Accuse a Marriage

In Article 2 of the preceding section, it was demonstrated that an accusation is the medium through which a judicial action is instituted. The exercise of a judicial action is not absolute. Only he can prosecute his case in court and exercise his action in defense of a right who is recognized by law as having the right to stand in court. Canon 1609, § 2 cites the obligation of the judge or the tribunal not only to investigate its competency but also to determine whether the plaintiff *in iudicio possit iure consistere.* The right to accuse a marriage, then, is the right to institute an action concerning the nullity of a marriage or the separation from a spouse, by means of the placing of the first act of judicial procedure before a competent tribunal.[27] One is able to bring a suit into court or to institute a judicial action only insofar as one has a legitimate right to stand in trial. Thus, the right to accuse a marriage is the right to stand in trial to place the first act of judicial procedure relating to a matrimonial cause.

Article 2. The Distinction between the Right to Accuse a Marriage and an Action

The right to accuse is really distinct from an action which is the faculty recognized by positive law to protect a substantive right in court. Since some authors [28] have adopted the terminology employed by Roberti when speaking of actions and accusa-

[27] Cappello, "Annotationes," *Periodica,* XXXV (1946), 195-198. Cf. Roberti, "De Jure Denuntiandi Nullitatem Matrimonii," *Apollinaris,* III (1930), 248-250.

[28] *Infra,* p. 66, note 33.

tions, the following is a list of some of the terms used by Roberti and the definitions he has given to them: *subjectum legis*, i.e., the general juridic capacity by which one is constituted a subject of ecclesiastical law; *capacitas partis*, i.e., the procedural juridic capacity by which one is constituted a subject as regards procedural law; *legitimatio ad processum*, i.e., the capacity to exercise one's rights and actions in judicial procedure; *legitimatio ad causam*, i.e., the right to action in some particular case.[29] One can be deprived of the right to accuse a marriage and yet retain an action. The deprivation of the right to accuse prevents the action from being exercised. An action is a faculty which is derived according to the principles of the natural law from a substantive right and which is recognized by public, positive law. This faculty embraces the juridical power to seek in court that which is one's due. But the exercise of this faculty depends upon one's juridical capacity to stand in court, the requirements for which are determined by the same public law which recognizes a judicial action. Thus, for example, one who has incurred the penalty of Canon 1971, § 1, 1° and who is thereby deprived of the right of accusation, still retains an action or the right to defend a controverted, substantive right. But he may not exercise that right because, by a positive disposition of law, he has been rendered incapable of placing before the court a regular accusation, the medium through which the action is instituted.[30]

In summary, Canon 87 establishes the general juridic capacity of all those who are validly baptized by which they are constituted as subjects of ecclesiastical law.[31] Canon 1667 confirms the judicial capacity of a baptized person to enforce his rights in court, unless the contrary is explicitly stated elsewhere in the law.[32] Canon 1646 gives to the baptized person the right to

[29] Roberti, *De Processibus*, 4. ed., nn. 215, 240. The earlier editions also include the above definitions.

[30] Canons 1971, 1972; Instr. *Provida*, Art. 55, § 1.

[31] Baptismate homo constituitur in Ecclesia Christi persona cum omnibus christianorum iuribus et officiis, nisi, ad iura quod attinet, obstet obex, ecclesiasticae communionis vinculum impediens, vel lata ab Ecclesia censura.

[32] Quodlibet ius non solum actione munitur, nisi aliud expresse cautum

exercise his judicial juridic capacity provided that he is not prohibited by the sacred canons.[33] The right of a person to exercise his judicial juridic capacity is also expressed as the right to stand in judgment or the right to exercise an action. In the Code of Canon Law, this juridic capacity or right is described not only as *potest in iudicio agere* (Canon 1646) but also in such terms as *is in iudicio possit iure consistere* (Canon 1609, § 2) and *legitimam personam esse standi in iudicio* (Canon 1709, § 1).[34]

It should be inserted here that it does not seem accurate to suggest that either the right to accuse or the *jus standi in iudicio* is immediately derived from Canon 87. It is true that Canon 87 recognizes one who is validly baptized as a *persona juridica.* But the right of this person to stand in judgment is derived from and qualified by Canon 1646.[35] This specification is indicated clearly by the Rota as regards matrimonial causes. On July 15, 1941, the Rota stated that the capacity of any *actor* to accuse

sit, sed etiam exceptione, quae semper competit et est suapte natura perpetua.

[33] Quilibet potest in iudicio agere, nisi a sacris canonibus prohibeatur . . . This capacity granted by Canon 1646 is also referred to by Roberti as the procedural capacity of a person or the *legitimatio ad processum.* Cf. *De Processibus,* 4. ed., nn. 215, 240. Authors also speak of a *legitimatio ad causam* or the capacity to exercise an action in a particular case. Cf. Cappello, "Annotationes," *Periodica,* XXXV (1946), 196; Doheny, *Canonical Procedure,* 2. ed., p. 129. The *legitimatio ad causam* is said to be the relation of a person to a determined cause and the condition that must be verified before an action can be prosecuted. Authors do not agree whether the notion *legitimatio ad causam* is really distinct from the *legitimatio ad processum* granted in Canon 1646. Cf. Hanssen, "De sanctione nullitatis in processu canonico," *Apollinaris,* XI (1938), 255; Cappello, "art. cit.," *Periodica,* XXXV (1946), 196; Roberti, *De Processibus,* 4. ed., n. 250; Conway, "Matrimonial Processes: Culpable Spouse," *The Irish Ecclesiastical Record,* LXIX (1947), 54-55.

[34] It is important to keep clearly distinguished the right to exercise an action and the exercise of the action itself. This distinction is exemplified in Canon 1609, § 2; "Eodemque modo antequam aliquem ad agendum (the exercise of the action) admittat, cognoscere tenetur num is in iudicio possit iure consistere (the right to exercise an action or the right to stand in judgment).

[35] Cf. Canon 1654, § 2.

is verified at least with solid probability if the *actor* can vindicate for himself his right of standing in judgment according to Canon 1646.[36] Canon 1971 represents a specific application of Canon 1646. Paragraph one of Canon 1971 defines precisely who is permitted and who is prohibited the exercise of procedural capacity to accuse a marriage before a competent tribunal. It is this capacity to institute an action concerning the nullity of a marriage that is properly termed the right to accuse a marriage.

Article 3. The Right to Accuse a Marriage and the Right to Stand in Judgment

Directly related to the topic under discussion is a reply of the Pontifical Commission for the Authentic Interpretation of the Code issued on January 4, 1946. The question proposed to the Code Commission was: "Whether the inability of a spouse to accuse a marriage according to the prescription of Canon 1971, § 1, 1° carries with it the incapacity to stand in judgment so that the sentence is vitiated by irremediable nullity according to canon 1892, 2°." The Code Commission answered: "In the negative." [37]

Attention is given here to two controverted questions relating to this reply. First, it may be asked, what is the relationship between the right of a spouse to accuse a marriage and the right of a spouse to stand in judgment? Second, what is the relationship between the juridic inability of a spouse to accuse a marriage and the juridic incapacity of a spouse to stand in judgment? In answer to the first question, two opinions are put forth by authors.

The first opinion is that the right to accuse marriage is the

[36] S.R.R. *Decisiones*, XXXIII (1941), p. 620, n. 2.

[37] "An inhabilitas coniugis ad accusandum matrimonium, a canone 1971, § 1, 1°, statuta, secumferat incapacitatem standi in iudicio, ita ut sententia vitio insanabilis nullitatis laboret iuxta canonem 1892, 2°." R. "Negative." —Pont. Comm., 4 Jan., 1946, AAS, XXXVIII (1946), 162.

Can. 1971, § 1, 1°—Habiles ad accusandum sunt: Coniuges in omnibus causis separationis et nullitatis, nisi ipsi fuerint impedimenti causa.

Can. 1892, 2°—Sententia vitio insanabilis nullitatis laborat, quando: Lata est inter partes, quarum altera saltem non habet personam standi in iudicio.

right to stand in judgment to institute an action relating to the nullity of marriage. The second opinion is that the right to accuse marriage is not the right to stand in judgment to introduce an action relating to the nullity of marriage. Rather, the right to accuse marriage is the right to propose a cause concerning the nullity of marriage to a competent tribunal and to request the tribunal to judge the cause and to declare the marriage null. The first opinion holds that an accusation of marriage is a judicial procedural act, that is, an act by means of which a person who has the right to stand in judgment introduces an action relating to the nullity of marriage. The second opinion holds that an accusation of marriage is an extrajudicial act, that is, an act which is preliminary to the exercise of an action in court, by means of which the court is requested to judge the cause and to declare the marriage null.

The following are the observations made by some of the authors who hold that an accusation is a judicial procedural act by means of which a person exercising the right to stand in judgment institutes an action to obtain a declaration of the nullity of a marriage.

Roberti asserts that an accusation is a strictly judicial act, because an accusation is the placing of an action in a judicial process. An accusation, according to Roberti, supposes that the accuser has a right to stand in court because he who proposes an action becomes an *actor*. As an *actor*, a person assumes the burden of proof and all other obligations which fall to a party to a trial.[38]

Sipos also asserts that an accusation institutes a judicial action.[39] According to Sipos, to accuse a marriage one must possess a juridic and procedural capacity. He defines the latter as the *"capacitatem per se et per alium standi in iudicio,"* according to Canon 1646.[40]

Beste simply declares that a person is capable of accusing

[38] "De Iure Denuntiandi Nullitatem Matrimonii," *Apollinaris*, III (1930), 249.

[39] *Enchiridion Iuris Canonici*, 6. ed., p. 785.

[40] *Enchiridion Iuris Canonici*, 6. ed., p. 729. Canon 1646 states that anyone is able to act in trial unless forbidden by the sacred canons.

marriage if he enjoys the right of standing in trial. Beste makes no attempt to elucidate his position.[41]

Cappello states that to accuse a marriage is to institute a judicial action. One may exercise a judicial action only insofar as he has a right to stand in judgment and provided that he is not prohibited by the sacred canons according to Canon 1646.[42] Cappello concludes that a spouse who is capable of accusing marriage enjoys, without a doubt, the capacity of acting and therefore has the right to stand in judgment.

Opposed to the foregoing opinion that the right to accuse is the right to stand in judgment to institute an action concerning a matrimonial cause of nullity is the proposition that the right to accuse a marriage is "the right to present or propose a marriage case concerning the nullity of a marriage to a competent tribunal and to request that tribunal to judge the case and declare the marriage null."[43] This definition of the right to accuse marriage is derived by Marquardt from the observations of three authors, Romani, Badii, and Lazzarato. Romani asserts that to accuse marriage is to propose a cause to a competent judge and to invoke his ministry to pass judgment.[44] Romani does not explain the definition. Badii defines an accusation as the exercise of a faculty conceded by law to invoke the authority of a judge for the defense of a right.[45] Lazzarato holds that an accusation is an extrajudicial act merely requesting that the tribunal be constituted for the purpose of passing judgment on a matrimonial cause of nullity.[46] Marquardt explains the definitions of Romani, Badii, and Lazzarato in the following manner.

a. The definition of an accusation of marriage may be derived from Article 55, § 2 of the *Provida* which states that he who

[41] *Introductio in Codicem*, 4. ed., p. 922.

[42] "Annotationes," *Periodica*, XXXV (1946), 195.

[43] Marquardt, *The Loss of Right to Accuse a Marriage*, p. 62.

[44] *Summa Juris Canonici Lineamenta* (Romae: Apud Auctorem, 1939), p. 226, n. 576.

[45] "Sul diritto di accusare il matrimonio," *Il Diritto Ecclesiastico*, XL (1929), 187 as cited by Marquardt, *op. cit.*, p. 53.

[46] "Azione matrimoniale ed accusa ex officio," *Rassegna di Morale e Diritto*, VI (1940), 117 as cited by Marquardt, *op. cit.*, p. 53.

wishes to accuse a marriage must present to the competent tribunal a *libellus* in which the object of the controversy is set forth and the services of the judge are requested to declare the nullity of marriage. An accusation of marriage, therefore, "is that act by which a person (the accuser) proposes to a competent tribunal facts pointing to the nullity of a marriage and invokes the ministry of that tribunal to declare the nullity."[47]

The right to accuse, then, is the right to propose a marriage case to a tribunal and to ask its official assistance, that is, to recognize the petition, admit the action, hear the case, and declare in favor of nullity.[48]

b. When one has the right to accuse marriage, his request that the tribunal consider his case is an effective request. According to Canons 1709 and 1710, the accuser has a right to be heard. His petition must be considered.[49]

c. "It is by means of the exercise of the right to accuse that one receives permission to bring his case into court and to exercise his action in defense of a right."[50]

d. The right to accuse is really distinct from the right to exercise an action in court. This distinction is based on the following consideration: "The right to accuse marriage is a natural right deriving ultimately from the right to contract a valid marriage. If a person has the right to contract a valid marriage, he has the right to action to obtain a declaration of nullity if he finds himself in an invalid marriage. Deriving from that right to action is the right to accuse, the right to bring his case to the attention of a tribunal and to invoke its ministry . . .[51] Since he cannot exercise his action in court without first invoking the ministry of the tribunal and having them consider his petition, his right to act as plaintiff (*jus agendi*) is necessarily accompanied by the right to accuse the marriage . . .[52] The

[47] Marquardt, *op. cit.*, p. 54; cf. Canon 1706.

[48] *Ibid.*, pp. 53, 62. Marquardt identifies a "marriage case" with an "action" on p. 64.

[49] *Ibid.*, p. 62.

[50] *Ibid.*, pp. 62-63.

[51] *Ibid.*, p. 75.

[52] *Ibid.*, p. 63.

right of accusation, then, which is exercised before the trial begins, is really distinct from the action, which is exercised during the trial. It is also distinct, though related to, processual capacity which is the ability or capacity to stand in judgment (capacitas standi in iudicio). . ." [53]

Finally, attention should be drawn to the observations of other authors who make no explicit reference to a relation between the right to accuse and the right to stand in judgment.

Vlaming states that to accuse a marriage is to bring before a judge a matrimonial cause for the purpose of exercising an action and of vindicating a right concerning it. He gives no reasons for his definition.[54]

Lega states that the accusation of marriage is the beginning of any formal, judicial process concerning the nullity of the marriage bond. Moreover, an accusation is governed according to the rules of true contentious procedure of Book IV of the Code.[55] Unlike a denunciation which is made to the Ordinary or to the promoter of justice, an accusation, Lega asserts, gives rise to a judicial process *per se.*[56]

Vermeersch-Creusen hold that to accuse a marriage is to attack judicially the validity of a marriage contract. These authors give no further explanation of their definition.[57]

Gasparri states that to be capable of accusing marriage is to possess the right to institute directly a judicial action in a matrimonial cause. Without attempting to elaborate, Gasparri notes that an accusation in a matrimonial cause is to be compared to an accusation in any contentious trial.[58]

DeSmet and Coronata look upon an accusation as the presentation of an action before a competent tribunal in order to vindicate a right.[59] According to Coronata, the specific differ-

[53] *Ibid.*, p. 64.

[54] *Praelectiones Iuris Matrimonii*, 4. ed., p. 544.

[55] *Iudicia Ecclesiastica*, III, 73 *.

[56] *Loc. cit.*

[57] *Epitome Iuris Canonici*, 6. ed., III, n. 286.

[58] *De Matrimonio*, II, n. 1256.

[59] *De Sponsalibus et Matrimonio*, 4. ed., p. 603; *Institutiones Iuris Canonici*, 4. ed., III, n. 1485.

ence between an accusation and denunciation is that an accuser presents an action, a denouncer does not.[60]

It should be noted that for the most part, the authors, whose opinions have been outlined above, have presented their ideas without citing the juridical bases or canonical reasons for their position. In the discussion that follows, an attempt will be made to establish canonically that the right to accuse marriage is precisely the right to stand in judgment to introduce an action to obtain a declaration of the nullity of the marriage. According to the canons of the Code and the articles of the instruction *Provida,* the view that the right to accuse marriage is an extrajudicial act by means of which the court is requested to judge the case and to declare the marriage null is, in the mind of the writer, an opinion that is devoid of juridic foundation.

Article 55, § 2 declares that one who wishes to impugn a marriage must present to the competent tribunal a *libellus* in which the object of the controversy is set forth and the services of the judge are demanded to declare the nullity of marriage. Article 55, § 2 restates Canon 1706 with one notable exception. In place of the words *"Qui aliquem convenire vult"* of Canon 1706, Article 55, § 2 substitutes *"Qui matrimonium accusare vult."* Since the expression employed in Canon 1706 refers to the introduction of a cause to a tribunal,[61] *a pari,* the accusation of a marriage refers to the introduction of a cause to a tribunal for the nullity of marriage. Article 55, § 1 of the *Provida* states that only those persons are able to introduce a cause for the nullity of marriage who have the right of accusing a marriage according to the regulations prescribed in Title III of the Provida.[62] Ac-

[60] *Institutiones Iuris Canonici,* 4. ed., III, n. 1485.

[61] Lega (ed. Bart.), *Iudicia Ecclesiatica,* II, 513.

[62] Title III of the *Provida* embraces Articles 34-41. In general, those who are capable of impugning marriage according to the regulations prescribed in Title III are the consorts unless they were the culpable cause of the impediment or of the nullity of the marriage, and the promoter of justice in his own right, and without any previous denunciation, in the case of impediments which are public of their very nature; and in the case of other impediments where a previous denunciation has preceded and when the party has lost his right of instituting an action, safeguarding the provisions of Articles 38 and 39.

cording to Article 55, §§ 1, 2, then, the least that can be said of the right to accuse a marriage is that the right to accuse a marriage is the right to introduce a cause for the nullity of marriage.

In order to determine the nature of this right of introducing a matrimonial cause, consideration must be given to the meaning of the expression "*causam de nullitate matrimonii introducere possunt,*" employed in Article 55, § 1 of the *Provida.*[63] The point at issue, the point on which the two foregoing opinions differ radically, is whether an introduction of a cause of the nullity of marriage is merely an extrajudicial *request* that the tribunal adjudicate the petition in which the object of the controversy is exposed and declare the nullity of the marriage, or whether the introduction of a cause of the nullity of marriage is a judicial *demand* that the tribunal adjudicate the petition and declare the nullity.[64] To answer this question it is necessary to understand that the law recognizes an action or right of a person, who discovers his marriage to be invalid, to obtain a declaration of nullity in an ecclesiastical court.[65] The ecclesiastical court, in turn, cannot take cognizance of a matrimonial cause of a person unless the person has made an accusation according to law.[66] It is through the medium of the accusation that the person takes the first step to exercise his action in court.[67] The accusation, then, is the first act that the person performs in his pursuit of the declaration of nullity. To accuse a marriage, therefore, is to place the first act of the exercise of the action or right that a person enjoys to obtain the declaration of

[63] Art. 55, § 1. "Illi tantum causam de nullitate matrimonii introducere possunt, qui accusandi matrimonium iure pollent, ad normam regularum, quae in Titulo III traditae sunt."

[64] Marquardt has not made his position altogether clear. In one place he asserts that an accusation is merely a request that the ministry of the tribunal be exercised. Later he states that this request is an effective request in the sense that the tribunal must consider the petition and either accept or reject it. In either case, Marquardt holds that an accusation is an extrajudicial act; cf. *The Loss of Right to Accuse a Marriage,* pp. 53, 62.

[65] Canons 1667, 1679.

[66] Canon 1970.

[67] Cf. Canon 1708.

nullity. But just as an action which is recognized by law is in every part of its being a right and not a mere request, so the introduction of the cause of nullity into court also partakes in the nature of a right since the introduction of the cause is simply the initial act of the exercise of the action. Hence, the accusation of marriage (the introduction of the cause of nullity of a marriage to a tribunal) is not in the nature of a mere request, but rather of an actual demand as of strict right based on the right of action, as effect from cause, that the cause be adjudicated and the declaration of nullity be granted.

According to the law of the Code, not everyone who possesses an action, or the right to demand of an ecclesiastical court a declaration of nullity, is permitted to exercise this right. Canon 1646 states that only those persons are able to act in court who are not forbidden by the sacred canons. Since the initial act of the exercise of an action is the act of accusation, only those who are not forbidden by the sacred canons may accuse a marriage. Therefore, not everyone who possesses an action has the right to accuse. If the sacred canons do not prohibit a person to act in court, he is said to have the right to stand in judgment or to possess a *legitima persona standi in iudicio*.[68] If the sacred canons do prohibit a person to act in court, he is said to lack the right to stand in judgment or to lack a *legitima persona standi in iudicio*.[69]

Canon 1971, § 1, 1°, which is elaborated upon in Title III of the *Provida*, declares the consorts are capable of accusing marriage in all cases of nullity, unless they were the culpable cause of the impediment or of the nullity of marriage.[70] Since the accusation of a marriage is the first act of the exercise of an action to obtain a declaration of nullity, Canon 1971, § 1, 1° is a specific application of Canon 1646. Those who are not forbidden by Canon 1971, § 1, 1° to accuse a marriage, that is, those who are recognized as juridically capable of accusing, have a right to

[68] Cf. Canon 1709, § 1.

[69] Cf. e.g., Canon 1652.

[70] Comm. Pont., 17 Julii, 1933, *AAS*, XXV (1933), 345.

stand in judgment to introduce a matrimonial cause before a competent tribunal. He who possesses the right to accuse a marriage thereby possesses the right to place the first act of the exercise of an action to obtain a declaration of the nullity of the marriage.

Observations should be made concerning some of the terminology employed by Marquardt. According to Marquardt, an accusation is an extrajudicial act,[71] by which a person proposes to a competent tribunal facts pointing to the nullity of a marriage and invokes the ministry of that tribunal to declare the nullity. The writer submits that formally to accuse a marriage is either an act of the *persona standi in iudicio* or is not such an act. If it is not such an act, having no essential relation thereto, then it necessarily is nothing other than a denunciation. The act of the proponent must be accounted as having some juridic recognition. There is no third category. The act of accusation, as described by Marquardt, must, therefore, be accounted as a denunciation under the provision of Canon 1971, § 2. Later, Marquardt equates the presentation of facts pointing to the nullity of a marriage with the proposing of an action.[72] An action, Marquardt admits, is the right to pursue in court that which is one's due.[73] The writer submits that there is here a confusion of concepts. Is an action the presentation of facts that point to the nullity of marriage, or is an action the right to pursue a declaration of the nullity of marriage? Moreover, what does the expression "propose an action" mean? According to the definition accepted by canonists,[74] it means to propose a right to pursue in judgment that which is one's due. Therefore, according to Marquardt, the right to accuse a marriage is the right to propose a right to a declaration of nullity. As such, this assertion is obscure in Marquardt's context. Marquardt adds that "it is by means of the exercise of the right to

[71] *The Loss of Right to Accuse a Marriage*, p. 53.

[72] *Ibid.*, pp. 54, 62.

[73] *Ibid.*, p. 54.

[74] *Supra*, p. 59.

accuse that one receives permission to bring his case into court and to exercise his action in defense of a right."[75] As such, this statement is superfluous and contradictory. For if one has a right to exercise, there is no need for "permission." Again, Marquardt's observation that the right of accusation is exercised before the trial begins is juridically unsound, for the right to accuse is itself a matter for judicial discussion and decision.[76]

From the foregoing considerations, it must be concluded that the right to accuse is not an extrajudicial act of a person requesting the ministry of a tribunal to declare the nullity of a marriage, but rather the first judicial act of a person who has the right to stand in judgment to exercise his action to obtain a declaration of the nullity of his marriage.

The second question relating to the reply of the Code Commission of January 4, 1946 concerns the relationship between the juridic inability of a spouse to accuse marriage and the juridic incapacity of a spouse to stand in judgment. It will be recalled that to the question whether the inability of a spouse to accuse marriage according to Canon 1971, § 1, 1° implies the incapacity to stand in judgment so that the sentence labors under irremediable nullity according to Canon 1892, 2°, the Code Commission replied, "in the negative."[77] Authors such as Bar-

[75] *Ibid.*, pp. 62-63.

[76] Cf. Canons 1708, 1°, 1971, § 1, 1°. The *libellus* introduces the litigation. There is, at least, potential litigation on the right to present the *libellus*.

[77] On January 18, 1938, a private response was given by the Sacred Congregation for the Discipline of the Sacraments to the Archbishop of Milan. The Congregation was asked whether a plaintiff, who was the cause of the nullity or of the impediment, is capable of accusing marriage when the accusation is based on two grounds, and when the plaintiff was the cause of the impediment or the nullity only as regards the second ground. The reply was that the plaintiff was not capable of accusing this marriage. The second question was asked whether a sentence declaring the nullity of the marriage on both grounds is valid, or is it to be considered null according to Canon 1892, 2°. The reply was that the sentence would be valid as regards the first ground but null as regards the second. In other words, the response of the Sacred Congregation implied that the incapacity to accuse a marriage was embraced under the notion of the inability to stand in judgment, and for that reason, the sentence was

toccetti, Vlaming, Beste, DeSmet, Coronata, and Sipos do not address themselves to this question. Cappello,[78] and Regatillo,[79] limit themselves to pertinent observations concerning the response of the Code Commission. Marquardt [80] and Conway [81] attempt a consideration of the juridic basis from which the response is derived.

Cappello called attention to this response shortly after its publication in 1946.[82] Cappello notes that, on the one hand, Canon 1971, § 1, 1° does not clearly and explicitly deny to the culpable spouse a right to stand in judgment and therefore it would seem that the prescription of Canon 1892, 2° would not apply.[83] He adds that it is not always clear whether the consort was truly the culpable cause, or whether he acted maliciously, or whether his sin was both objectively and subjectively grave. It will happen, therefore, that doubts will inevitably arise for or against the culpability of the consort and, therefore, for or against the validity of the process and the judicial acts, and the validity of the sentence itself. The reason

---

vitiated with incurable nullity according to Canon 1892, 2°.—Bouscaren, *Canon Law Digest* (4 vols. and Supplements through 1958 and 1959, Milwaukee: Bruce and Company, 1934-1959), II, 545. This decision of the Congregation of the Sacraments was abrogated by the January 4, 1946 response of the Code Commission which alone has the right to interpret authentically the Canons of the Code; cf. Pope Benedict XV, *Motu Proprio*, AAS, IX (1917), 483.

78 "Annotationes," *Periodica*, XXXV (1946), 195.

79 *Interpretatio et Iurisprudentia Codicis Iuris Canonici* (Santander: Sal Terrae, 1949), p. 538 (hereafter cited *Interpretatio et Iurisprudentia C.I.C.*).

80 *The Loss of Right to Accuse a Marriage*, p. 64; cf. Graziani, "De Iure Accusandi Matrimonium," *Ephemerides Iuris Canonici*, II (1946), 145-147.

81 "Matrimonial Processes: Culpable Spouse," *The Irish Ecclesiastical Record*, LXIX (1947), 54.

82 "Annotationes," *Periodica*, XXXV (1946), 195.

83 "Si res obiective consideretur et argumenta hinc inde allata mature perpendantur, ingenue fatendum varias opiniones et sententias solidis niti rationibus. Ex una parte can. 1971, § 1, 1° clare et explicite nullatenus denegat coniugi culpabili legitimam personam standi in iudicio, ideoque non videtur applicandum praescriptum can. 1892, 2°." *Ibid.*, p. 197.

for the response of the Code Commission, then, is to relieve the tribunal of the many and most grave disadvantages of passing a sentence that would be irremediably null and subject to the complaint of nullity because of the doubt of the culpability of the spouse who brought the action.[84] Cappello observes that, on the other hand, Canon 1971, § 1, 1°, considered with Canons 1646 and 1648 and the canons that follow, seems to deprive the culpable spouse of the right of acting, that is, to declare him as not having a right to stand in judgment.[85] Otherwise, he asks, what do the words *"habilis," "inhabilis," "capax,"* and *"incapax,"* mean? Cappello continues that if a spouse who is the culpable cause of the impediment is, nevertheless, able to stand in judgment to exercise an action, what is the force of the prescription of Canon 1971, § 1, 1° and what would be the juridical effects of the penalty that is established and the privation that is decreed? He answers that they would be of little or of no significance.[86] Cappello concludes that though the reason and importance of the reply of the Code Commission are clear, there are yet many questions and difficulties concerning it that remain to be resolved.

Regatillo, after concluding from the response of the Code Commission that a spouse who is incapable of accusing is not thereby deprived of the right to stand in judgment cries out in wonder. Regatillo insists that the response of the Code Commission practically reduces to nothing the previous replies of the Commission concerning the interpretation of Canon 1971, § 1, 1° and Canon 1971, § 1, 1° itself.[87] He continues that he had always understood the words *"habilis"* and *"inhabilis"* to have in law the precise meaning of the capacity or the incapacity to place validly

[84] *Ibid.*, pp. 197-198.

[85] "Ex alia parte can. 1971, § 1, 1°, collatus cum can. 1646 et 1647 ss., videtur coniugem culpabilem iure agendi privare, seu decernere eumdem personam standi in iudicio non habere."—*Ibid.*, p. 198.

[86] *Loc. cit.*

[87] "Mira responsio CI. quae practice in nihilum redigit responsa praecedentia et fere ipsum c. 1971, § 1, n. 1."—*Interpretatio et Iurisprudentia C.I.C.*, p. 538.

a juridic act and thus, according to Canon 11, he concluded that a spouse incapable of accusing marriage did not have the right to stand in judgment. And if one who was incapable of accusing marriage were admitted as an *actor,* the sentence would be null, according to Canon 1892, 2°. In this latter sense were the preceding responses of the Code Commission issued. But by virtue of the response of January 4, 1946, Regatillo asserts that the words *"habilis"* and *"inhabilis"* should be struck from Canon 1971, § 1, 1° because the spouse who is incapable of accusing remains recognized as having the *persona standi in iudicio.*[88]

Regatillo suggests that the reason for the negative response of the Code Commission is based on practical rather than on juridic considerations.[89] He rejects the notion that the Church is willing to have any spouse, culpable or inculpable of the nullity of a marriage, accuse his marriage because he would otherwise be forced to live in perpetual concubinage or, at least, because he would be forbidden to contract a new marriage.[90] Regatillo states that if this were true, it would be sufficient for the Code Commission simply to suppress Canon 1971, § 1, 1° in respect to the inability of the culpable spouse to accuse marriage. For the inability to accuse marriage at least impedes an accusation, so that the tribunal, knowing of the incapacity of the spouse to accuse a marriage, must forbid the spouse the exercise of his action. Regatillo agrees with Cappello in stating that the reason underlying the response is based on the grave inconveniences that would otherwise follow. Thus, an accuser in presenting his *libellus* may conceal his culpability. The fact that the accuser was the cause of the impediment may not be revealed until the trial is well in progress or nearing the end or even after the sentence. If the accusation was null, argues Regatillo, all of the expense and labor involved would be useless, time would be wasted, and displeasure on the part of all would be rampant. Therefore, natural equity urges that the process be continued

[88] *Loc. cit.*

[89] "Interpretatio haec, potius quam iuridica, videtur inniti rationibus practicis, quae certe vim habent."—*Loc. cit.*

[90] Cf. Restrepo, "Annotationes," *Periodica,* XXXII (1943), 115.

and the sentence be passed regardless of the validity or the invalidity of the accusation.[91]

Marquardt, it will be recalled, holds that an accusation is merely an extrajudicial act by which the accuser presents to a competent tribunal facts pointing to the nullity of a marriage and requests the ministry of that tribunal to declare the nullity. He concludes that it is possible for someone to have the capacity of validly exercising an action in court (*legitimatio ad causam*) and nevertheless be deprived of the right and the capacity of accusing his marriage.[92] He asserts that "we cannot, therefore, speak now of the 'processual incapacity' of parties who have been deprived of the right of accusing their marriage. They have complete processual capacity. They are merely prohibited from exercising this capacity, since they are incapable of taking the preliminary step necessary to exercise this action, i.e., they are incapable of making a regular accusation of their marriage." [93]

Conway expresses the opinion that the relationship between the inability of a spouse to accuse a marriage and the incapacity of a spouse to stand in judgment is based on a distinction between a lack of processual capacity *per se* and the inability to exercise an action in a particular case. According to Conway, it was generally agreed by canonists before January 4, 1946 that there was no distinction between processual capacity *per se* and the inability to exercise an action in a particular case as far as their effects were concerned.[94] Both concepts were included under the expression *persona standi in iudicio*. Since the Code Commission has declared that if a culpable spouse accuses marriage, the sentence is not incurably null, only one conclusion can be drawn, namely, although a culpable spouse has no right to bring an action into court, he, nevertheless, has a *persona standi in iudicio*.[95] Therefore, according to Conway, it must further be

[91] *Loc. cit.*

[92] *The Loss of Right to Accuse a Marriage*, p. 64.

[93] *Ibid.*, p. 113.

[94] "Matrimonial Processes: Culpable Spouse," *The Irish Ecclesiastical Record*, LXIX (1947), 54.

[95] Cf. Cruesen, "De Iure Accusandi Matrimonium," *Nouvelle Revue Theologique*, LXVIII (1946), 344; Mahoney, "De Iure Accusandi Matri-

concluded that contrary to that which was heretofore believed, the term *persona standi in iudicio* refers only to processual capacity *per se*. *Persona standi in iudicio* does not refer to the capacity to exercise an action in a particular case.[96]

Conway explains that a person may lack the right to bring a particular action to an ecclesiastical court for one of two reasons. First, he may lack processual capacity *per se,* that is, he may be incapable in law of being a party to a judicial process. A minor, for example, *per se* cannot act in court. If through error or negligence the minor is permitted to stand in trial, the entire process is invalid and incurably null. Secondly, a person may lack the right to bring a particular action to an ecclesiastical court not because he lacks processual capacity but rather because the law will not allow him to exercise it in regard to a particular class of actions. A priest, for example, who has contracted invalidly because of substantial error, may not bring an action to court after the lapse of two years according to Canon 1684. Thus, he possesses processual capacity *per se* but he may not exercise it in relation to this particular action. If, however, he succeeds in bringing this action to court after the lapse of two years from the signing of the contract, the process would be valid. Applying this explanation to the reply of the Code Commission, Conway concludes that though the culpable spouse has no right to bring the action to court for a declaration of the nullity of his marriage, the spouse nevertheless has the right to stand in judgment. And contrary to what was heretofore thought by canonists, the term *legitima persona standi in iudicio* refers only to processual capacity *per se* and not to *legitimatio ad causam* as well.[97]

The following observations may be made concerning the con-

---

monium," *Clergy Review*, XXVI (1946), 660; Ellis, "Notes on Canon Law," *Theological Studies*, VIII (1947), 123; Doheny, *Canonical Procedure*, 2. ed., I, 124.

[96] *Loc. cit.;* cf. Doheny, *Canonical Procedure,* 2. ed., I, 124; Noone, *Nullity in Judicial Acts*, The Catholic University of America Canon Law Studies, n. 297 (Washington, D. C.: The Catholic University of America Press, 1950), p. 65.

[97] Conway, "art. cit.," *IER*, LXIX (1947), 55-56; cf. Roberti, *De Processibus,* 4. ed., nn. 215, 240.

siderations given to the response of the Code Commission by the foregoing authors.

Both Cappello and Regatillo lay stress on the practical consequences that accrue from the negative reply of January 4, 1946. In this regard, an allusion may be made here to certain animadversions written by Trezzi, a Defender of the Bond of the Sacred Roman Rota. It is to be noted that the observations of Trezzi were written before the response of the Code Commission of January 4, 1946. Anticipating the question proposed to the Code Commission, Trezzi asks rhetorically whether the inability of a culpable spouse to accuse marriage is to be understood as the same as the incapacity to stand in judgment so that, according to Canon 1892, 2° the sentence is irremediably null. Trezzi suggests that the sentence demands a negative answer. Among the reasons he gives are the purpose of the law-giver and disadvantages that would otherwise follow.[98] It was not the mind of the legislator, argues Trezzi, to permit that the decisions handed down by tribunals be filled with the greatest uncertainty regarding their validity. Otherwise, doubts over their irremediable nullity could be raised at any time. Torre agrees with Trezzi that the legislator did not intend to place such unbearable burdens on both the tribunal and the parties themselves.[99] Moreover, according to Trezzi, if the validity of the sentences passed by the tribunal were to remain uncertain because of a question concerning the culpability of a spouse, a great detriment would befall the public good and the salvation of souls.[100] Trezzi's remarks made before the reply of the Code Commission, are almost identical to those of Cappello and Regatillo written after the response. Nevertheless, both Cappello and Regatillo seem to view the response as somewhat of a canonical anomaly. Cappello makes no serious attempt to sound the juridical foundation of the response. He leaves the question open. Regatillo resorts to an interpretation based on natural equity asserting that the negative

[98] As reported by Torre, *Processus Matrimonialis*, 3. ed., p. 380.

[99] *Ibid.*, p. 382.

[100] *Loc. cit.*

reply of the Code Commission was based more on practical reasons than on juridic considerations. It may be admitted that the answer of the Code Commission is of much practical significance. It contributes immeasurably toward easing the burdens of ecclesiastical judges and to contributing to the peace of mind of the parties affected by a judicial sentence. But it must also be admitted that to interpret a penal law in terms of "natural equity," rather than according to the strict literal meaning of the words,[101] seems to be unwarranted, at least, until some effort has been made to interpret the response according to the canons of the Code and canonical jurisprudence. The generality of canonists have failed to make this effort. Marquardt and Conway are two notable exceptions.

Marquardt asserts that the response of the Code Commission necessitates the conclusion that the deprivation of the right to accuse marriage is nothing more than the deprivation of the right to place an extrajudicial act by which a plaintiff proposes to a tribunal facts pointing to the nullity of marriage and requests the ministry of that tribunal to declare the nullity. Therefore, one can be deprived of the right to accuse a marriage and still possess completely the right to stand in judgment.[102] The writer submits that this conclusion is not necessitated by the reply of the Code Commission. On the contrary, this conclusion seems to reduce the reply to an absurdity. Again, it must be understood that an act of accusation must be accounted as having some juridic recognition. If it is not recognized as an act of one who has a *legitima persona standi in iudicio,* then it must be recognized as a denunciation under the provision of Canon 1971, § 2. There is no third category. Hence, the response of the Code Commission which refers to the incapacity to stand in judgment according to Canon 1892, 2° becomes, in the light of Marquardt's explanation, totally irrelevant, since the inability to denounce a marriage bears no relationship whatsoever to the incapacity to stand in judgment.

The interpretation of Conway is based on a distinction be-

[101] Canon 19.

[102] *The Loss of Right to Accuse a Marriage,* pp. 110-113.

tween the right *per se* to exercise an action in judicial procedure (*legitimatio ad processum*), and the right to exercise an action in a particular case (*legitimatio ad causam*). Conway holds that the response reveals an abandonment of hitherto accepted principles of Roman law governing the right to stand in judgment in favor of those of Continental and German law which attributes different effects to each.[103]

The opinion of Conway is summarized in his statement that the reply of the Code Commission necessitates the conclusion that, contrary to what was heretofore thought, the term *persona standi in iudicio* refers only to processual capacity *per se* and not to the capacity to exercise an action in a particular case, at least, as far as their effects are concerned.[104] This opinion does not appear to be in absolute accord with Canons 1646-1654 which treat of the right to stand in judgment. Canon 1646 states the general principle that every person is able to exercise an action in court unless he is prohibited by the Sacred Canons. The right to stand in judgment is determined by Canon 1646 and not by the distinction between *legitimatio per se* and *legitimatio ad causam*. The canons that follow Canon 1646 consider the right to stand in judgment not only in relation to the persons who are permitted and who are forbidden to exercise their actions but also in relation to the particular cases in which these actions may be exercised. Thus, Canon 1652, for example, states that religious, without the consent of their superiors have no right to stand in court, "except in the following cases." The writer suggests that the reply of the Code Commission does not necessarily indicate a distinction between processual capacity *per se* and the right to exercise an action in a particular case in respect to the effects of each. The following reasons are presented to support this opinion.

It has been established that the right to accuse marriage is the right to introduce into court a cause of the nullity of marriage.[105] The right to introduce into court a cause of the nullity of mar-

103 "Art. cit," *IER*, LXIX (1947), 55.

104 *Supra*, p. 81.

105 Instr. *Provida*, Art. 55, § 1.

riage signifies precisely the right to place the first procedural act (the act of an accusation) in the exercise of an action to obtain a declaration of nullity.[106] According to the strict interpretation of Canon 1971, § 1, 1° demanded by Canon 19, and according to the principle of law "odia restringi et favores convenit ampliari,"[107] the juridic inability of a spouse to accuse a marriage extends only to the act of accusation itself, which is merely one (the first) of many acts which a plaintiff places in the exercise of his action. This conclusion is confirmed in a Rota decision handed down on January 30, 1936.[108] The penalty of Canon 1971, § 1, 1°, according to the strict interpretation of the canon, does not extend to the other procedural acts of the plaintiff which follow thereupon.[109] The right to stand in judgment, on the other hand, is a far broader concept than the right to accuse. The right to stand in judgment comprises not only the right to accuse or to place the first act of the exercise of an action but also the right to place all other acts that culminate in a judicial sentence. Therefore, the deprivation of the right to accuse a marriage, which is a most restricted concept, does not imply the deprivation of the right to stand in judgment as such, which includes not only the right to accuse but also the right to place all other judicial acts in the course of the trial. Thus, Trezzi who, it will be recalled, wrote before the negative response of the Code Commission was issued, insists that the law says what it wants to say.[110] Canon 1971, § 1, 1° declares that a spouse who was the culpable cause of the impediment or of the nullity of marriage is incapable of *accusing*. Canon 1971, § 1, 1° does not declare that the culpable consort is incapable of

106 Canons 1646, 1667, 1679, 1970, 1971, § 1, 1°; Instr. *Provida*, Art. 34, 35, § 1, 1°.

107 R.J. in VI°, 15.

108 ". . . inhabilitas (canonis 1971, § 1, 1°) restringenda est ad ipsum actum accusationis . . ."—S.R.R. *Decisiones*, XXVIII (1936), 78, n. 10.

109 ". . . non autem extendi potest ad alios actus processuales . . ."—*Loc. cit.*

110 "Lex autem quod voluit dixit."—Cf. Torre, *Processus Matrimonialis*, 3. ed., p. 383.

standing in judgment[111] in respect to the procedural acts which follow the act of accusation.

Therefore, the reply of the Code Commission may be interpreted in the following manner. The inability to place the act of accusation (the first act of procedure) in the exercise of an action for the nullity of marriage does not imply the incapacity to perform all other procedural acts subsequent to the act of accusation so that the sentence does not labor under irremediable nullity. The Code Commission is declaring, then, that an accusation which is placed invalidly[112] by a spouse who is juridically incapable of accusing according to Canon 1971, § 1, 1°, affects only the integrity and licitness, not the essence and validity of the judicial process and sentence.[113] Canon 1680, § 2 states that the nullity of any act does not comprise the nullity of those acts which precede or follow it and which do not depend upon the invalid act. Hence, the Code Commission is asserting that the judicial process and the sentence of the tribunal which follow upon the invalid accusation of a culpable spouse[114] are not affected according to the prescription of Canon 1680, § 2. It would seem that the juridic reason is based on the fact that even though the accusation is invalid in law, it *de facto* reveals the object of the controversy as claimed by the plaintiff[115] which, as far as the essence of the process is concerned, is sufficient for the tribunal to cite the defendant[116] and to effect the joinder of issue.[117] Both Noone and Marquardt agree that nowhere in

[111] *Ibid.*, p. 382; cf. Cappello, "Annotationes," *Periodica*, XXXV (1946), 197; *supra*, p. 85.

[112] Canon 11.

[113] Canons 1680, § 2, 1892, 2°.

[114] Canons 11, 1971, § 1, 1°.

[115] Canon 1706.

[116] Canon 1711, § 1.

[117] Canon 1726; cf. Noone, *Nullity in Judicial Acts*, pp. 65, 80, 81, 93; Marquardt, *The Loss of Right to Accuse a Marriage*, pp. 58-61. "Requiruntur (ad validitatem iudicii) vero actoris petitio reique contradictio, ut de obiecto iudicii determinato fiat disceptatio utque iudex de eo pronuntiare possit."—S.R.R. *Decisiones*, XXVIII (1936), 120.

the Code can it be conclusively proved that an invalid accusation renders the process and sentence invalid.[118]

Prescinding from the obvious practical consequences that issue from this response, the opinion of the writer regarding the juridical basis of the response itself may be summarized in the following assertions. In the reply of January 4, 1946, the Code Commission:

1. explicitly asserted that the juridic inability of the culpable spouse to place the first act (an accusation) of the exercise of an action to obtain a declaration of nullity does not imply the incapacity to place all other procedural acts that follow thereupon and which culminate in a valid judicial sentence.

2. implicitly asserted that all of the procedural acts subsequent to the invalid accusation of a culpable spouse are not affected by the invalidity of the accusation.

3. did not deny that the inability to accuse a marriage involves the incapacity to stand in judgment to accuse a marriage.

4. did not affirm that the culpable spouse can legally proffer a demand, based on the right of action, that his cause be heard and adjudicated and that a declaration of nullity be granted.

118 *Nullity in Judicial Acts*, p. 81; *The Loss of Right to Accuse a Marriage*, p. 59.

CHAPTER V

THE RIGHT OF THE SPOUSES TO ACCUSE A MARRIAGE

SECTION I. THE JURIDIC RECOGNITION OF THE RIGHT OF THE SPOUSES TO ACCUSE A MARRIAGE

Article 1. The Right of Catholic Spouses to Accuse a Marriage

To establish juridically the right of Catholic spouses to accuse a marriage of invalidity, it must first be recalled that the law of the Church in Canon 1035 recognizes the natural right of all persons to contract a marriage unless they are prohibited by law. The natural law demands that all persons who contract marriage must contract validly. From the natural duty to contract a valid marriage arises a natural right to a valid marriage. The law of the Church recognizes every right as fortified with an action, unless a provision is expressly made to the contrary, according to Canon 1667. Specifically, Canon 1679 further declares that if an act or a contract is invalid by law, the parties whose rights are affected may pursue in an ecclesiastical court [1] a declaration of the nullity of the act or the contract. Canon 1646 states that anyone can exercise an action unless he is forbidden by the Sacred Canons. Canon 1971, § 1, 1° applies the principles of Canons 1667, 1679, and 1646 to marriage contracts which are entered into invalidly. Canon 1971, § 1, 1° states that spouses who have contracted marriage invalidly have the right to accuse their marriage of invalidity. According to Canon 87, however, the right to pursue in an ecclesiastical court a declaration by the Church of the nullity of a marriage is possessed only by those validly baptized persons who are not impeded from the bond of communion with the Catholic Church because of some obstacle, or who have not incurred a censure inflicted by the Church.[2]

[1] Canon 1552, § 1.

[2] Cf. Instr. *Provida*, Art. 35, § 3. The right of non-Catholics to accuse marriage is discussed in the following article.

In respect to the right of a person to accuse a marriage, those persons are within the bond of communion of the Catholic Church who were validly baptized in or converted to the Catholic Church and who have not apostatized from the Catholic Faith.[3] Therefore, those persons who after being born and baptized in the Catholic Church or who have been converted to the Catholic Church, and who have not fallen away from the Catholic Church, that is, who have not joined a non-Catholic sect or have declared themselves as having no religion at all, are the spouses referred to in Canon 1971, § 1, 1°.

Clearly, the ultimate formal object of the right of a Catholic spouse to accuse a marriage is a declaration of nullity according to Canon 1679. The question to be answered here is, what is the material object (*materia circa quam*) of the right of the Catholic spouse to accuse marriage? How far does this right to accuse marriage extend?

Canon 1680, § 1 states that an act is null and void only when the essential constituents of the act are lacking or when some formalities or conditions are wanting which the Sacred Canons require under the pain of nullity. According to Canon 1038, § 2, the Supreme Authority of the Church alone has the exclusive right of constituting impedient or diriment impediments of marriage for baptized persons either by universal or particular law.

[3] On January 15, 1940, the Sacred Congregation of the Holy Office, with the approval and confirmation of Pope Pius XII, declared that "apostates from the faith" are included among non-Catholics who are forbidden to accuse marriage; cf. S.C.S. Officii, 18 Januarii, 1928, *AAS*, XX (1928), 75; Bouscaren, *Canon Law Digest*, I, 762; S.C.S. Officii, 15 Januarii, 1940, *AAS*, XXXII (1940), 52; Bouscaren, *Canon Law Digest*, II, 534. This reply of the Holy Office is unintelligible in this context if the expression "*apostatae a fide*" must be interpreted according to the definition of apostate provided in Canon 1325, § 2, namely, "(*qui*) *a fide christiana totaliter recedit.*" It seems certain that the reply of the Holy Office of January 15, 1940 must be understood in the light of an earlier private declaration in which the Holy Office defined apostates as "*ii scilicet qui nati et baptizati in Ecclesia Catholica postea a vera Fide deficientes.*"—S.C.S. Officii, 27 Februaurii, 1937, *Periodica*, XXVI (1937), 400; Bouscaren, *Canon Law Digest*, II, 530-531; cf. Instr. *Provida*, Art. 231, § 1 ("... *si apostatae a fide catholica*"); Canon 1065, 1 ("qui ... catholicam fidem abiecerunt"); Comm. Pont., 30 Julii, 1934, *AAS*, XXVI (1934), 494; Bouscaren, *Canon Law Digest*, II, 287; *infra*, p. 94.

Attention is directed here to the diriment impediments of marriage, that is, those circumstances which attach to a person which not only render a marriage illicit but also make its celebration null and void according to Canon 1036, § 2. According to a response of the Code Commission of March 12, 1929,[4] the impediments which constitute the material cause of an accusation by a Catholic spouse include not only those which are determined by the Code in Canons 1067-1080[5] but also the impediments understood in the wide sense of the term, namely, the impediments of defect of consent and defect of form. These impediments are considered by the Code in Canons 1081-1103.[6]

It will be recalled that immediately prior to the Code of Canon Law in 1917, the impediments to marriage were divided not only *ratione notitiae* but also *ratione iuris accusandi vinculum matrimoniale.*[7] *Ratione iuris accusandi,* impediments were divided into impediments of private right (*impedimenta iuris privati*) and impediments of public right (*impedimenta iuris publici*).[8] Those impediments were of public right which have as their end the sanctity of the Sacrament of Matrimony, the purity of Christian marriage, and the preservation of the common

[4] *AAS,* XXI (1929), 171.

[5] In general, the impediments of marriage fall under the concepts ot age, impotence, *ligamen,* disparity of cult, sacred orders, solemn vows, abduction, *crimen,* consanguinity, affinity, public decency, spiritual relationship, and legal relationship if so prescribed by civil law.

[6] In respect to the impediment of defect or form, it must be remembered that according to Article 231 of the *Provida,* if a person was certainly obliged to observe the canonical form in the celebration of marriage and, nevertheless, contracted only a civil marriage, or was married before a non-Catholic minister, or if apostates from the Catholic Faith, contracted civil marriage in apostacy or in a foreign rite, neither judicial formalities nor the intervention of the defender of the bond are required to establish the fact such persons are free to marry. Such cases are to be settled by the Ordinary himself or by the pastor after consultation with the Ordinary as indicated in Canon 1019 and subsequent Canons. But if there is any doubt as to the existence of the conditions indicated above, the question is to be decided according to the rules of judicial procedure.

[7] Feije, *De Impedimentis,* nn. 85, 584; cf. *supra,* p. 47.

[8] *Loc. cit.*

good.[9] Among the impediments of public right were *impubertas, defectus aptitudinis ad consentiendum, disparitatis cultus, ligamen, ordo sacer et votum solemne, crimen, raptus, cognatio naturalis et spiritualis et legalis, consanguinitas, affinitas, et publica honestas.*[10] Because such impediments were related directly to the good of the Church and to society as well, the law recognized the right of the "public" to accuse a marriage in which these impediments were verified. Thus, the right of accusing a marriage invalid by force of an impediment of public right was in no way reserved to the Catholic spouses themselves but was extended to the ecclesiastical judge or to the *promotor fiscalis, ex officio,* and to any other Catholic who was capable of accusing marriage.[11]

The impediments of private right were impediments of *erroris substantialis personae vel conditionis servilis, vis et metus, defectus conditionis appositae, et impotentiae occultae.*[12] Because these impediments were principally but not exclusively constituted for the welfare of the parties themselves,[13] marriages that were contracted invalidly because of the existence of such an impediment could be accused only at the instance of the contracting parties themselves. Only a Catholic party could present the accusation.[14] As a rule, impediments of private right could not be accused by the *promotor fiscalis ex officio* or by any other Catholic.[15] If, however, the impediment of private right was certain and notorious, the ecclesiastical judge had the power and the obligation to declare the marriage null.[16] Thus,

[9] Wernz, *Ius Decretalium,* IV, n. 216; *supra,* p. 48.

[10] Aichner, *Compendium Iuris Ecclesiastici,* pp. 570-578; Wernz, *Ius Decretalium,* IV, n. 216; cf. *supra,* p. 48.

[11] Cf. *supra,* p. 48; *Instr. Austr.,* §§ 115, 122.

[12] Wernz, *Ius Decretalium,* IV, n. 216; Feije, *De Impedimentis,* n. 85; Aichner, *Compendium Iuris Ecclesiastici,* p. 569.

[13] Wernz, *Ius Decretalium,* IV, n. 216.

[14] *Instr. Austr.,* § 115.

[15] S.C. Prop. de Fide, Instr. *Causae Matrimoniales,* 1883—*Fontes,* n. 4901, § 3; *Instr. Austr.,* §§ 115, 122.

[16] C. 3, X, *de divortiis,* IV, 19; Reiffenstuel, Lib. IV, tit. 19, n. 19.

paragraph 118 of the Austrian Instruction ruled that in cases in which the marriage was not capable of being consummated because of the impediment of impotence, only the spouses could accuse the marriage unless the fact of the impotence was notorious. Moreover, the impediments of substantial error, servile condition, force and fear, and unfulfilled condition were not to be considered of private right if they were, *de facto*, publicly known in a locale in which the Tridentine form was prescribed.[17] For an impediment was of private right in the old law only insofar as it could not be determined by the public whether the parties themselves had removed the impediment and had convalidated their marriage by a renewal of consent, if such consent was permitted without the Tridentine form.[18] Obviously, a marriage invalid by reason of an impediment *iuris privati* which was publicly known was a source of scandal in a locale embraced by the form decreed by *Tametsi.*

Under the Code of Canon Law, the Catholic spouses retain the right to accuse the invalidity of marriage in all cases of nullity, whether the impediment is of private or public right.[19] Moreover, the promoter of justice retains the right to accuse, *iure proprio,*[20] in all cases in which the impediment is of public right, that is, an impediment *publicum natura sua,* according to Canon 1971, § 1, 2°.[21] The difference between the old law and the new law in respect to the right to accuse marriage may be found in the following consideration. In the old law, the right to accuse marriage in cases in which the impediment was of public right was possessed cumulatively by the Catholic spouses, the *promotor fiscalis ex officio,* and any other Catholic who was not otherwise forbidden by law.[22] In the law of the Code, the

[17] Lega, *De Judiciis,* IV, n. 453; Gasparri, *De Matrimonio* (ed. 1891), n. 1182; cf. *supra,* p. 45.

[18] Reiffenstuel, Lib. IV, tit. 18, nn. 3, 4; Schmalzgrueber, Lib. IV, tit. 18, nn. 14, 15; *Instr. Austr.,* §§ 116-121; Lega, *De Judiciis,* IV, n. 453.

[19] Canons 87, 1646, 1667, 1679, 1971, § 1, 1°; Instr. *Provida,* Art. 35, § 1, 1°.

[20] Instr. *Provida,* Art. 35, § 1, 2°.

[21] Instr. *Provida,* Art. 35, § 1, 2°; Wernz-Vidal, *Ius Canonicum,* V (3. ed. a Aguirre, 1946), p. 181 ad VIII; Doheny, *Canonical Procedure,* 2. ed., I, 108, 109; S.R.R. *Decisiones,* XX (1928), 402, n. 2.

[22] *Instr. Austr.,* §§ 115, 122.

right to accuse marriage in cases in which the impediment is of public right (*impedimentum natura sua publicum*) is possessed cumulatively only by the Catholic spouses and the promoter of justice *iure proprio*.[23] Therefore, the new law of the Code withdrew from all Catholics, other than the spouses themselves and the promoter of justice the right to accuse marriages.[24] All other persons, even though they are the blood relatives of the consorts, do not have the right to accuse a marriage under the new law. At most, they are permitted merely to denounce the marriage to the Ordinary or to the promoter of justice.[25] Finally, in the law of the Code as in the old law,[26] the right of Catholic consorts to accuse a marriage is juridically withdrawn if they themselves are the culpable cause of the impediment or of the nullity of the marriage.[27] The juridic withdrawal of the right to accuse a marriage will be discussed in detail in Section II of this Chapter.

Article 2. The Right of Excommunicates to Accuse a Marriage

The first paragraph of Canon 1654 states that excommunicated persons who are to be shunned (*excommunicati vitandi*) [28] and other persons excommunicated by a declaratory or a condemnatory sentence [29] may personally institute an action only to impugn the justice or the legality of their excommunication; through a proxy, they may act in court to avert whatever may be prejudicial to their souls; in any other cause, they are to be rejected from exercising an action. The second paragraph prescribes that other excommunicated persons generally may stand in judgment.[30] Thus, as regards the right to stand in judgment,

23 Canon 1971, § 1, 1°, 2°; Instr. *Provida,* Art. 35, § 1, 1°, 2°. The role of the promoter of justice in accusing marriage shall be considered in detail in a later Chapter; cf. *infra,* p. 190.

24 Doheny, *Canonical Procedure,* 2. ed., I, 108.

25 Canon 1971, § 2; Instr. *Provida,* Art. 35, § 2.

26 *Instr. Austr.,* §§ 116-121.

27 Canon 1971, § 1, 1°; Instr. *Provida, Art.* 35, § 1, 1°; Comm. Pont., 17 Julii, 1933, *AAS,* XXV (1933), 345.

28 Canon 2258, § 1.

29 Canon 2232, § 2.

30 Cf. Canons 19, 1646, 2256, 2°; 2263.

the Code distinguishes between two classes of excommunicates. The right to accuse a marriage to be exercised by a member of the first group, namely, the *vitandi* and *tolerati* against whom a declaratory or condemnatory sentence has been passed, is determined by the clause, "*per procuratorem, ad aliud quodvis animae suae praeiudicium avertendum.*" It seems certain that excommunicates who compose the first group have the right to stand in judgment to accuse an invalid marriage. The reason is that to be bound by the ties of an invalid marriage, not yet declared such by the Church, whether one does or does not live with the consort, is certainly prejudicial and detrimental to the good of one's soul. Lega and Roberti both affirm the right of excommunicates of the first group to accuse a marriage.[31] This right must be exercised, however, through the agency of a procurator or proxy, the norms for which are determined in Canons 1655-1666, and in the Instruction *Provida,* Articles 43-54.

The second group of excommunicates comprises all those who are excommunicated, but who are not *vitandi* or *tolerati* after a condemnatory or declaratory sentence. Canon 1654, § 2 states that all such excommunicates can generally stand in judgment. They possess the right to accuse a marriage unless they are prohibited from accusing for some other reason prescribed by law.[32] The agency of a procurator would not be necessary for excommunicates of the second group.[33]

Article 3. The Right of Apostates and Non-Catholics[34] *to Accuse a Marriage*

A. *Pertinent Documents of the Holy See*

In view of the importance of this topic and the questions and difficulties that so frequently arise concerning the admission of a non-Catholic as an *actor* in a matrimonial cause before a competent ecclesiastical tribunal, the decrees of the Holy Office

[31] *Iudicia Ecclesiastica,* I, 330; *De Processibus,* 4. ed., n. 227.

[32] Cf. Canons 1646, 2256, 2°; 2263.

[33] Cf. Canon 1654, § 2.

[34] As indicated above (p. 89), the expression "non-Catholics" in this context includes those who are not baptized and those who are baptized outside of the Catholic Church and who have not converted to the

and of the Code Commission, relating to the right of a non-Catholic in formal matrimonial causes involving ordinary judicial procedure, are first presented here in chronological order.

On January 18, 1928, the Holy Office answered the question:

I. Whether in matrimonial causes a non-Catholic, whether baptized or non-baptized, can be a plaintiff. Reply. In the negative, that is, the Code, especially Canon 87 is to be observed. But if there are special reasons for admitting non-Catholics as plaintiffs in such cases, recourse must be had in each case to the Supreme Sacred Congregation of the Holy Office.

II. Whether the Supreme Sacred Congregation of the Holy Office has exclusive competence in all matrimonial causes between a Catholic party and a non-Catholic party, whether baptized or unbaptized, which are in any way brought before the Holy See. Reply. In the affirmative, especially in consideration of Canon 247, § 3, and without prejudice to the prescription of Canon 1557, § 1, 1°.[35]

On July 30, 1934, the Code Commission answered the question: Whether according to the Code of Canon Law, persons

---

Catholic Faith, or who have abandoned the Catholic Faith and who have joined a non-Catholic sect or who claim no religious affiliation whatsoever. The term "non-Catholics" is also to be predicated of catechumens according to the present practise of the Holy Office and the traditional attitude of the Church; cf. Canon 1239, § 2; McCloskey, *The Subject of Ecclesiastical Law According to Canon 12,* The Catholic University of America Canon Law Studies, n. 165 (Washington, D. C.: The Catholic University of America Press, 1943), 49-50; Doheny, *Canonical Procedure,* I, 114, note 20.

[35] "I. Utrum in causis matrimonialibus acatholicus sive baptizatus, sive non baptizatus, actoris partes gerere possit. Resp. Negative, seu standum est Codici I. C., praesertim can. 87. Siquidem autem speciales occurrant rationes ad admittendos acatholicos ut actores in huiusmodi causis, recurrendum ad Supremam Sacram Congregationem Sancti Officii in singulis casibus.

"II. Utrum in quibuslibet causis matrimonialibus inter partem catholicam et partem acatholicam, sive baptizatam sive non baptizatam, quocumque modo ad Sanctem Sedam delatis, Suprema Sacra Congregatio Sancti Officii exclusivam habeat competentiam. Resp. Affirmative, habita praesertim ratione can. 247, § 3, et salvo praescripto can. 1557, § 1, 1°."—S.C.S. Officii, 27 Januarii, 1928, *AAS,* XX (1928), 75; Bouscaren, *Canon Law Digest,* I, 762-763.

who belong or have belonged to an atheistic sect are to be considered, as regards all legal effects, even those which concern sacred ordination and marriage, the same as persons who belong or have belonged to a non-Catholic sect. Reply. In the affirmative.[36]

On February 27, 1937, the Holy Office in a private response answered the question of the Bishop of Salzburg: Whether apostates, namely, persons who, after being born and baptized in the Catholic Church, have fallen away from the true Faith, or joined a non-Catholic sect, or declared themselves "of no religion," are to be considered as non-Catholics as regards the right to act as plaintiff in marriage cases. Reply. In the affirmative; that is, apostates from the Faith are to be considered non-Catholics as regards the effects concerned in the declaration of the Holy Office of 18 January, 1928.[37]

On March 22, 1939, the Holy Office answered the question: Whether the decision of the Supreme Sacred Congregation of the Holy Office given on 18 January, 1928, ad I, by which it was declared that non-Catholics cannot act as plaintiffs in marriage cases, refers only to the tribunal of the Sacred Roman Rota, or also to diocesan courts. Reply. In the negative to the first part, in the affirmative to the second; that is, it refers also to diocesan courts.[38]

[36] "An ad normam Codicis iuris canonici, qui sectae atheisticae adscripti sunt vel fuerunt, habendi sint quoad omnes iuris effectus etiam in ordine ad sacram ordinationem et matrimonium, ad instar eorum qui sectae acatholicae adhaerent vel adhaeserunt. Resp. Affirmative."—Comm. Pont., 30 Julii, 1934, *AAS,* XXVI (1934), 494; Bouscaren, *Canon Law Digest,* II, 286-287.

[37] "Utrum etiam apostatae, ii scilicet qui nati et baptizati in Ecclesia Catholica postea a vera fide deficientes vel nomen dederint sectae acatholicae, vel 'sine religione' esse sese declaraverint, sint recensendi, in ordine ad jus accusationis in causis matrimonialibus inter acatholicos. Resp. Affirmative seu apostatas a Fide ad effectum declarationis S. Officii diei 18. 1. 1928 recensendos esse inter acatholicos."—*Periodica,* XXVI (1937), 400; Bouscaren, *Canon Law Digest,* II, 530-531.

[38] "Utrum decisio Supremae S. Congregationis S. Officii data die 18 Januarii 1928 ad I., qua nempe declaratum fuit acatholicos in causis matrimonialibus actoris partes agere non posse, spectet tantum Tribunal S. Romanae Rotae, an etiam Tribunalia dioecesana. Resp. Negative ad

On January 15, 1940, the Holy Office answered the question: Whether apostates from the faith are also included among the non-Catholics who, according to the decree of the Holy Office of 18 January, 1928, are forbidden to act as plaintiffs in matrimonial cases. Reply. In the affirmative.[39]

B. *Observations Relative to the Documents of the Holy See*

In the one hundred and fifteenth paragraph of the Austrian Instruction [40] of 1855, there is stated the general principle that the right to accuse marriage may be exercised by any Catholic. No provision was made in the Austrian Instruction or in the Instruction *Causae Matrimoniales* of the Sacred Congragation for the Propagation of the Faith in 1883 for an accusation of marriage to be made by a non-Catholic.

On January 18, 1928, the Supreme S. Congregation of the Holy Office declared that a non-Catholic, whether baptized or unbaptized, was unable to be a plaintiff in a matrimonial cause according to the law of the Code, especially Canon 87.[41] Canon 87 declares that all baptized persons are subject to the laws of the Church with all the rights and duties of a Christian. No distinction is made in Canon 87 between persons who are baptized into the Catholic Church and those who are validly baptized into non-Catholic sects.[42] Canon 87 adds, however, that in regard to rights, there may be some obstacle that impedes the bond of communion with the Church. Thus, though a baptized

primam partem; affirmative ad alterum, seu: spectare etiam Tribunalia dioecesana."—S.C.S. Officii, 22 Martii, 1939, *AAS,* XXXI (1939), 131; Bouscaren, *Canon Law Digest,* II, 547.

39 "An inter acatholicos qui, juxta decretum S. Officii diei 18 Januarii, 1928, in causis matrimonialibus agere prohibentur, connumerandi sint etiam apostatae a fide. Resp. Affirmative."—S.C.S. Officii, 15 Januarii, 1940, *AAS,* XXXII (1940), 52; Bouscaren, *Canon Law Digest,* II, 534.

40 The Fathers of the III Council of Baltimore, held in 1884, recommended the procedural norms of the Austrian Instruction to the Bishops of the United States; *supra,* p. 39.

41 *AAS,* XX (1928), 75.

42 Cf. Cappello, "De Acatholicorum Incapacitate Agendi in Foro Ecclesiastico," *Miscellanea Vermeersch* (2 vols., Romae: Pontificia Università Gregoriana, 1935), I, 394.

non-Catholic may be the subject of ecclesiastical rights according to Canon 87, and though these rights may be fortified by an action according to Canon 1667, the Holy Office declared that such a person is unable to institute an action regarding the nullity of his marriage, because he is impeded by the obstacle of being outside the communion of the Church. Therefore, a baptized non-Catholic, though he retains his basic juridic capacity as a subject of the Church, lacks the procedural capacity or the right to stand in judgment to accuse a marriage. An infidel, on the other hand, possesses neither the juridic nor the procedural capacity to accuse a marriage, according to Canon 87.

Having stated the principle that non-Catholics, whether baptized or non-baptized, are unable to accuse a marriage, the Holy Office added that if there are special reasons for admitting non-Catholics as plaintiffs in matrimonial causes, recourse must be made to the Holy Office in each case. It will be observed that the response of the Holy Office of January 18, 1928 is repeated almost word for word in Article 35, § 3 of the Instruction *Provida*. It would seem that in cases in which the plaintiff is a baptized non-Catholic, the authorization granted by the Holy Office to admit such a person to accuse a marriage amounts to a permission for the non-Catholic to exercise a right which is radically recognized in Canon 87. But in cases in which the plaintiff is an infidel, the authorization of the Holy Office would seem to consist in a permission to exercise a right granted by the natural law, but lacking in juridic recognition by the Church.

It is of great importance to note that the response of the Holy Office of January 18, 1928 to the first question relates to a non-Catholic's right to institute an action in a matrimonial cause. This reply concerns the right of a non-Catholic to stand in judgment to accuse a marriage. The response of the Holy Office of January 18, 1928 in answer to the second question relates to the exclusive competence of the Holy Office in any matrimonial cause which involves a non-Catholic. Difficulties concerning the interpretation of the responses to these two questions can be avoided if it is remembered that the right to accuse and the competence of a tribunal are two distinct concepts. The response of the Holy Office to the first question is embodied by Article 35, § 3 of the Instruction *Provida* under the title *De*

Jure Accusandi Matrimonium. The response of the Holy Office to the second question constitutes the basis of Article 12 of the *Provida* under the title *De Foro Competenti.* Article 12 of the *Provida* reads: Cases between a Catholic party and a non-Catholic party, whether the latter be baptized or not baptized, can be adjudged in the first and second instance by diocesan tribunals; but if they are referred to the Holy See, they belong exclusively to the Sacred Congregation of the Holy Office, which may, if it wishes and the cause suggests it, remand the case to the Tribunal of the Sacred Roman Rota.

Article 12 of the *Provida* leaves no doubt that the diocesan tribunal has competence over its non-Catholic subjects, whether baptized or unbaptized in the marriage cases mentioned. The exclusive competence of the Holy Office indicated in the response of the Holy Office of January 18, 1928 and in Article 12 of the *Provida* obtains only in the instance when the matrimonial cause involving a non-Catholic, is referred, for one reason or another, to the Holy See. The relationship between Article 12 and Article 35, § 3 is this. The diocesan tribunal is competent to try a formal matrimonial cause of a non-Catholic subject without seeking permission of the Holy Office. But a non-Catholic subject lacks the right to stand in judgment to accuse his marriage before the competent tribunal. Therefore, even though the tribunal is competent to hear the case, before the tribunal can admit the non-Catholic as an *actor,* authorization is needed from the Holy Office.[43] The significance of this distinction between a diocesan tribunal's competence over its non-Catholic subjects and the inability of a non-Catholic to accuse without authorization from the Holy Office is more clearly appreciated when related to cases in which the promoter of justice and not the non-Catholic is the *actor.* Thus, if a non-Catholic, whether baptized or unbaptized, presents to the tribunal of the diocese in which his or her marriage was celebrated, a case in which the nullity of the marriage was detrimental to the public

[43] On March 22, 1939, the Congregation of the Holy Office declared that the decision of January 18, 1928, *ad* I, wherein it was declared that non-Catholics cannot act as plaintiffs in marriage cases, applied not only to the Tribunal of the Sacred Roman Rota but also to diocesan tribunals.—*AAS,* XXXI (1939), 131.

good, the promoter of justice, authorized by his Ordinary, can stand in judgment to accuse the marriage without applying to the Holy See.[44] This conclusion may be derived from the response of the Holy Office of March 22, 1939, in which the Holy Office declared that the promoter of justice in virtue of Canon 1971 can impugn a marriage without any previous authorization from the Sacred Congregation of the Holy Office, if he has been apprised of the invalidity of the marriage by the non-Catholic consort in cases in which, in the judgment of the Ordinary, the public good demands it.[45]

Another question that may well be raised here is whether the prohibition of non-Catholics to accuse a marriage without authorization from the Holy Office extends to cases envisaged under Canon 1990? Canon 1990 states that without observing the formalities of an ordinary trial, the Ordinary may declare the nullity of a marriage after consultation with the defender of the bond and the summoning of the parties, if an impediment of ligamen, disparity of cult, consanguinity, affinity, orders, solemn vow, or spiritual relationship rendered the marriage null, provided the existence of the impediment can be proved from a certain and authentic document, and there is certainty that no dispensation from the impediment was granted. The cases with which Canon 1990 is concerned are described by the Code as *"De casibus exceptis a regulis hucusque traditis."*[46]

On April 20, 1931, the Holy Office, in a private reply to the Bishop of Harrisburg, answered the following difficulty. An unbaptized person contracted marriage with a baptized non-Catholic in 1917. Later, the parties separated and the unbaptized person sought to obtain from the ecclesiastical tribunal a declaration of nullity of the marriage on the ground that, at the time of the marriage, the impediment of disparity of cult existed. According to the decision of the Holy Office of January 18, 1928,

[44] *Infra*, p. 239; cf. Canon 1964; Instr. *Provida*, Art. 3, § 1; Canon 1971, § 1, 2°; see also Instr. *Provida*, Art. 35, § 1, 2°; Canon 1586.

[45] *AAS*, XXXI (1939), 131; cf. the reply of the Congregation of the Sacraments to the Bishop of Berlin on November 3, 1931—*Apollinaris*, VII (1934), 279-280; Bouscaren, *Canon Law Digest*, II, 542; *infra*, pp. 231-237.

[46] C.I.C., Liber IV, titulus xx, caput vii.

the Bishop of Harrisburg referred the case to the Holy Office. The Holy Office responded that the aforesaid case could be handled by the Ordinary himself according to Canons 1990-1992.[47]

The reply of the Holy Office to the Bishop of Harrisburg seemed to indicate that no recourse to the Holy Office was necessary in cases considered under Canon 1990 involving non-Catholic petitioners. Twelve years later, however, on December 6, 1943, the Code Commission settled a long-standing controversy when it declared that the process of Canon 1990 was judicial, not administrative.[48] This decree of the Code Commission which ruled that Canon 1990 cases must be adjudged according to the principles of judicial procedure coupled with the reply of the Holy Office of January 18, 1928 prompted some authors to conclude that non-Catholics are incapable of acting as plaintiffs in the summary cases of Canon 1990 without authorization of the Holy Office.[49] This conclusion enjoys a modicum of probability. The contrary opinion, however, seems to be more solidly probable for the following reasons.

1. Canon 1990 was incorporated into the Code almost word for word from decrees of the Holy Office issued between March 20, 1889 and June 21, 1912.[50] The decree of June 5, 1889, for example, indicated that it was sufficient that one party be baptized and the other be unbaptized for the Ordinary to conduct a summary process to declare on the existence of the impediment of disparity of cult according to the old law. Nothing in the decree pointed to the inability of the unbaptized party to be a plaintiff, when the invalidity of the marriage was evident from a certain and authentic document, or other evidence.

> Quando agitur de impedimento disparitatis cultus, et evidenter constat unam partem esse baptizatam et alteram

[47] Bouscaren, *Canon Law Digest,* II, 552-553.

[48] *AAS,* XXXVI, (1943), 94.

[49] Doheny, *Canonical Procedure,* II, 152, 162; Hannan, "Non-Catholic Petitioners and Plaintiffs," *The Jurist,* IV (1944), 623.

[50] S.C.S. Officii, 20 Martii, 1889, *Fontes,* IV, n. 1114; 5 Junii, 1889, *Fontes,* IV, n. 1118; 10 Junii, 1896, *Fontes,* IV, n. 1180; 23 Junii, 1903, *Fontes,* IV, n. 1266; 21 Junii, 1912, *Fontes,* IV, n. 1293 ad 2.

> non fuisse baptizatam . . . dummodo ex certo et authentico documento vel in hujus defectu ex certis argumentis evidenter constet de existentis hujusmodi impedimentorum . . . praetermissis solemnitatibus . . . requisitis, matrimonium poterit ab Ordinariis declarari nullum, cum interventu tamen defensoris vinculi matrimonialis . . .[51]

In view of the silence of the pre-Code commentators concerning the inability of the non-Catholic to be a plaintiff in such cases[52] it would seem that, according to Canon 6, 2°,[53] the Ordinary has the right to admit non-Catholics as petitioners in a summary process without any authorization from the Holy Office.[54]

2. As is evident from the first paragraph of the *Motu Proprio* of Pope Benedict XV in which the Roman Pontiff instituted the Pontifical Commission for the Authentic Interpretation of the Code,[55] the Code Commission alone has the power to interpret the Code so as to extend or restrict it. Therefore, the reply of the Holy Office of January 18, 1928, in which the Holy Office reserved the right to admit non-Catholics in matrimonial causes, cannot be interpreted as a restriction of the right of the Ordinary to declare the nullity of marriage according to the prescription of Canon 1990. If it is objected that the response of the Holy Office prohibiting non-Catholics to accuse a marriage did not distinguish between formal and summary procedure,[56] it may be answered that the crucial point at issue is that Canon 1990 does not distinguish or place any restrictions on the right of the Ordinary as regards Catholic or non-Catholic petitioners. Certainly, the response of the Holy Office cannot be interpreted as

[51] *Fontes,* IV, n. 1118; cf. n. 1180.

[52] Regatillo, *Interpretatio et Iurisprudentia C.I.C.,* 534.

[53] Canones qui jus vetus ex integro referunt, ex veteris iuris auctoritate, atque ideo ex receptis apud probatos auctores interpretationibus, sunt aestimandi.

[54] Park, "Competence of the Ordinary in a Case under Canon 1990," *American Ecclesiastical Review,* LXXXVI (1932), 69 (hereafter cited "Canon 1990," *AER*); Beste, *Introductio in Codicem,* 4. ed., p. 914.

[55] *AAS,* IX (1917), 483.

[56] Doheny, *Canonical Procedure,* II, 152.

restricting or distinguishing the right granted to the Ordinary by Canon 1990 because the Holy Office does not have the authority so to interpret the Code.[57]

3. Though it is true that an interpretation of law given by a rescript in a particular case, such as that addressed to the Bishop of Harrisburg by the Holy Office in 1931, affects only those to whom it was given,[58] it is also true that the Holy Office did declare, albeit privately, the meaning of the law of Canon 1990. Certainly, it is difficult to deny that such a declaration can serve as a guide to other tribunals confronted, at least, by the same case without having the meaning of the law reiterated by the Holy Office every time the question arises in a different diocese. It is of interest to note that Gasparri, writing just four years after the reply of the Holy Office of 1928, held that the prohibition of non-Catholics to act as plaintiffs in formal causes should not be extended to the *casibus exceptis* of Canon 1990.[59]

4. Since the non-Catholic is restricted in the free exercise of a right to stand in judgment to accuse a marriage, according to Canon 87, the response of the Holy Office relating to this restriction must be interpreted strictly, according to Canon 19. The question to which the Holy Office addressed itself related only to "*causis matrimonialibus.*" This expression is a technical term which, when understood in its strict sense, refers only to causes tried in formal procedure. But cases under Canon 1990 are referred to not as "causes" but as "cases" which are explicitly excepted from the solemnities and formal procedure which accompany an ordinary trial. Therefore, the response of the Holy Office which affirms the incapacity of a non-Catholic to be an *actor* applies only to formal causes and not to cases tried according to Canon 1990.[60]

In the absence of a pronouncement from the Code Commission, the opinion that restricts the decree of the Holy Office of Janu-

57 Regatillo, *Interpretatio C.I.C.*, p. 534; Park, "Canon 1990," *AER*, LXXXVI (1932), pp. 68-71.

58 Canons 49; 17, § 3.

59 Gasparri, *De Matrimonio*, II, n. 1260.

60 Cf. Bevilacqua, "Competence of the Ordinary in the Documentary Process of Canons 1990-1992," *The Jurist*, XXII (1961), 248.

ary 18, 1928 to formal causes is not without extrinsic[61] and intrinsic probability and hence, in accordance with Canon 15, a tribunal would be permitted to admit a non-Catholic as a plaintiff under Canon 1990. Doheny, who opposes this opinion, admits that it is, nevertheless, the generally accepted opinion.[62]

In any event, if the nullity of a marriage relates to the common good,[63] the promoter of justice, upon the non-Catholic's denunciation of the marriage which is invalid because of an impediment under Canon 1990, could immediately institute an action against the marriage.[64] But if during the course of a summary trial, it is discovered, for example, that the impediment cannot be proved from a certain and authentic document, and that the case must be remanded to a collegiate tribunal to be tried according to the requirements of formal procedure, it seems certain that permission must be sought from the Holy Office to admit the non-Catholic plaintiff to stand in judgment. Again, however, if the public good is at stake in the judgment of the Ordinary, the promoter of justice could impugn the validity of the marriage without authorization from the Holy Office.[65]

[61] Abbo-Hannan, *The Sacred Canons* (2. ed., 2 vols., St. Louis: Herder, 1957), I, 127; Beste, *Introductio in Codicem,* 4. ed., pp. 915, 923, 934; Gasparri, *De Matrimonio,* II, n. 1260; Johnson, *De Processibus Matrimonialibus Exceptis* (Romae: Apud Custodiam Librariam Pont. Instituti Utriusque Iuris, 1937), p. 52-53; Park, "Canon 1990," *AER,* LXXXVI (1932), pp. 69-71; Regatillo, *Interpretatio C.I.C.*, p. 534: Ayrinhac, *Marriage Legislation in the New Code of Canon Law* (Revised and enlarged by P. J. Lydon, New York: Benziger, 1952), p. 362; Mahoney, "Marriage Causes of Non-Catholics," *The Clergy Review,* XXXVIII (1953), 748-749; Sipos, *Enchiridion Iuris Canonici,* 6. ed., p. 783; Bevilacqua, "art. cit.," *The Jurist,* XXII (1961), 258.

[62] Doheny, *Canonical Procedure,* II, 152. Monsignor Doheny admits that his own opinion is "extremely rigorous" but that it is demanded by the "inexorable rules of logic." Cf. Doheny, "Procedure in Summary Cases," *The Jurist,* IV (1944), p. 33.

[63] *Infra,* p. 231; cf. Lega (ed. Bart.), *Iudicia Ecclesiastica,* III, 89*.

[64] Cf. S.C.S. Officii, 22 Martii, 1939, *AAS,* XXXI (1939), 131; cf. Canon 1586.

[65] *AAS,* XXXI (1939), 131; cf. Doheny, *Canonical Procedure,* II, 161-162; cf. Canon 1586.

Section II. The Juridic Withdrawal of the Right to Accuse a Marriage

Article 1. The Incapacitating Character of the Juridic Withdrawal of the Right to Accuse a Marriage

Canon 11 states that only those laws are considered invalidating or incapacitating which explicitly or equivalently state that an action is null and void, or that a person is incapable of acting. An invalidating law is one which renders juridically void an act which by the natural law and the general principles of human positive law would otherwise be valid.[66] An example of an invalidating law can be found in Canon 1094 in which it is stated that those marriages only are valid which are contracted either before a pastor or the local Ordinary or a priest delegated by either and at least two witnesses, saving the exceptions mentioned in Canon 1098 and 1099. An incapacitating law is one that renders a person incapable of performing certain acts. An example of an incapacitating law is that of Canon 1072 which prescribes that clerics in major orders cannot contract a valid marriage. The distinction between an invalidating law and an incapacitating law lies in the fact that the latter is a species of the former, at least in relation to its effects.[67] An invalidating law affects an act directly. An incapacitating law affects an act indirectly by directly depriving a person of the exercise of a right enjoyed by virtue of the natural or positive human law. An incapacitating law directly affects the person, in the sense that it declares the person absolutely or relatively lacking in the capacity to place certain juridic acts, in such a manner, that if the person places such acts, they are viewed by law as juridically ineffectual and invalid.[68] Because of the serious consequences that attach to invalidating or incapacitating laws, Canon 11 sets up a presumption against such laws unless they

[66] Cicognani, *Canon Law,* 2. ed., p. 558; Michiels, *Normae Generales Iuris Canonici* (2 vols., ed. altera, Parisiis-Tornaci-Romae: Desclée, 1949), I, 343.

[67] Roelker, "The Concept of Invalidating Laws," *The Jurist,* III (1943), p. 36.

[68] Michiels, *Normae Generales Iuris Canonici,* 2. ed., I, 342-343.

are expressly or equivalently mentioned. Express mention is made if the words of the law, understood according to their proper signification, directly state that an act is invalid or that a person is incapable of acting. Equivalent mention is made if the words of the law, understood according to their proper signification, do not directly indicate the invalidity of an act or the incapacity of a person, but do so indirectly. Invalidity or incapacity is indicated indirectly through the use of other words which, nevertheless, convey the same meaning.[69]

From the explanation that has been given above, it is apparent that Canon 1971, § 1, 1° is an inhabilitating law, that is, a law which directly affects not an act but a person in such a manner that it declares the person incapable of placing a juridic act. Canon 1971, § 1, 1° first states the general positive principle that spouses are capable of accusing marriage. The declaration of the deprivation of the juridic capacity of the spouses is contained in the adversative subordinate clause, *"nisi ipsi fuerint impedimenti causa."* In other words, there is expressly stated by Canon 1971, § 1, 1° that spouses who have caused the impediment are incapable of accusing marriage. The fact that Canon 1971, § 1, 1° is an incapacitating law carries with it significant consequences regarding its interpretation.

Canon 19 states that laws which decree a penalty, or restrict the free exercise of one's rights, or establish an exception to the law, are subject to strict interpretation. The incapacitating law of Canon 1971, §1, 1° does, indeed, restrict the free exercise of one's rights. The right to accuse marriage is precisely the right to institute an action relating to the nullity of marriage. This right is founded remotely on man's duty established by the natural law to contract a valid marriage and proximately on the provision of the ecclesiastical law that if a contract is invalid by law, the parties whose rights are affected may pursue in an ecclesiastical court a declaration of the nullity of the contract.[70] Any law which restricts this right must be interpreted strictly.

[69] An example of express declaration of juridic incapacity may be found in Canon 504. An example of an equivalent expression of inability can be seen in Canon 765.

[70] Cf. Canons 1679, 1646, 1667; cf. *supra*, p. 88.

By strict interpretation is meant that the words used in the law are to be understood according to their literal and proper meaning as opposed to a liberal interpretation which amplifies the meaning of the words to the fullest possible extent within their proper signification.[71] The words of Canon 1971, § 1, 1° are to be understood, then, according to their strictest, literal, and proper signification.

Canon 16, § 1 states that ignorance does not excuse from the observance of an invalidating or incapacitating law, unless the law expressly declares otherwise. Canon 1971, § 1, 1° makes no reference to the matter of ignorance. Therefore, viewed simply as nothing more than an incapacitating law, Canon 1971, § 1, 1° binds even though the spouses are ignorant of its existence, provided, of course, that all of the conditions necessary to be rendered incapable of accusing marriage are fulfilled.[72]

Canon 15 states that all laws including invalidating and incapacitating laws lose their binding force in a doubt of law. A doubt is an uncertain state of mind between two contradictory decisions which is based on a reasonable cause.[73] A doubt of law is present when the doubt relates to the existence, the meaning, the scope, or the cessation of the law.[74] For example, a tribunal may doubt whether the prohibition of Canon 1971, § 1, 1° actually applies to the circumstances and facts that have been presented in the depositions during the course of a trial. If an expert and reasonable investigation and review of the law fails to induce moral certainty [75] as to the course which the tribunal should take, Canon 15 would apply. Canon 15 also

[71] Cf. Cicognani, *Canon Law,* p. 615; Michiels, *Normae Generales Iuris Canonici,* 2. ed., I, 480-481; Canon 18.

[72] Cf. *infra,* pp. 143, 170-171.

[73] Michiels, *Normae Generales Iuris Canonici,* 2. ed., I, 416.

[74] Michiels, *op. cit.,* 419-420.

[75] Moral certainty may be defined as the firm assent of the mind to propositions accepted from evidence taken from the normal manner of human conduct which the mind finds sufficient to win its full consent. Cf. The Allocution to the Rota by Pope Pius XII on October 1, 1942 translated into English in Bouscaren, *Canon Law Digest,* III, 605; Caron, "Moral Certitude in Canonical Decisions," *The Jurist,* XIX (1959), 14.

makes provision for a doubt of fact but this matter in relation to the prohibition of Canon 1971, § 1, 1° may be more properly considered in the discussion of the elements necessary to constitute a crime.[76]

Article 2. The Penal Character of the Juridic Withdrawal of the Right to Accuse a Marriage

In the preceding Article, it was demonstrated that Canon 1971, § 1, 1° is an incapacitating law, that is, a law that renders a person incapable of accusing marriage if that person has been the cause of the impediment. The purpose of the legislator in establishing incapacitating laws is to protect the common good. Incapacitating laws are made to protect the public welfare from fraud, danger, or injury.[77] It is important to understand that in themselves, incapacitating laws are not penal laws in the strict sense of the term. In other words, the fact that the law deprives a person of the free exercise of a right is not always to be considered as a punishment. Otherwise, any restriction of a person's freedom to act, in order to regulate the public or private order of society, would be a penalty.[78] The question to be considered here is whether the deprivation of the right to accuse marriage according to Canon 1971 § 1, 1° is merely an incapacitating provision of the law designed to safeguard the purity of marriage and the social structure of the community, or whether it is also to be considered as a penalty in the strict canonical sense of the term. Is the incapacitating clause *"nisi ipsi fuerint impedimenti causa"* also a penal prescript? The answer to this question is of singular significance, because upon it rest the norms according to which the clause is to be interpreted throughout the analysis that is to follow.

A penal law is a law to which there is attached at least an indeterminate penalty. A penalty is the privation of some temporal or spiritual benefit for the correction of the criminal and

[76] Cf. *infra*, p. 144.

[77] Cicognani, *Canon Law*, p. 558.

[78] Roelker, "The Concept of Invalidating Laws," *The Jurist*, III (1943) pp. 37-39.

for the punishment of crime.[79] A crime can be defined as a grave, external, morally imputable violation of a law to which there is attached at least an indeterminate penalty.[80] Basing their opinions on recent responses of the Code Commission and on many decisions of the Rota, the overwhelming majority of authors hold that Canon 1971, § 1, 1° is to be interpreted as a vindicative penalty. A vindicative penalty is one that has for its primary purpose the expiation of the crime committed. The secondary purpose of a vindicative penalty is the correction or amendment of the offender.[81] However, there are some who think that the clause *"nisi ipsi fuerint impedimenti causa"* is not a penal sanction.[82] Vermeersch-Creusen state simply that the privation of Canon 1971 is merely a restriction of rights and not a penalty properly so-called. They give as their reason for this opinion the "end and nature of the law" embraced under Canon 1971.[83] Bartoccetti also denies that Canon 1971, § 1, 1° is a penalty. Bartoccetti asserts that the sole purpose of Canon 1971, §1, 1° is to protect the dignity of the Sacrament of Matrimony and to ward off the danger of divorce. The purpose of this canon is not to penalize. The sanction involved arises from the common good itself. Therefore, in its application to a given person, the restrictive principles which accompany penal law are not to be applied. Rather, the criteria to be employed are "equity and opportunity" which favor the public good and not the convenience of the parties.[84] Because the purpose of this canon

79 Canons 2195, 2215.

80 Canons 2195, 2218.

81 Canon 2286.

82 Vermeersch-Creusen, *Epitome Iuris Canonici*, 6. ed., III, n. 286; Bartoccetti, "De iure et officio promotoris justitiae," *Apollinaris*, X (1937), 587.

83 "Ex fine et natura hujus legis censemus non esse poenam proprie dictam . . ."—*Epitome Iuris Canonici*, 6. ed., III, n. 286.

84 "Haec inhabilitas agendi coniugis culpabilis, cum suum fontem inveniat in tuitione dignitatis magni sacramenti et in necessitate divortii periculi vitandi, non iam ut poena sed ut sanctio ob commune bonum inducta concipienda est; proindeque in eius applicatione non iam principia restrictiva, quae obtinet in iure poenali, applicari debent sed potius criteria

is to provide a means by which the common good will be safeguarded; because the purpose of this canon is to remove the venom of divorce from society, the restrictions prescribed by the canon are to be applied with "notable amplitude and generous liberality." [85] It should be noted that when Bartoccetti uses the term divorce in this context, he seems to be referring to those "divorces" which, he claims, are creeping into marriage tribunals under the guise of declarations of nullity.[86] In any event, to apply a strict interpretation to the *nisi* clause of Canon 1971 is, according to Bartoccetti, to frustrate the clear intention of the legislator. The intention of the legislator is to stamp out the abuse heaped on the Sacrament of Matrimony and, therefore, the remedy provided by Canon 1971, § 1, 1° is to be applied liberally and in a manner that will be most effective in achieving the end for which the law was made.[87]

The more common opinion [88] and, indeed, the opinion that is based on the legislation of the right to accuse marriage enacted before the Code and on the responses of the Code Commission and the jurisprudence of the Rota after the Code is that Canon 1971, § 1, 1° is a penal canon.

It will be recalled that in the law of the Decretals, it was determined that one who was the *causa dolosa* of an impediment to

---

aequitatis et opportunitatis, quae favent bono publico potiusquam privatorum commodis."—Bartoccetti, "*art. cit.*," *Apollinaris*, X (1937), p. 587.

[85] ". . . restrictiones et cautelae tunc privatis impositae . . . licet sint quandoque summe onerosae, sed ut medium pro universorum salute tutanda, ideoque intelliguntur et applicantur notabili amplitudine et moderato tutiorismo. Hic vero lues removenda est, ut dixi, divortii venenum summe perniciosum."—*Loc. cit.*

[86] " . . . agitur in nostro casu de eliminando periculo ne divortium—tecto quidem sub nomine—in nostro foro subrepat . . ."—Bartoccetti, "Circa inhabilitatem coniugum accusandi matrimonium," *Apollinaris*, XI (1938), p. 201.

[87] ". . . si in casu dubii in re nascentis adhiberentur interpretationes strictae, quae debent applicari in poenalibus, intentio legis penitus frustraretur."—*Loc. cit.*

[88] Gasparri, *De Matrimonio*, n. 1260; Noval, *De Judiciis*, n. 850; Beste, *Introductio in Codicem*, 4. ed., p. 923; Regatillo, *Institutiones Iuris Canonici*, II, n. 751; Doheny, *Canonical Procedure*, 2. ed., I, 121; Cappello, *De Matrimonio*, 5. ed., p. 883.

a marriage was not admitted to accuse that marriage. Pope Alexander III cited the reason for such a prohibition and made it clear that the restriction was primarily penal in character. The Pope declared that it was not fitting that a man who knowingly contravened the law of the church should thereby profit from his own guilt.[89] Sanchez applied the principle of Pope Alexander III to a case in which a person was aware of his own impotence at the time when he contracted marriage. Because of the deceitfulness of the person in not revealing the impediment, Sanchez argued that the court should give no hearing to his accusation against the marriage on the grounds that no one should profit from his own delinquency.[90] Pirhing and Schmalzgrueber reiterated the same principle of Pope Alexander III with its vindicative implications.[91]

The penal character of the deprivation of the right to accuse according to Canon 1971, § 1, 1° of the current Code is confirmed by the replies of the Code Commission which have defined the concept of *causa impedimenti* in the most strict and limited manner. Of particular significance in this regard is the terminology employed by the Code Commission in a response issued on July 27, 1942.[92] The Code Commission in this response described the *causa impedimenti* as that which is *directa et dolosa. Dolosa* is a term the significance of which cannot be understood without resorting to the Fifth Book of the Code which embodies the law of ecclesiastical penalties. *Dolus,* it will be remembered, is one of the foundations of the imputability of a delict or crime. A crime is the material cause of a penalty.[93] Referring explicitly to the interpretation of the Code Commission of July 27, 1942, the Rota in 1944 declared in definitive language that the privation of the

89 " . . . nec dignum est, ut . . . vir, qui scienter contra canones venerat, lucrum de suo dolo reportet . . ."—c. 1, X, *de eo, qui duxit in matrimonium quam polluit per adulterium,* IV, 7; JE, n. 12636; cf. *Glossa Ordinaria,* ad c. 1, X, IV, 7, s. v. *nisi mulier.*

90 "Cum enim dolus nemini patrocinari debeat minime audietur, si illam tunc norit. Argumento ex c. 1, *de eo, qui duxit.*"—Sanchez, *De Sancto Matrimonii Sacramento Disputationum,* Lib. VII, d. 114, n. 4.

91 Pirhing, Lib. IV, tit. 18, n. 2; Schmalzgrueber, Lib. IV, tit. 15, n. 71.

92 *AAS,* XXXIV (1942), 241.

93 Canons 2199, 2215.

right of accusing is a penalty which presupposes a delict with its three fold element: *dolus,* an external act, and a penal law, according to Canon 2195, § 1 which states that in Canon Law, the term delict implies an external and morally imputable violation of law, to which at least an indeterminate sanction is attached.[94] One year later, the Rota again stated that the *appositio dolosa* of the cause of the nullity of the marriage constituted a delict and that the incapacity to accuse the marriage was the penalty for this offense.[95]

Thus, though it is unquestionably true to say with Bartoccetti that the purpose of Canon 1971, § 1, 1° is to safeguard the purity of marriage, and to protect the common good of both the Church and civil society, and to forestall the abuse of the laws of the Church concerning the marriage contract, it is also true that the means that the Church has chosen to accomplish these ends is a law to which there is attached a vindicative penalty.[96] And since Canon 1971, § 1, 1° is a penal law vindicative in character, it must be interpreted according to the prescriptions of Book V which relate to penalties in general and to vindicative punishment in particular.

Section III. The Interpretation of the Clause, *"nisi ipsi fuerint impedimenti causa"*

Article 1. The Interpretation of "Impedimenti"

Canon 1971, § 1, 1° states that the spouses, in all cases of separation and nullity, have the right to accuse their marriage

[94] "Quaestio ideo definita est: privatio iuris accusandi est poena quae praesupponit delictum cum suo triplici elemento: doli, actus externi ac legis penalis, iuxta c. 2195, § 1: 'Nomine delicti, iure ecclesiastico, intelligitur externa et moraliter imputabilis legis violatio cui addita sit sanctio canonica saltem indeterminata.' "—S.R.R. *Decisiones,* XXXVI (1944), 352, n. 6.

[95] "In casibus consideratis in can. 1971, § 1, 1°, appositio dolosa causae nullitatis matrimonii constituit delictum; inhabilitas accusandi, huius delicti poena."—S.R.R. *Decisiones,* XXXVII (1945), 394, n. 18; cf. XX (1928), 405, nn. 4, 5; XXVII (1935), 453, n. 2; XXVIII (1936), 78, n. 10; XXIX (1937), 517, n. 2.

[96] *Supra,* p. 25; cf. Marquardt, *The Loss of Right to Accuse a Marriage,* p. 82.

unless they themselves were the cause of the impediment.[97] The proper and literal signification of the word "impediment," as it is related to the nullity of marriage, is determined by the Code from Canons 1067 to 1080. These canons are grouped under the chapter head of, *"De impedimentis dirimentibus,"* diriment impediments.[98]

A diriment impediment may be defined as a circumstance attaching to the person which, according to law, renders a marriage invalid. The common opinion of authors, who wrote even before March 12, 1929, was that the word impediment of Canon 1971, § 1, 1° should be interpreted to include not only the diriment impediments listed in Canons 1067-1080, but also the impediments of defect of consent and defect of form which are considered by the Code in Canons 1081-1103.[99] On March 12, 1929, the Commission for the Authentic Interpretation of the Code was asked whether the word "impediment" of Canon 1971, § 1, 1° is to be understood as embracing only those impediments properly so-called (Canons 1067-1080), or also those diriment impediments of marriage improperly so-called (Canons 1081-1103). The Code Commission answered, in the negative to the first part; in the affirmative to the second.[100]

It is interesting to note that this response of the Code Commission was not a declarative but an extensive interpretation of

[97] "Habiles ad accusandum sunt: Conjuges, in omnibus causis separationis et nullitatis, nisi ipsi fuerint impedimenti causa."

[98] In general, the diriment impediments of marriage fall under the concepts of age, impotence, ligamen, disparity of cult, sacred orders, solemn vows, abduction, *crimen,* consanguinity, affinity, public decency, spiritual relationship, and legal relationship if so prescribed by civil law.

[99] Among those who held this opinion were Noval, *De Judiciis,* n. 850, and Cappello, "De iure accusandi matrimonium," *Periodica,* XVI (1927), 231. Cappello cites DeSmet, Chelodi, Wernz-Vidal, Vermeersch-Creusen, and Pruemmer as being in agreement with him. Cf. Vermeersch-Creusen, *Epitome Iuris Canonici,* III, 6. ed., n. 286.

[100] Utrum vox impedimenti canonis 1971, § 1, n. 1 intelligenda sit tantum de impedimentis proprie dictis (cann. 1067-1080), an etiam de impedimentis improprie dictis matrimonium dirimentibus (cann. 1081-1103). R. Negative ad primam partem; affirmative ad secundum."—*AAS,* XXI (1929), 171.

the law. In other words, this response actually extended the meaning of Canon 1971, § 1, 1° so as to include the cases of defect of consent and defect of form. These cases would not otherwise be included according to the proper meaning of the word *impedimenti* in Canon 1971, § 1, 1°.[101] In an audience with the Dean of the Sacred Roman Rota on April 26, 1929, Pope Pius XI expressly declared that the Interpretation of the Code Commission of March 12, 1929 did not have retroactive force, and therefore, did not, at that time (April 26, 1929), apply to matrimonial cases in which the spouses themselves were the cause of the impediments improperly so-called.[102] As a matter of fact, according to Canon 17, § 2 and Canon 9, the extensive interpretation by the Code Commission of the word, impediment, did not apply until July 6, 1929 since the response was not published in the *Acta Apostolicae Sedis* until April 5, 1929.[103] Hence, there existed an anomalous situation in which the Code Commission issued an interpretation which was the same as the opinion expressed by a substantial number of authors as private interpreters of the law, and yet, these same authors were, as a matter of fact, incorrect in their opinion. The reason is that these authors were not interpreting the law according to its proper meaning prior to July 12, 1929.[104] As late as December

[101] Canon 18.

[102] Holböck, *Tractatus de Iurisprudentia Sacrae Romanae Rotae* (Graetiae, Austria: Universitats-Buchdruckerei Styria, 1952), p. 362; cf. Jemolo, *Il Matrimonio nel Diritto Canonico* (Milano: Casa Editrice Dott. Francesco Vallardi, 1949), p. 381, note, 2; S.R.R. *Decisiones,* XXIII (1931), 47, n. 3; XXVIII (1936), 61, n. 2.

[103] Canon 17, § 2 states that an authentic interpretation which restricts or extends an original law does not have retroactive effect, and it must be promulgated to be binding. Canon 9 states that laws issued by the Holy See are promulgated by being published in the *Acta Apostolicae Sedis,* unless another manner of promulgation is prescribed. Thus promulgated, the laws do not begin to bind until three months have elapsed after the date of issue of the *Acta* unless the nature of the law is such that its immediate enforcement is evident, or the law itself explicitly or specially provides for a longer or shorter period of suspension. See also Canon 34, § 3, 3°.

[104] Canon 18.

7, 1931, the Rota reminded the defenders of the bond of inferior courts that spouses who had been the culpable cause of the nullity of a marriage because of defect of consent before July 6, 1929 did not incur the penalty of Canon 1971, § 1, 1°, and therefore, were not to be deprived of the right to accuse their marriage.[105]

Article 2. The Distinction between the Cause of the Impediment and the Cause of the Nullity of Marriage

Four years after the authentic, extensive interpretation of the word, *impedimentum,* the Code Commission was asked whether a spouse who, according to Canon 1971, § 1, 1°, was the culpable cause of the impediment or of the nullity of the marriage, was capable of accusing marriage. The Code Commission answered: "In the negative." [106] The substance of this response is repeated word for word in Article 37, § 1 of the *Provida.*[107] In general, the authors hold three different opinions concerning the interpretation of the expression *"sive impedimenti sive nullitatis matrimonii."*

The first opinion is that the two terms contained in the clause *"sive impedimenti sive nullitatis matrimonii,"* are to be understood conjunctively.[108] According to this opinion, the response of the Code Commission is to be interpreted to mean that a person is to be deprived of the right to accuse the marriage only if he had caused the impediment for the purpose of contracting a marriage that was null.[109]

The second opinion interprets the words *"sive impedimenti*

105 Cf. S.R.R. *Decisiones,* XXII (1930), 670, n. 2; XXIII (1931), 47, n. 3.

106 "An ad normam eiusdem canonis 1971, § 1, 1°, habilis sit ad accusandum matrimonium coniux, qui fuerit causa culpabilis sive impedimenti sive nullitatis matrimonii. R. Negative."—Comm. Pont., 17 Julii, 1933, *AAS,* XXV (1933), 345.

107 "Coniux inhabilis est ad accusandum matrimonium, si fuit ipse causa culpabilis sive impedimenti sive nullitatis matrimonii."

108 "Grammaticalis enim adhibita copulativa constructio (. . . sive . . . sive) hoc exigit."—Roberti, "De matrimonii accusatione," *Apollinaris,* VI (1933), 443.

109 *Loc. cit.*

sive nullitatis" in the light of the response of the Code Commission of March 12, 1929 in which the meaning of the term *impedimenti* was extended to include cases involving impediments improperly so-called.[110] Thus, "*sive impedimenti*" refers to cases involving impediments properly so called (Canons 1067-1080). The expression "*sive nullitatis*" refers to those cases involving impediments improperly so-called, namely, defect of consent and defect of form (Canons 1081-1103).

The foregoing opinions do not seem to give a satisfactory explanation to the meaning of the expression, *sive impedimenti sive nullitatis*. Against the opinion that holds that the construction . . . *sive* . . . *sive* is to be interpreted in a copulative or conjunctive sense, it may be replied that such grammatical usage is strictly classical in character and is not to be found in the language of the Code or in the language of modern canonists.[111] Against the opinion that relates "*sive impedimenti*" to impediments properly so-called and "*sive nullitatis*" to impediments improperly so-called, it may be replied that the response of the Code Commmission of March 12, 1929 had already interpreted "*impedimenti*" to include impediments in the wide sense. Therefore, it would seem unlikely that the Code Commission would ignore in 1933 the interpretative significance it had given to the term "*impedimenti*" in 1929 and add the words *sive nullitatis* as a reminder that impediments in the wide sense were also included.[112] Redundancy and irrelevant terminology are not characteristics of the responses of the Code Commission.

The third opinion, which appears to be the correct opinion, holds that the terms "*impedimenti*" and "*nullitatis*" are to be understood disjunctively. Thus, the response, according to the proper signification of the words it has employed, can be elabo-

[110] Graziani, "Limitazioni al Diritto del Coniuge di Accusare la Nullità del Matrimonio," *Il Diritto Ecclesiastico,* XLVI (1935), 118.

[111] Bertola, "Ius Accusandi Matrimonium," *Miscellanea Vermeersch,* I (1935), 446.

[112] Marquardt, *The Loss of Right to Accuse a Marriage,* p. 87; Donnelly, "Fraud and the Estoppel of Canon 1971, § 1, 1°, *The Jurist,* VI (1946), 389.

rated to read: Whether according to Canon 1971, § 1, 1°, a spouse who was the culpable cause of the impediment, or a spouse who was the culpable cause of the nullity of the marriage, is capable of accusing marriage.[113] It would seem that the response of the Code Commission looked toward those marriage cases in which a person could be the culpable cause of the nullity of the marriage and yet not be a guilty cause of the impediment. Such situations can arise, for example, if a man knows with certainty that the girl he wishes to marry is not of canonical age, or is impotent, or is related to him by invalidating degrees of consanguinity or affinity, or is bound by a prior bond. This man cannot be said to be the cause of the impediment, much less the culpable cause. But if he directly and maliciously wills to contract an invalid marriage with this girl, he is most certainly the culpable cause of the nullity of the marriage. Cappello suggests that one can also be the culpable cause of the nullity of the marriage without being the culpable cause of the impediment if he directly and maliciously fails to fulfill a licit and innocent condition placed by the other contracting party.[114] It would seem, therefore, that the response of the Code Commission of July 17, 1933 and Article 37, § 1 of the *Provida* make it clear that the law intends to render juridically incapable of accusing marriage any spouse who was the culpable cause of the impediment of the marriage understood in both its strict and wide signification. And even though the spouse is not the culpable cause of the impediment, he is nevertheless rendered juridically incapable of accusing marriage if he was the culpable cause of the nullity of the marriage. The meaning of the expression *"sive impedimenti sive nullitatis"* was not the only element of this response that occasioned controversies among the authors. Also disputed was the interpretation of the words *"causa culpabilis."* This matter is treated in the Article that follows.

[113] Cappello, *De Matrimonio,* 5. ed., p. 882; Marquardt, *The Loss of Right to Accuse a Marriage,* p. 88; Donnelly, "art. cit.," *The Jurist,* VI (1946), 390.

[114] *De Matrimonio,* 5 ed., p. 882.

Article 3. Principles on the Culpable Cause

A. *Introduction*

In a decision issued on May 20, 1944, the Sacred Roman Rota [115] outlined four different interpretations of the meaning of "culpable cause" offered by authors between July 17, 1933 and July 27, 1942.[116] The four interpretations were as follows:

1. A spouse is the culpable cause of the impediment or of the nullity of marriage if he intends the impediment or the nullity in order to make way for a possible future marriage.

2. A spouse is the culpable cause of the impediment or of the nullity of marriage if he merely has a knowledge of the impediment or of the nullity. It is not necessary that the spouse intend to vitiate the contract of marriage.

3. A spouse is the culpable cause of the impediment or of the nullity of marriage if he is not only aware of the impediment or of the nullity of marriage but also intends the impediment or the nullity.

4. A spouse is the culpable cause of the impediment or of the nullity of marriage if he wilfully places the cause of the impediment while aware of the mortal sinfulness of his action even though he was ignorant that the effect of his action rendered the marriage contract invalid.

It will be observed that one characteristic is common to all four interpretations, namely, that the culpable cause is a free agent who is morally responsible for the goodness or evil of his acts. A second characteristic is common to three of the four interpretations, [117] namely, that the culpable cause is not only a morally responsible agent but also, in one degree or another, the formal voluntary cause of the impediment or of the nullity of

[115] *Decisiones,* XXXVI (1944), 351, n. 2.

[116] Cf. Restrepo, "Annotationes," *Periodica,* XXXII (1943), 116; Roberti, "Quando coniux dicendus sit dubie habilis ad accusandum matrimonium," *Apollinaris,* XII (1939), 267-269. On July 27, 1942, the meaning of the expression, *causa culpabilis* as employed in the response of the Code Commission of July 27, 1933, was authentically interpreted by the Code Commission as a *causa et directa et dolosa.*

[117] See numbers 1, 3, 4.

marriage. These common characteristics were preserved, perhaps, by virtue of two additional responses of the Code Commission which accompanied the reply relating to the culpable cause and which are considered in the two subtitles immediately following.

B. *The Innocent and Licit Cause of the Impediment*

The Code Commission was asked whether an innocent and licit cause of the impediment, placed by a spouse, is an obstacle to the right of that spouse to impugn the marriage according to Canon 1971, § 1, 1°. The reply of the Code Commission was in the negative.[118] This response of the Code Commission is repeated in the Instruction *Provida* at Article 37, § 2.[119] In cases in which an innocent and licit cause is placed against the marriage and the marriage is thereby rendered invalid because the condition is not fulfilled or is not verified, the non-realization of the condition rather than the placing of the condition is the cause of the nullity of the marriage.[120] Thus, if a man places the condition, "I will marry you, provided you are now a virgin," the marriage will be valid or invalid depending on whether the woman is or is not a virgin at the time when the marriage is contracted.[121] If the woman is not a virgin, the man is not the culpable cause of the nullity of the marriage. The condition he has placed occasions the invalidity of the marriage. The fact that the condition is not verified causes the nullity.[122] On the other hand, if the man maliciously placed the condition, "I will marry you, provided you are now a virgin," though he knew, *de facto*, that the girl was not a virgin, he would then be considered the culpable cause of the nullity of the marriage.

118 "An causa impedimenti honesta et licita a coniuge apposita obstet quominus coniux ipse habilis sit ad accusandum matrimonium, ad normam canonis 1971, § 1, n. 1? R. Negative."—17 Julii, 1933, *AAS*, XXV (1933), 345.

119 "Qui causam impedimenti honestam et licitam apposuit, habilis est ad accusandum matrimonii."

120 S.R.R. *Decisiones*, XXXII (1940), 893, n. 3; XXVIII (1936), 75, n. 5.

121 Canon 1092, § 4.

122 S.R.R. *Decisiones*, XXXII (1940), 893, n. 3; XXVIII (1936), 75, n. 5.

Here the question arises whether a party is to be considered the culpable cause of the impediment or of the nullity of marriage, if he has placed an innocent and licit condition against marriage without the permission of the Ordinary, contrary to the Instruction of the Sacred Congregation of the Sacraments of June 29, 1941.[123] On at least two occasions, the Rota has declared that the failure to obtain such permission would not deprive the party who placed the condition of the right to accuse the marriage.[124] Holböck suggests that the reason that the right of accusing would not be lost in the case of a spouse who failed to obtain the required permission of the Ordinary may be found in the strict interpretation demanded by Canon 1971, § 1, 1°.[125] The reason of Holböck appears to be sufficiently cogent.

C. *The Victim of Force and Fear*

The second response of the Code Commission which assisted authors, in some measure, to determine the meaning of "culpable cause," concerned a spouse whose consent was elicited through fear and coercion. The Code Commission was asked whether, according to Canon 1971, § 1, 1° a spouse who was the victim of fear or coercion was capable of accusing marriage. The reply was in the affirmative.[126] This response of the Code Commission is repeated in the Instruction *Provida* at Article 37, § 3.[127] It should be clear that the right to accuse the invalidity of a marriage on the grounds of force and fear is not exclusively reserved to the party who was the victim of the force and fear. Thus,

[123] *AAS,* XXXIII (1941), 304, n. 9; cf. Bouscaren, *Canon Law Digest,* II, 262.

[124] S.R.R. *Decisiones,* XXX (1938), 406, n. 5; XXXII (1940), 893, n. 2; cf. Doheny, *Canonical Procedure,* 2. ed., I, 133, 134.

[125] *Iurisprudentia S.R.R.*, pp. 364, 368.

[126] "An ad normam canonis 1971, § 1, n. 1 habilis sit accusandum matrimonium coniux, qui metum aut coactionem passus sit. R. Affirmative."—17 Julii, 1933, *AAS* (1933), 345.

[127] "Habilis est ad accusandum matrimonium coniux qui metum aut coactionem passus est."

a case may be visualized in which a third party was the cause of the fear in only one of the contracting parties. In this case not only the party who suffered the fear but also the other innocent consort has the right to accuse the marriage.[128]

It is not within the scope of this study to elaborate on the influence of fear on matrimonial consent. It is sufficient to recall that fear which invalidates a marriage is determined by Canon 1087, § 1, which states that marriage is invalid if contracted under the influence of force or grave fear inflicted unjustly and by an external agent, so that one is forced to choose marriage in order to free himself. The matter of this article is concerned with a right of the spouse to accuse a marriage which is alleged to have been invalid because consent to the marriage was given under duress. Just as Canon 1087 relates to the influence of fear on the validity of marital consent, so Canon 2205, § 2 and Canon 2229, § 3, 3° determine the effect of fear on delictual imputability in general and *latae sententiae* penalties in particular. (The incapacity to accuse a marriage, it must always be remembered, is a *latae sententiae* penalty.) The response of the Code Commission is merely the statement of a general principle[129] which has long been recognized in the law of the Church.[130] It must be interpreted in the light of those canons which treat of force and fear in relation to delictual imputability. In this regard, the following considerations are presented.

D. *Force, Fear, Necessity, Grave Inconvenience, and Mental Affliction and Delictual Imputability*

Force may be defined as the using of violence to compel another to perform an action against his will.[131] Force as visualized by the canons of the Code is usually understood as the

[128] "Adnotandum est matrimonium ex capite vis et metus posse accusari non tantum a coniuge, qui metum passus est, sed etiam a comparte, nisi haec fuerit causa invocati metus."—S.R.R. *Decisiones,* XXIII (1931), 33, n. 2.

[129] Roberti, "De matrimonii accusatione," *Apollinaris,* VI (1933), 442.

[130] Pirhing, Lib. IV, tit. 18, n. 1.

[131] Cf. Canon 2205, § 1.

"external force that cannot be resisted" described in Canon 103, § 1.[132] Absolute physical force is opposed to relative force, namely, that found in fear or moral necessity.

The classical definition of fear is the concern or perturbation of mind caused by an imminent or future danger.[133] Fear is essentially a matter of the mind, not of the emotions. Emotion may be a manifestation of fear, but emotion need not be present. Fear is present when the mind, being disturbed by the dread of some imminent or future evil, which it desires to avoid, is moved or compelled to will something which it would not otherwise will. Grave fear is described as that which would certainly influence and deter a prudent and resolute man from his resolve.[134] Though some evils are considered to be "absolutely" grave so that they would influence any man regardless of the circumstances, most evils are relatively grave in respect to a determined person. Fear is essentially a subjective affection of the mind. The gravity of the subjective state depends, almost entirely, on the physical and psychological constitution of the individual. Hence, the gravity of the fear must be measured according to the person's age, sex, health, strength of mind, integrity of character, range of education, and other similar considerations.[135]

Closely allied to the concepts of force and fear and governed by the same fundamental principles of imputability are the notions of necessity and grave incovenience.[136] Necessity, in the present context, is defined as that objective condition of things, brought about in any manner whatsoever, in which an act, according to penal law, is posited or omitted because of an absolute

[132] McCoy, *Force and Fear in Relation to Delictual Imputability and Penal Responsibility,* The Catholic University of America Canon Law Studies, n. 200 (Washington, D. C.: The Catholic University of America Press, 1944), p. 83.

[133] D. (4.2) 1.

[134] Alphonsus Liquori, *Theologia Moralis* (ed. L. Gaudé, 4 vols., Romae: Typis Polyglottis Vaticanis, 1905-1912), Lib. III, Tract V, Cap. III, n. 718.

[135] McCoy, *Force and Fear in Relation to Delictual Imputability and Penal Responsibility,* p. 83.

[136] Canon 2205, § 2.

or moral powerlessness, physical or spiritual.[137] Absolute physical necessity is present when one lacks absolutely the strength or the natural means for fulfilling the law. Absolute spiritual necessity is present when one cannot observe a penal law without disobeying a command enjoined by a legitimate superior. Moral physical necessity is present when a person is faced with the choice between violating the law and suffering some grave physical hardship or serious damage to his natural goods such as health, status, or fortune. Moral spiritual necessity is present when one cannot observe the law without suffering serious harm to his own soul or to the soul of another because of scruples or because of some scandal.[138] Necessity is grave when an impending evil cannot be avoided without serious absolute or relative difficulty. Necessity is slight when an imminent evil can be avoided without serious difficulty or hardship.[139]

The grave inconvenience spoken of in Canon 2205, § 2 may be equated with relative necessity or moral impossibility.[140] Having examined the notions of force, fear, necessity, and grave inconvenience, it remains to determine how they affect the imputability of a crime, and specifically, the *latae sententiae* penalty of Canon 1971, § 1, 1°.

According to Canon 2205, § 1, physical violence which deprives

[137] Michiels, *De Delictis et Poenis,* I, 199.

[138] *Ibid.,* I, 200.

[139] Wernz-Vidal, *Ius Canonicum,* VII, 107.

[140] Michiels, *De Delictis et Poenis,* I, 204. It should be carefully noted in this regard that in the observance of almost every law there arise a certain intrinsic difficulty. Almost every law and every obligation imposes some hardship upon the subject. "Inconvenience" relates to the difficulty that is, *per accidens,* involved in obeying the law, that is, the hardship that is over and above that which the law, of its nature, requires for its ordinary observance. The gravity of the inconvenience or hardship is measured according to the common estimation of prudent men, the practice of the Church, and the gravity of the law to be observed. Furthermore, the application of these norms must always be executed in the light of the subjective physico-psychological constitution of the person who suffered the inconvenience.—Michiels, *De Delictis et Poenis,* I, 206-207; Wernz-Vidal, *Ius Canonicum,* VII, 107-109; McCoy, *Force and Fear in Relation to Delictual Imputability and Penal Responsibility,* p. 99.

a person of all freedom of action absolutely excuses from imputability, and, therefore, precludes the existence of a delict.[141] Such force which precludes a delict completely is had only when it cannot be resisted[142] and provided that the victim did not expose himself to such circumstances through the lack of due diligence.[143] In the latter case, *culpa juridica* not *dolus* would be present. Slight or moderate force would diminish imputability but would not itself preclude *dolus*.[144]

In order to analyze the effect of fear on the delictual imputability of *latae sententiae* penalties, it is necessary to refer to Canons 2205, § 2, 2229, § 3, 3°, and a response of the Pontifical Commission for the Authentic Interpretation of the Code issued on December 30, 1937.[145] Canon 2205, § 2 prescribes the general rule of delictual imputability in cases in which fear is involved. Canon 2229, § 3, 3° applies this rule specifically to *latae sententiae* penalties, and in so doing, modifies Canon 2205, § 2 to some extent. Canon 2205, § 2 states that grave fear, even though relative, necessity, and grave inconvenience very often take away all liability if there is a question of purely ecclesiastical laws.[146] If, however, an act is intrinsically evil or involves contempt of the faith or of ecclesiastical authority, or works to the detriment of souls, grave fear diminishes but does not destroy imputability.[147] Canon 2229, § 3, 3° rules that if the law does

141 "Vis physica quae omnem adimit agendi facultatem, delictum prorsus excludit."

142 Canon 103, § 1.

143 Canon 2199.

144 McCoy, *Force and Fear in Relation to Delictual Imputability and Penal Responsibility*, p. 87.

145 *AAS*, XXX (1938), 73.

146 "Metus quoque gravis, etiam relative tantum, necessitas imo et grave incommodum, plerumque delictum, si agatur de legibus mere ecclesiasticis penitus tollunt."

147 "Si vero actus intrinsece malus aut vergat in contemptum fidei vel ecclesiasticae auctoritatis vel in animarum damnum, causae, de quibus in § 2, delictum imputabilitatem minuunt quidem, sed non auferunt."—Canon 2205, § 3.

not demand perfect *dolus,*[148] grave fear does not exempt from *latae sententiae* penalties if the offense tends toward a contempt of the faith or ecclesiastical authority, or begets a public injury to souls. Clearly, then, if the act placed under grave fear did not tend toward the contempt of the faith, or ecclesiastical authority, or if the act did not beget public injury to souls, no penalty would be warranted. Note should be made that in Canon 2229, §3, 3°,[149] no mention is made of the clause *actus sit intrinsece malus* as found in Canon 2205, § 3. It can be concluded that grave fear exempts from *latae sententiae* penalties even if the act is intrinsically evil and gravely culpable provided that it does not tend toward the contempt of the faith or ecclesiastical authority or to the public harm of souls. This conclusion was expressly verified by the Code Commission on December 30, 1937.[150]

Without exploring the nature of intrinsically evil acts, it may be stated that, in general, all acts contrary to the funda-

148 Perfect *dolus* is had when the law is expressed in such terms as *praesumpserit, ausus fuerit, scienter, studiose, temerarie, consulto egerit;* cf. Canon 2229, § 2.

149 Metus gravis, si delictum vergat in contemptum fidei aut ecclesiasticae aut auctoritatis vel in publicum in animarum damnum, a poenis latae sententiae nullatenus eximit.

150 *AAS,* XXX (1937), 73; cf. Bouscaren, *Canon Law Digest,* II, 570-571. It should also be observed that Canon 2229, § 3, 3° adds the modifier *publicum* to the *animarum damnum* of Canon 2205, § 3. The term, public, of Canon 2229, § 3, 3° is used in opposition to the term "occult" rather than "private." The reason is that harm to souls can scarcely be considered a private matter in the Church; cf. Wernz-Vidal, *Ius Canonicum,* VII, 215; McCoy, *Force and Fear in Relation to Delictual Imputability and Penal Responsibility,* p. 128. Moreover, since there is a question of a *latae sententiae* penalty, that is, a penalty that is incurred at the very moment that the crime is committed, Canon 2229, § 3, 3° refers only to cases in which the harm to souls is a matter which is public at the time of the actual commission of the criminal act. Otherwise, the delinquent may forever be uncertain whether the crime actually became public or whether, *de facto,* it remained occult over the years. Hence, it would seem that the term, public, in Canon 2229, § 3, 3° is to be interpreted according to the definition of public *ratione notitiae* in Canon 2197, 1°; cf. McCoy, *op. cit.,* p. 129.

mental precepts of the natural law are intrinsically evil.[151] Lying (concealing an impediment or giving fictitious consent) is an intrinsically evil act. Thus, if a consort was deceitful in concealing an impediment or in feigning consent, the penalty of Canon 1971, § 1, 1° would not be incurred if the party caused the impediment or the nullity under the influence of, at least, relatively grave fear,[152] provided the act did not tend toward the contempt of the faith or ecclesiastical authority or to the public harm of souls.[153]

[151] Noldin, *Summa Theologiae Moralis* (recognovit A. Schmitt, Vol. I-II, 31 ed.; paravit G. Heinzel, Vol. III, 30 ed., Oeniponte: Typis et Sumptibus Feliciani Rauch. 1950-1956) I, 78; Michiels, *De Delictis et Poenis*, I, 210.

[152] "Simulans, utpote causa culpabilis nullitatis matrimonii, per se non hábet jus accusandi matrimonium. . . . Haec tamen dispositio in toto suo rigore non solet applicari . . . apparet contrahentem metu sibi incusso graviter turbatum et ita ad simulandum adductum fuisse."—*S.R.R. Decisiones*, XXIX (1937), 100, n. 3; cf. XXIV (1932), 349, n. 2; Lega (ed. Bart.), *Iudicia Ecclesiastica*, III, 95*.

[153] The law is not altogether clear in the determination of whether this principle also applies if the deceitful act was placed under the influence of grave necessity or grave inconvenience. On the one hand, it may be argued that in the response of the Code Commission of December 30, 1937 which declared that grave fear excuses from penalties *latae sententiae* even if the crime is intrinsically evil and gravely culpable, provided that it does not tend to the contempt of the faith or of ecclesiastical authority or to the public harm of souls according to Canon 2229, § 3, 3°, there is implied an exception to Canon 2205, § 3 and to the provision of Canon 2229, § 3, 3°. According to the strict interpretation demanded by Canon 19, grave fear only, and not necessity and grave inconvenience, excuses from the penalty of Canon 1971, § 1, 1° if the act was intrinsically evil and gravely culpable. On the other hand, it may be said that if the deceitful act (simulation of consent) was placed under grave necessity or grave inconvenience the penalty of Canon 1971, § 1, 1° would not be incurred; first, because Canon 2205, § 2, 3° places necessity and grave inconvenience on the same juridic level as grave fear in relation to delictual imputability in general; and second, because the response of the Code Commission is merely an explanation of Canon 2229, § 3, 3° which, in turn, is a determination of and not an exception to Canon 2205, § 3. There seems to be a sufficient doubt of law here to warrant the application of Canon 15. Moreover, the latter opinion is in accord not only with Canon 2219, § 1, which urges the more benign interpretation in matters

It should be asked here whether the placing of an act which causes the impediment or the nullity of a marriage is to be considered as an act which tends toward the contempt of the faith or of ecclesiastical authority. Before answering this question it must first be understood that the contempt here mentioned relates not to a subjective contempt of the agent but to an objective contempt which derives from the very nature of the external act or from the external circumstances in which the act is placed.[154] Not every contravention of the law of the Code is to be interpreted as contempt of the faith or of ecclesiastical authority in the sense of Canon 2229, § 3, 3°.[155]

In the context of Canon 1971, § 1, 1° contempt of the faith or of ecclesiastical authority would be verified only *per accidens*, that is, by force of aggravating circumstances which of themselves tended toward this special contempt. For example, if the spouse deliberately feigned true marital consent for the overt purpose of mocking the sacramental character of matrimony or to evidence belligerence against the jurisdiction of the Church over matrimony, the simulated consent in this case would be in contempt of the faith.

In summary, grave fear, necessity, and grave inconvenience

---

penal, but also with the jurisprudence of the Rota in this matter; cf. *Decisiones*, XXXVI (1944), 355, n. 4.

[154] Michiels, *De Delictis et Poenis*, I, 210.

[155] The Code itself in Titles XI and XII of the Fifth Book indicates some of the acts which of their very nature involve contempt of the faith. Among these acts are the crimes of apostasy, heresy, schism (Canon 2314, § 1), defamation of the Sacred Species (Canon 2320), superstition and sacrilege (Canon 2325), and the making of false relics (Canon 2326). Title XIII of the Fifth Book lists certain acts which of their nature tend toward contempt of ecclesiastical authority. Such crimes are the commanding or forcing ecclesiastical burial against the prohibition of the Church (Canon 2339), violating the privilege of the forum (Canon 2341), violating the privilege of the canon by assaulting the Pope, a legate of the Pope, or one's own Ordinary, etc. (Canon 2343). Though the list of crimes included in Titles XI, XXI, and XIII of the Fifth Book is not intended to be exhaustive, it should be clear from the examples presented that the placing of an impediment or the causing of the nullity of marriage in some other way is not envisioned by the legislator as an act which of its nature is in contempt of the faith of or ecclesiastical authority.

excuse from the penalty of Canon 1971, § 1, 1° even if the act which caused the nullity or the impediment was intrinsically evil, provided the act, *per accidens,* does not tend toward the contempt of the faith or ecclesiastical authority, or provided that the act is not committed under such circumstances in which it is immediately known and in which its divulgation may and must be prudently considered as easily possible, and is of such a kind as to cause harm to souls.[156]

One final observation should be made concerning the effect of drunkenness, mental debility, and passion on the imputability of the penalty of Canon 1971, § 1, 1°. Canon 2229, § 3, 2° states that drunkenness, mental debility, and passion do not excuse from penalties *latae sententiae* if notwithstanding the diminution of the imputability, the action is gravely sinful.[157] If, due to the extent of the intoxication, or to the nature of the mental debility, or to the ardor of the passion, deliberation by the intellect or freedom of the will is so impaired as to diminish imputability so that the act ceased to be gravely sinful, the *latae sententiae* penalty of Canon 1971, § 1, 1° would not be incurred.[158]

Article 4. The Causa et Directa et Dolosa *of the Impediment or of the Nullity of Marriage*

A. *Introduction*

In spite of the responses of the Code Commission which defined the cause of the impediment or of the nullity of a marriage as the "culpable cause," and which illustrated two instances in which a party was capable of accusing marriage, the lack of unanimity among the authors concerning the interpretation of the expression "culpable cause" continued until July 27, 1942. On this date, the Code Commission was asked whether, according to Canon 1971, § 1, 1° and the reply of July 17, 1933,

[156] Cf. Canons 2205, § 3; 2229, § 3, 3°; 2197, 1°; *AAS*, XXX (1937), 73.

[157] "Ebrietas, omissio debitae diligentiae, mentis debilitas, impetus passionis, si, non obstante imputabilitatis deminutione, actio sit adhuc graviter culpabilis, a poenis latae sententiae non excusant." Cf. Canons 2201, §§ 3, 4; 2206.

[158] Cf. Canons 2195, § 1; 2199; 2218, § 2.

ad II,[159] only the consort who was both the direct and malicious case of the impediment or of the nullity of the marriage is to be considered as incapable of accusing marriage; or whether the consort who was either the indirect or non-malicious cause of the impediment or of the nullity of the marriage is also (to be considered as incapable of accusing marriage). The Code Commission replied in the affirmative to the first part; in the negative to the second part.[160] As will be seen, not even this additional clarification of the Code Commission proved sufficient to resolve permanently the difficulties and disagreements among canonists.

Before examining the meaning of the operative words contained in this response, namely, *et directa et dolosa* (dolose) [161] note should be made of the grammatical construction in which these words are enframed. The clause, *causa fuit et directa et dolosa,* contains the double conjunction, . . . *et* . . . *et* . . . There is here an unmistakable indication that the adjective *directa* and the adjective *dolosa* modify the predicate nominative, *causa. Directa* does not modify *dolosa.* Moreover, in the second part of the question, the two adjectives are most definitely presented as indicating two separate concepts. The response reads: " . . . *causa exstitit vel indirecta vel doli expers.*" Therefore, it must be concluded that a person who is the direct cause but not the dolose cause of the impediment or of the nullity of marriage is

[159] In this reply, the Code Commission declared that the culpable cause of the impediment or of the nullity of marriage was incapable of accusing marriage.

[160] "Utrum secundum canonem 1971, § 1, 1°, et responsum diei 17 Iulii, 1933, ad II (*AAS,* XXV [1933], 345), inhabilis ad accusandum matrimonium habendus sit tantum coniux, qui sive impedimenti sive nullitatis matrimonii causa fuit et directa et dolosa, an etiam coniux, qui impedimenti vel nullitatis matrimonii causa exstitit vel indirecta vel doli expers. R. Affirmative ad primam partem; negative ad secundam."—Comm. Pont., 27 Julii, 1942, *AAS,* XXXIV (1942), 241.

[161] In order to avoid any misunderstanding in the course of this analysis, the writer will employ the adjective "dolose" to express in English the technical denotation of the Latin term *"dolosa"*; cf. *Webster's New International Dictionary of the English Language* (5 vols., 2. ed. by W. Neilson, T. Knott, P. Carhart, G. & C. Merriam, 1957), II, 767; cf. *infra,* p. 143.

not deprived of the right to accuse his marriage. Only he who is both the direct and dolose cause of the impediment or of the nullity of marriage is juridically incapable of accusing his marriage.[162]

B. *The* Causa Directa *of the Impediment or of the Nullity of Marriage*

In no canon of the law of the Code are the words "direct" and "indirect" specifically defined. From principles and definitions adopted from moral theology, it will be found that these words can be interpreted in several ways. In this discussion, there will be presented five diverse, interpretative approaches to the meaning of the terms, direct and indirect.

1. Interpretations Adopted by Some Authors

According to the first interpretation, a direct cause is one which in itself or in cooperation with another cause produces its effect immediately. An indirect cause is one which in itself or together with another cause does not produce its effect immediately but rather mediately, that is, through the medium of another cause.[163] In other words, direct and immediate are understood as synonymous. This interpretation seems to suffer from the difficulty that the distinction between a direct and indirect cause, which is based on whether or not the cause produces its effect immediately or mediately, is not commonly employed by moral theologians.[164]

For a thing to be willed directly, it is not necessary that it be willed because of itself or as an end in itself. Something may be willed directly as a means to an end. In a directly voluntary act, the will tends toward the act and wants to perform it, whether the act is intended as an end in itself or whether the

[162] Cf. Marquardt, *The Loss of Right to Accuse a Marriage*, p. 94.

[163] Cf. Reh, "Guilt of the Plaintiff in a Marriage Case," *The Jurist*, III (1943), 410.

[164] Merkelbach, *Summa Theologiae Moralis* (10. ed., 3 vols., Brugis, Belgica: Desclée de Brouwer, 1954), I, n. 62; Noldin, *Summa Theologiae Moralis*, I, 31. ed., n. 43.

act is intended as a means to a further end.[165] The first interpretation seems to be unacceptable, therefore, because it is unlikely that the Code Commission would have based its interpretation of the words "direct" and "indirect" on a distinction that is not commonly cited by moral theologians in their divisions of the voluntariness and involuntariness of human acts.

The second interpretation is based on a distinction which was made by St. Thomas in his answer to the question whether sin is aggravated by reason of its causing more harm.[166] St. Thomas declares that when harm resulting from sin is foreseen and intended, the quality of harm aggravates the sin directly because then the harm is the direct (*per se*) object of the sin.[167] When the harm is foreseen but not intended, the quantity of the harm aggravates the sin indirectly.[168] When the harm is neither foreseen nor intended, it does not aggravate the sin directly if this harm is connected with the sin accidentally (*per accidens*).[169] In this context, a cause *per se* is a cause which produces a determined effect which is both foreseen and voluntary. A cause *per accidens* is a cause which produces an effect that is neither foreseen nor voluntary. According to this interpretation, the Code Commission intended that a *causa directa* be understood as a *causa per se,* and that a *causa indirecta* be understood as a *causa per accidens.*

This interpretation of the term "direct" as employed by the Code Commission is not cogent for the following reason. The

[165] *Loc. cit.*

[166] *Summa Theologiae,* Ia, IIae, q. 73, a. 8; cf. Marquardt, *The Loss of Right to Accuse a Marriage,* p. 99.

[167] "Quandoque enim nocumentum quod provenit ex peccato, est praevisum et intentum . . . tunc directe quantitas nocumenti adauget gravitatem peccati, quia tunc nocumentum est per se obiectum peccati."—*Summa Theologiae,* Ia, IIae, q. 73, a. 8.

[168] "Quandoque autem nocumentum est praevisum sed non intentum . . . quanitas nocumenti aggravat peccatum sed indirecte."—*Loc. cit.*

[169] "Quandoque autem nocumentum nec est praevisum nec intentum . . . tunc si per accidens se habeat ad peccatum, non aggravat peccatum directe."—*Loc. cit.*

term "direct" as employed by St. Thomas in the context mentioned above embraces a broader concept than that which is presented by those who espouse the second interpretation. A direct cause, according to St. Thomas in Ia, IIae, q. 73, a. 8, is not only one that produces a determined effect that is foreseen and voluntary but also one that produces an effect that is neither foreseen nor intended, if the effect follows *per se* from the sinful act. This effect, according to St. Thomas, aggravates the sin directly because what is directly consequent to the sin belongs, in a manner, to the very species of that sin.[170]

Basing his opinion on the definition of "direct" as that which produces an effect which is foreseen and voluntary, Marquardt concludes that "no one can be considered a direct cause of the impediment or the nullity if he did not know that his action was actually causing an impediment as such or the nullity as such of his marriage. . . . He must, if he is to incur the punishment (of the deprivation of the right to accuse) place that fact knowing and intending the impediment or the nullity. Otherwise, the full effect of his act is unforeseen and consequently unintended and he is only an indirect cause of the impediment or the nullity."[171] This conclusion is logically correct. It appears, however, to be based on a faulty premise. The term "direct" employed by St. Thomas in this context does not refer merely to an effect which is foreseen and intended. The term "direct" also refers to an effect which is not foreseen and not intended if this effect flows directly from a sinful act which is foreseen and intended. Therefore, it would seem that Marquardt should have concluded that if the impediment or the nullity of the marriage followed directly (*per se*) from the sinful act, even if the impediment or the nullity were not foreseen and not intended, the punishment of the deprivation of the right to accuse would be incurred. The second interpretation of the word "di-

[170] "Si vero nocumentum per se sequatur ex actu peccati, licet non sit intentum neque praevisum directe peccatum aggravat; quia quaecumque per se consequuntur ad peccatum pertinent quodammodo ad ipsam peccati speciem."—Ia, IIae, q. 73, a. 8.

[171] *The Loss of Right to Accuse a Marriage*, pp. 100-101.

rect" is unacceptable because it does not appear to be in accord with the meaning of the word "direct" as used by St. Thomas.

The third interpretation of the expression *causa directa* is based on the distinction drawn by authors[172] between *dolus directus* and *dolus indirectus*. According to Michiels, *dolus directus* is present when one positively intends an anti-juridic effect forbidden by penal law. *Dolus indirectus* is present when one foresees that the effect of his action is in violation of the law, but through culpable negligence, takes no measures to preclude the anti-juridic effect.[173]

This opinion should not be accepted because it is based on a distinction which has no foundation in Canon Law. According to Canon 2200, § 1, which defines *dolus* as the deliberate will to violate the law, a *causa dolosa* cannot be conceived as being other than a direct cause. Thus, Roberti correctly observes that indirect *dolus* is unknown in Canon Law.[174] Michiels concurs with Roberti and adds that the term indirect *dolus* is more accurately described by the Code as *culpa iuridica*.[175]

2. Interpretations Adopted by the S. Roman Rota

a. *Voluntarium Secundum Se.*—The fourth interpretation of *causa directa* is made in the light of the distinction drawn by St. Thomas between *voluntarium secundum se* and *voluntarium secundum suam causam*.[176] According to this distinction, a direct cause (*voluntarium secundum se*) is verified if the intention

[172] Michiels, *De Delictis et Poenis,* I, 105; Roberti, *De Delictis et Poenis,* I, n. 65; Wernz-Vidal, *Ius Canonicum,* VII, 95; cf. Donnelly, "Fraud and the Estoppel of Canon 1971, § 1, 1°," *The Jurist,* VI (1946), 412; Reh, "art. cit.," *The Jurist,* III (1943), 411.

[173] *De Delictis et Poenis,* I, 105.

[174] *De Delictis et Poenis,* I, n. 65.

[175] *De Delictis et Poenis,* I, 105; cf. Canon 2199.

[176] *Summa Theologiae,* Ia, IIae, q. 77, a. 7. *Voluntarium* is defined as that which proceeds from the will as an effect from a cause with previous knowledge of the intellect. Cf. Torre, *Processus Matrimonialis,* 3. ed., p. 106; Sipos, *Enchiridion Iuris Canonici,* 6. ed., p. 786; S.R.R. *Decisiones,* XXXVI (1944), 353, n. 4; Reh, "art. cit.," *The Jurist,* III (1943), 411.

is borne directly on a specific object or effect as a means to a further end or as an end in itself.[177] An indirect cause (*voluntarium secundum suam causam*) is had when the will is directed toward the cause but not the object or effect as a means or as an end.[178] The object or effect is foreseen and permitted to follow from an act of commission or omission which is directly willed.[179]

It would be well to cite here a decision of the Rota (*coram* Canestri) handed down on May 29, 1944. In this decision, the Rota explicitly addressed itself to the question of the concept of a direct cause and of an indirect cause. The Rota stated emphatically that the distinction between a direct and indirect cause was based on the distinction between *voluntarium in se* and *voluntarium in causa*. Thus, according to the Rota, an act that proceeds from the will directly is one that is intended in itself and is the immediately intended object of the will. An act that proceeds indirectly from the will is not the immediately intended object of the will; rather, the act is repelled and merely permitted because it is inseparably conjoined with another object which is actually sought after.[180] In the light of this interpretation, a person is the direct cause of the impediment or of the nullity of marriage if he makes either the impediment or the nullity the immediately intended object of his will. This interpre-

177 ". . . quod aliquid potest esse voluntarium . . . secundum se, sicut quando voluntas directe in ipsum fertur . . ."—St. Thomas Aquinas, *Summa Theologiae,* Ia, IIae, q. 77, a. 7; cf. Noldin, *Summa Theologiae Moralis,* I, 31. ed., n. 43.

178 ". . . secundum suam causam, quando voluntas fertur in causam et non in effectum . . ."—St. Thomas Aquinas, *loc. cit.;* Noldin, *loc. cit.*

179 Noldin, *loc. cit.;* Zalba, *Theologiae Moralis Summa* (3 vols., Matriti: Biblioteca de Auctores Cristianos, 1952), I, 83; Merkelbach, *Summa Theologiae Moralis,* I, 10, ed., n. 62.

180 "Quid per causam directam venit? Nomen opponitur causae indirectae, et distinctio respondet voluntario in se ac voluntario in alio seu in causa. Primum illud est, quod in seipso intenditur et est immediatum objectum intentum a voluntate, alterum vero est illud, quod non intenditur immediate et ratione sui, sed potius repellitur et solummodo admittitur, quia est inseparabiliter conjunctum cum aliquo alio, quod efficaciter appetitur."—S.R.R. *Decisiones,* XXXVI (1944), 353, n. 4.

tation represents one of two different approaches by the Rota to the question of the interpretation of a direct cause.[181] It will become apparent that a difference exists between the interpretation mentioned above and that of May 30, 1949, which will be discussed in the paragraphs that follow. There are, however, two minor objections that can be placed against the Rotal interpretation of May 20, 1944.

Before a party is rendered by law incapable of accusing marriage, it must be established that he was not only the *causa directa* but also the *causa dolosa* of the impediment or of the nullity of marriage. As will be demonstrated in a later analysis of the *causa dolosa, dolus* as a source of criminal imputability always and without exception necessarily supposes a direct causal act as defined according to the Thomistic concept of *voluntarium secundum se.* Therefore, according to the interpretation that relates a direct cause to *voluntarium secundum se,* the word *directa* as employed by the Code Commission is either a mere redundancy or it is intended to reinforce the meaning of the term *dolosa* in order to distinguish unmistakenly between *dolus* and *culpa iuridica.* The customary conciseness of the replies of the Code Commission prompts a rejection of the notion that the word *directa* is a mere redundancy. On the other hand, the grammatical construction of the reply of the Code Commission of July 27, 1942,[182] namely, . . . *et directa et dolosa* . . . , seems to preclude the conclusion that the word *directa* has no other role than that of reinforcing the already obvious signification of the word *dolosa.* Rather, the grammatical construction of the answer of the Code Commission seems to reveal a conscious attempt to indicate that the two terms are conceptually distinct and separable.[183] The fifth and final interpretation of the *causa directa* of the impediment or of the nullity of marriage preserves this distinction.

[181] Cf. Rotal decision of May 30, 1949 published in *Monitor Ecclesiasticus,* LXXXVI (1951), 274; Bouscaren, *Canon Law Digest,* III, 639-640.

[182] *AAS,* XXXIV (1942), 241.

[183] Cf. Donnelly, "Fraud and the Estoppel of Canon 1971, § 1, 1°," *The Jurist,* VI (1946), 391; Marquardt, *The Loss of Right to Accuse a Marriage,* p. 98.

b. *Voluntarium Directe.*—The fifth interpretation of the *causa directa* was presented by the Rota in a decision handed down on May 30, 1949. On this date, the Rota (*coram* Jullien) again assayed the concepts contained in the reply of the Code Commission of July 27, 1942.[184] To appreciate the manner in which the Rota described the direct cause of the impediment or of the nullity of marriage in this decision, it is necessary to review the Thomistic concepts of *voluntarium directe* and *voluntarium indirecte.*[185] The *voluntarium directe* as proposed by St. Thomas is described by some authors [186] as *positive voluntarium.* The *voluntarium indirecte* is correspondingly called *negative voluntarium.* It is of equal necessity to realize that St. Thomas did not identify *voluntarium secundum se* with *voluntarium directe.* Nor did he equate *voluntarium secundum causam* with *voluntarium indirecte.* St. Thomas elaborated on the *voluntarium secundum se et secundum causam* in Ia, IIae, q. 77, a. 7. He introduced the distinction between *voluntarium directe et indirecte* in Ia, IIae, q. 77 a. 7 and explained it in Ia, IIae, q. 6, a. 3. Merkelbach deplores the confusion engendered by authors who identified *secundum se* with *directe* and *secundum causam* with *indirecte.*[187] In its decision of 1949, the Rota also called attention to the fact that the two distinctions were not to be identified.[188]

St. Thomas actually employed both distinctions in Ia, IIae, q. 77, a. 7 of the *Summa* in which he answered the question whether passion altogether excuses from sin. By way of explanation to his answer, St. Thomas draws two distinctions. The first distinction is that of *voluntarium secundum se* and *voluntarium*

[184] Cf. *Monitor Ecclesiasticus,* LXXXVI (1951), 274; Bouscaren, *Canon Law Digest,* III, 639.

[185] *Summa Theologiae,* Ia, IIae, q. 77, a. 7; Ia, IIae, q. 6, a. 3.

[186] Zalba, *Theologiae Moralis Summa,* I, 82; Noldin, *Summa Theologiae Moralis,* I, 31. ed., n. 43.

[187] *Summa Theologiae Moralis,* I, 10. ed., n. 62.

[188] "Voluntarium autem directum (quod verius non est confundendum cum voluntario in se, quemadmodum voluntarium indirectum distat a voluntario in causa . . .)."—*Monitor Ecclesiasticus,* LXXVI (1951), 274, n. 2.

secundum suam causam. The second distinction is that of *voluntarium directe* and *voluntarium indirecte.* Attention is given here to the second distinction of *voluntarium* by St. Thomas,[189] namely, as to the manner in which the effect exists in relation to the will. This distinction is to be considered in the following respect. The effect (*voluntarium*) is considered and said to exist (*esse*) as from the will precisely and only in regard to the activity or non-activity of the will in respect to it (*voluntarium*).[190]

An effect is voluntary directly if the will tends toward it. An effect is voluntary indirectly, if the will is able to prevent it but does not.[191] An effect is voluntary directly if it proceeds from another inasmuch as the other acts, just as heating proceeds from heat.[192] An effect is voluntary indirectly in the sense that it proceeds from another as not acting, just as the sinking of a boat is attributed to the helmsman inasmuch as he ceased to steer.[193] An effect is voluntary directly if it proceeds from the will as from a positive cause, that is, inasmuch as it proceeds from an act of the will which positively begets an effect. An effect is voluntary indirectly if it proceeds from the will as from a negative cause, that is, inasmuch as the will is able to act but abstains from acting and thereby does not prevent the effect.[194]

It is to be noted that an effect that follows from the want of action is not always imputed to the agent when he could have acted but did not. The effect that follows from the absence of

[189] "Secundo considerandum est quod aliquod dicitur voluntarium directe vel indirecte. . . ." *Summa Theologiae,* Ia, IIae, q. 77, a. 1; cf. Ia, IIae, q. 6, a. 3.

[190] ". . . voluntarium dicitur quod est a voluntate . . . uno modo directe, quod scilicet procedit ab aliquo in quantum est agens . . . indirecte, ex hoc ipso quod non agit."—Ia, IIae, q. 6, a. 3.

[191] ". . . directe quidem, id in quod voluntas fertur; indirecte autem, illud quod voluntas potuit prohibere, sed non prohibet."—*Loc. cit.*

[192] ". . . directe, quod scilicet procedit ab aliquo in quantum est agens sicut calefactio a calore."—*Loc. cit.*

[193] ". . . indirecte, ex hoc ipso quod non agit, sicut submersio navis dicitur esse a gubernatore, in quantum desistit a gubernando."—*Loc. cit.*

[194] Zalba, *Theologiae Moralis Summa,* I, 82; Noldin, *Summa Theologiae Moralis,* I, 31. ed., n. 43.

action by the will is imputed to the agent only when he could have acted and should have acted.[195] Thus, St. Thomas concludes that since by willing and acting the will is able and sometimes must prevent that which is not-willing and not-acting, not-willing and not-acting are imputed to one as if they issued from the will as effects from a cause.[196] And hence it is possible to have *voluntarium* without an act; sometimes without an exterior act but with an interior act, for example, when one wills not to act, and sometimes without even an interior act as when one does not will to act.[197]

In its decision of May 30, 1949, the Rota applied these principles to elucidate the meaning of the words "direct" and "indirect" employed in the response of the Code Commission of July 27, 1942. According to the explanation of the Rota in this decision, a person is the direct cause of the impediment or of the nullity of marriage if the impediment or the nullity proceeds from the will directly, that is, inasmuch as the will positively places an impediment or procures the nullity of marriage.[198] A person is the indirect cause of the impediment or of the nullity of the marriage if the impediment or the nullity proceeds from the will as not acting.[199] So that these concepts may be better understood, the Rota recalled the four-fold relation of the will

[195] Sed sciendum quod non semper id quod sequitur ad defectum actionis, reducitur sicut in causam in agens, ex eo quod non agit; sed solum tunc cum potest et debet agere."—*Summa Theologiae,* Ia, IIae, q. 6, a. 3.

[196] "Quia igitur voluntas volendo et agendo potest impedire hoc quod est non velle et non agere, et aliquando debet; hoc quod est non velle et non agere, imputatur ei, quasi ab ipsa existens."—*Loc. cit.*

[197] "Et sic voluntarium potest esse absque actu; quandoque quidem absque actu exteriori, cum actu interiori, sicut cum vult non agere; aliquando autem etiam absque actu interiori, sicut cum non vult agere."—*Loc. cit.*

[198] "Causa directa alicuius rei is dicitur qui per voluntarium directum hanc rem efficit, et, in casu nostro, qui per voluntarium directum impedimentum ponit vel matrimonii nullitatem procurat."—*Monitor Ecclesiasticus,* LXXXVI (1951), 274, n. 2.

[199] ". . . id quod a voluntate est sicut a non agente . . ."—*Loc. cit.*

toward a given object, namely, intention, choice, passive permission, and active permission.[200]

The writer here suggests that to introduce these notions as explanatory concepts of a direct and indirect cause visualized by St. Thomas in Ia, IIae, q. 77, a. 7 and in Ia, IIae, q. 6, a. 3 of the *Summa* is to identify, respectively, *voluntarium directum* and *indirectum* with *voluntarium secundum se* and *secundum suam causam,* which the Rota asserted, and correctly, are not to be confused.[201] The reason for this suggestion is found in the following consideration. The distinction between *voluntarium directum* and *indirectum* as drawn by St. Thomas is based on nothing more than a difference of manner in which an effect proceeds from the will which produces it.[202] The distinction between *voluntarium secundum se* and *secundum suam causam* is based on the manner in which the will attains its object or, in other words, the attitude of the will toward the effect produced by it.[203] The first distinction looks to the question whether the effect has proceeded from the will as from a positive cause which has produced the effect or whether the effect has proceeded from the will as a negative cause inasmuch as the will failed to act, when it could have and should have prevented the effect. The latter distinction looks to the question whether the will tended toward the effect in the manner of an intention (*voluntarium secundum se*) or in the manner of permission (*voluntarium secundum suam causam*). To speak in terms of "intention" and "permission," then, is to speak in terms of the attitude with which the will tends toward its object (*voluntarium secundum se* and *secundum suam causam*) which it directly produces and not in terms of the manner in which the effect is produced (*vol-*

[200] "Quod ut melius intelligatur, recolendum est circa aliquod obiectum quadruplicem voluntatis actum considerari posse . . . intentionem . . . electionem . . . permissionem passivam . . . permissionem activam."—*Loc. cit.*

[201] *Supra,* p. 136.

[202] *Summa Theologiae,* Ia, IIae, q. 77, a. 7; Ia, IIae, q. 6, a. 3; Zalba, *Theologiae Moralis Summa,* I, 82; Merkelbach, *Summa Theologiae Moralis* I, 10. ed., n. 59.

[203] *Summa Theologiae,* Ia, IIae, q. 77, a. 7; Zalba, *loc. cit.;* Merkelbach, *loc. cit.*

untarium directum and *indirectum*). It must be remembered that the words *directum* and *indirectum* as predicated of *voluntarium* merely represent, respectively, the will in respect to the production of the fact or effect as acting or as not acting when the will can and should act. Whether the will as acting in the production of the effect actually intends or only permits the effect of its positive influence is another question, which St. Thomas considers when he distinguishes between *voluntarium secundum se* and *voluntarium secundum suam causam.*[204]

Thus, according to the Rota in its decision of May 30, 1949, the direct cause of the impediment is one who places the impediment or who procures the nullity of marriage *"per voluntarium directum,"* [205] that is, in so far as the impediment or the nullity of marriage proceeds from the will as acting.[206] It is to be kept in mind that an effect that is *voluntarium directum* may be *voluntarium secundum se,* that is, intended by the agent; or, the effect may be *voluntarium secundum suam causam,* that is, permitted by the agent.[207] The Rota continues that one is only an

[204] ". . . quod aliquid potest esse voluntarium vel secundum se, sicut quando voluntas directe in ipsum fertur; vel secundum suam causam, quando voluntas fertur in causam et non in effectum . . ."—*Summa Theologiae,* Ia, IIae, q. 77, a. 7.

Voluntarium directum may be predicated of both *voluntarium secundum se* and *voluntarium secundum suam causam.* The same may be said of *voluntarium indirectum.* "Porro comparatione instituta inter utramque partitionem voluntarii in se et in causa, et voluntarii directi et indirecti, et in doctrina Angelici Doctoris insistendo, dicendum est, voluntarium directum complecti sub se tum voluntarium in se tum voluntarium in causa nam voluntarium directum dicitur ab A. D., 'quod procedit a voluntate sicut ab agente.' Atqui tum voluntarium in se, tum voluntarium in causa, a voluntate, procedit, in quantum est agens et volens. . . . Voluntarium autem indirectum, tum ad voluntarium in se, tum ad voluntarium in causa reduci potest."—Bucceroni, *Institutiones Theologiae Moralis* (6. ed., Romae: Ex Typographia in Instituto Pii X, 1914-1915), I, n. 34.

[205] Cf. *supra,* p. 137, note 192.

[206] ". . . directi, id in quod voluntas fertur . . ."—St. Thomas Aquinas, *Summa Theologiae,* Ia, IIae, q. 77, a. 7; ". . . directe quod scilicet procedit ab aliquo in quantum est agens . . ."—*Ibid.,* Ia, IIae, q. 6, a. 3.

[207] St. Thomas Aquinas, *Summa Theologiae,* Ia, IIae, q. 77, a. 7; Ia, IIae, q. 6, a. 3; cf. Bucceroni, *op. cit.,* I, n. 34.

indirect cause of the impediment or of the nullity of marriage if, to the best of his ability, he duly contracts marriage with a partner who to his knowledge is placing an obstacle to the validity of the marriage: in this case he foresees and permits the invalid marriage but does not directly will it (*voluntarium secundam suam causam!*).[208]

In the mind of the writer, there appears to be a notable discrepancy between the Thomistic explanation of the *voluntarium indirectum* in the *Summa,* Ia, IIae, q. 77, a. 7 and in Ia, IIae, q. 6, a. 3, and the Rotal explanation of this term in the decision of May 30, 1949. An act, i.e., effect, which is *voluntarium indirectum* is considered by St. Thomas as proceeding from the will inasmuch as the will does not act when the will can and must act to prohibit the effect.[209] St. Thomas here is considering the manner in which the effect proceeds from the will, and not the manner in which the will tends toward the effect. The Rota on the other hand, in introducing the notion of the person foreseeing and permitting the nullity of the marirage is not considering the manner in which the nullity proceeds from the will, but rather the manner in which the will tends toward the nullity of the marriage (merely permitting it). But this is to speak in terms of *voluntarium secundum suam causam*[210] and not in terms of *voluntarium indirectum.* Accordingly, in applying the Thomistic concepts of *voluntarium directum* and *voluntarium indirectum,* the Rota appears to be in error when it states that a party (A), who attempts to the best of his ability to contract marriage correctly with a person (B) who to his knowledge is placing an obstacle to the validity of the marriage, is only an indirect cause

208 ". . . patet esse causam impedimenti vel nullitatis matrimonii tantum indirectam eum qui rite suo pro marte nuptias ineat cum comparte quam valido connubio obicem apponere noverit: hic enim invalidas nuptias praevidit et permittit, non tamen vult directe."—*Monitor Ecclesiasticus,* LXXXVI (1951), 274, n. 2.

209 ". . . indirecte, ex hoc ipso quod non agit . . . cum potest et debet agere . . . indirecte autem, illud quod voluntas potuit prohibere, sed non prohibet."—*Summa Theologiae,* Ia, IIae, q. 77, a. 7; Ia, IIae, q. 6, a. 3.

210 ". . . quando voluntas fertur in causam et non in effectum . . ."—*Summa Theologiae,* Ia, IIae, q. 77, a. 7.

of the impediment or of the nullity of marriage. The writer suggests that a distinction is in order here, based on the following considerations.

If party (A) to the best of his ability attempts to prohibit party (B) from placing an obstacle to the marriage, party (A) is neither a direct nor indirect cause of the impediment, since the impediment neither proceeds from the will of party (A) as acting (*voluntarium directum*) nor from the will of party (A) as not acting when he was able and should have acted to prevent the effect (*voluntarium indirectum*). However, party (A) is the direct cause of the nullity of the marriage inasmuch as the invalidity of the marriage proceeds from the will of party (A) as acting as opposed to not acting when he could and should have acted to prevent the effect of the invalidity.[211]

If party (A) makes no attempt to prohibit party (B) from placing an impediment to the marriage, party (A) is an indirect cause of the impediment to the extent that he could and should have prevented the impediment but did not. On the other hand, party (A) is the direct cause of the nullity of the marriage, because the nullity of the marriage is an effect which proceeds from the will of party (A) as acting (*voluntarium directum*), and not as an effect which proceeds from the will as not acting (*voluntarium indirectum*).

3. Conclusion

In conclusion, therefore, a person is to be considered the direct cause of the impediment of marriage if the impediment proceeds from the will as an effect from a cause inasmuch as the will has, by its act, exercised a positive influence on the production of the impediment. A person is to be considered the direct cause of the nullity of marriage if the nullity of the marriage proceeds from the will as an effect from a cause inasmuch as the will has, by its act, exercised a positive influence in effecting the nullity of the marriage.

[211] It may or may not be of significance that the Rotal decision of May 30, 1949 was not published in the *Decisiones seu Sententiae inter Eas Quae Anno 1949 Prodierunt Cura Eiusdem Apostolici Tribunalis Editae;* cf. S.R.R. *Decisiones*, XLI (1949).

Prescinding from any consideration of the deliberate intention of a person to violate the law (*causa dolosa*),[212] the following cases are instances of direct causes of the impediment or of the nullity of marriage:

a) a party who deliberately simulates consent is the direct cause of the impediment (in the wide sense) of the marriage.
b) a party who deliberately places an honorable and licit condition against the marriage bond is the direct cause of the impediment (in the wide sense) of marriage.
c) a party who deliberately contracts marriage with a consort who is under the influence of invalidating force and fear is the direct cause (co-cause) of the nullity of marriage.
d) a party who deliberately places an invalidating intention against the substance of marriage is the direct cause of the impediment (in the wide sense) of marriage.
e) a party who deliberately attempts to contract marriage with a person who is impotent is the direct cause (co-cause) of the nullity of marriage.

The concept of the *causa directa* in relation to the incapacity of accusing marriage can scarcely be understood without a simultaneous appreciation of the significance of the expression, *causa dolosa*. As a matter of fact, the solution to many of the difficulties concerning the interpretation of the phrase, *causa et directa et dolosa* are rooted principally in the proper understanding of the concept of the *causa dolosa*. The explanation of this concept is presented in the paragraphs that follow.

C. *The* Causa Dolosa *of the Impediment or of the Nullity of Marriage*

1. The Concept of *Dolus* in the Code of Canon Law

The Code of Canon Law speaks of *dolus* in relation to the quality of juridic acts in general,[213] and in relation to contracts[214] and to crimes in particular.[215] When the Code treats

212 Canon 2200, § 1.

213 Canon 103, § 2.

214 Canon 1684, § 1.

215 Canon 2200, § 1.

of *dolus* in relation to juridic acts in general and in relation to contracts, the word *dolus* is understood to mean some form of deceit which leads a person into error. In the context of criminal law, however, the word *dolus* has a more specific and technical signification. In criminal law, *dolus* is one of the measures, indeed the strictest measure, by which the imputability of a crime is determined. It will be recalled that in 1944, the Rota declared that the deprivation of the right to accuse marriage is a penalty which presupposes a crime composed of the three elements determined in Canon 2195, § 1.[216] Before attempting to assay the concept of *dolus*, it would be well to review briefly the three essential elements of a crime as determined in Canon 2195, § 1. They are described by authors as the objective, subjective, and juridicial elements of a crime.[217]

a. *The Objective Element of a Crime.*—The objective element of a crime (*delictum*) consists in the external violation of the law which either forbids or commands an act. Not all transgressions of the moral or ethical order are crimes. Penal law is primarily intended to prevent any disturbance of the public and external spiritual welfare of the Christian community. Therefore, a criminal act must be, in some way, external. The criminal act must be capable of being perceived by the senses.[218] Thus, if a spouse in contracting marriage placed a condition *contra bonum prolis* which was purely internal and never expressed in any way, a serious sin would be committed. The placing of this condition, however, would not constitute a criminal act. According to law of the Code, there would be no crime and, therefore, there should be no penalty. Only if the internal dissent was expressed or uttered vocally or in writing or in some other manner, even though no one was present at the time to

[216] S.R.R. *Decisiones,* XXXVI (1944), 352, n. 6; *supra,* pp. 111-112; cf. XXXVII (1945), 394-395, nn. 17, 18.

[217] Michiels, *De Delictis et Poenis* (Lublin: Universitas Catholica, 1934), I, 57-59; Roberti, *De Delictis et Poenis* (Romae: Libraria Pontificii Instituti Utriusque Iuris, 1938), I, 53-55.

[218] Michiels, *De Delictis et Poenis,* I, 65-66; Chelodi, *Jus Poenale* (Tridenti, 1925), p. 12.

hear or to see the dissent externalized, would the objective element of a crime be verified.[219]

b. *The Subjective Element of a Crime.*—The subject element of a crime relates to the moral imputability of the criminal act to the alleged delinquent. By moral imputability is meant that property of an act whereby the act is attributed to a human agent who acted with knowledge and free will.[220] Subjectively, for an act to be a criminal act, it must proceed from the free will of the agent by way of malice (*dolus*) or negligence (*culpa*) with advertence to the fact that what is being done is mortally sinful.[221] Two elements constitute the basis of the imputability of a crime. They are: deliberation by the intellect and freedom of the will. Any cause that increases, or diminishes, or destroys the deliberation by the intellect or the freedom of the will correspondingly increases, diminishes, or destroys imputability.[222] The gravity of a crime and the severity of the penalty depend not only upon the gravity of the law violated and the damage inflicted upon the social order, but also upon the subjective guilt of the delinquent.[223] It is well to keep in mind throughout this discussion that punishment is always and only directed toward the guilty will of the wrong-doer. No one is guilty unless he has guilty intent. "*Non est reus nisi mens sit rea.*"[224] Hence, criminal imputability always relates to the mortally sinful will. The Code distinguishes between two degrees of imputability. They are called *dolus* and *culpa*.

1°. *Dolus*

Dolus or malice is the deliberate will to violate a law.[225] A crime committed with the deliberate will to violate a law is

[219] Cf. Pendola, "De Iure Accusandi Matrimonium," *Periodica,* XXXVIII (1949), 240-241.

[220] Wernz-Vidal, *Ius Canonicum,* 2. ed., VII, 43.

[221] Michiels, *De Delictis et Poenis,* I, 84-85.

[222] Canon 2199.

[223] Canons 2196, 2218, § 1.

[224] Wernz, *Ius Decretalium,* IV, n. 21.

[225] Canon 2200, § 1.

called a *delictum dolosum*. For a person to be a *causa dolosa*, two things are necessary. First, there must be a direct intention to violate the law. The direct will to violate the law does not imply the direct intention to commit a crime. It is sufficient that the act by which the law is violated be directly willed.[226] Second, on the part of the intellect, there must be a conscious advertence to the illicit character or mortal sinfulness of the act to be performed. For *dolus* to be present, it is not necessary that there be knowledge of the penal character of the law violater. Much less is it necessary that the specific penalty imposed by the law be known by the offender.[227] It is sufficient and necessary that the person actually advert both to the law which he is about to violate and to the fact that that action that he is to place is a grave violation of the law. Thus, according to Canon 2200, § 1 for a person to be the *causa dolosa* of some effect, there must be a conscious advertence to the illicit character of the act to be performed and a deliberate willingness to perform it.

It should be clear that *dolus* can be verified either in a positive act of commission against a contrary prohibitive law, or in a negative act of omission against a contrary preceptive law. It is important to note here that if a spouse has placed an act of commission or omission to cause the impediment or the nullity of the marriage, *dolus* is presumed in the external forum until the contrary is proved.[228] The prescription of Canon 2200, § 2

[226] Michiels, *De Delictis et Poenis,* I, 103.

[227] Wernz-Vidal, *Ius Canonicum,* VII, 58; Michiels, *De Delictis et Poenis,* I, 102, note 14. Canonists distinguish between *dolus* as defined in Canon 2200, § 1 and *dolus* as described in Canon 2229, § 2 which demands full knowledge and complete deliberation. Canon 2229, § 2 enumerates certain terms which, if expressed by the law, demand on the part of the subject not merely a direct intention to violate the law (*dolus*) but a direct intention that is absolutely free and posited with perfect deliberation (perfect *dolus*), otherwise no penalty is incurred. Canon 1971, § 1, 1° demands *dolus* but not perfect *dolus*. Cf. Vermeersch-Creusen, *Epitome Iuris Canonici,* 6. ed., III, n. 421; Wernz-Vidal, *Ius Canonicum,* VII, 214; Berutti, *Institutiones Iuris Canonici* (6 vols., Taurini-Romae: Marietti, 1938), VI, 91; Roberti, *De Delictis et Poenis,* I, 276; S.R.R. *Decisiones,* XXXVI (1944), 354, 4 b; *Monitor Ecclesiasticus,* LXXVI (1951), 275, n. 5.

[228] Canon 2200, § 2; cf. canon 16, § 2.

does not imply that the law presumes a particular person guilty before he has been proved guilty. Rather, it does presume that in the ordinary course of human affairs, the average man is accustomed to act reasonably, that is, that he knows what he is doing and realizes the ordinary implications, both physical and moral, of his voluntary conduct. Thus, when a law is violated, it is presumed that the person who is proven to have violated it did so deliberately and freely. And since *dolus* is verified precisely in the deliberate will to violate the law, *dolus* is presumed in the external forum. The presumption of *dolus* is overthrown if the person who has violated the law can prove that because of circumstances surrounding the objectively criminal act, there is present merely juridic negligence or on moral fault at all.[229]

Finally, Michiels observes that some authors distinguish between *dolus directus* and *dolus indirectus*. *Dolus directus* is present when one positively intends an anti-juridic effect forbidden by penal law. In so doing, one adverts to the causal connection between his action or omission and the anti-juridic effect. *Dolus indirectus* is had when one simply foresees the anti-juridic effect of his own action and does nothing about it, though he does not positively desire the anti-juridic effect.[230] Michiels and Roberti concur in the opinion that in the Code the notion of *dolus indirectus* is more correctly described by the expression, *culpa juridica*.[231]

2°. *Culpa*

The second source of imputability is *culpa* or culpable negligence. A brief analysis of *culpa* is in order here for no other reason than to assist in bringing into sharper focus the notion of a *causa dolosa*. *Culpa* is the morally imputable neglect to avoid

[229] Michiels, *De Delicitis et Poenis*, I, 113.

[230] Dolus directus habetur, cum quis positive intendit effectus antijuridicos vi poenalis vitandos, quos animadvertit relatione causalitatis cum sua actione vel omissione conjunctos; . . . Dolus indirectus . . . quando quis simpliciter praevidet anti-juridicum propriae actionis effectum et ab eo non refugit, quin tamen eum positive velit.—*De Poenis et Delictis*, I, 105.

[231] Michiels, *De Delictis et Poenis*, I, 105; Roberti, *De Delictis et Poenis*, I, n. 65; cf. *supra*, p. 133.

violating a criminal law. *Culpa* is rooted either in culpable ignorance of the law violated or in the omission of due diligence in failing to foresee the injurious effects of an action or in failing to prevent a foreseen criminal effect when one has the duty to do so.[232] As regards the culpable ignorance of the law violated, it is necessary and sufficient for criminal negligence to be present, that a person foresee, at least in an uncertain way, that he is exposing himself to a violation of penal law. In this state of mental uncertainty, that is, knowing that he is ignorant of the law and that there is a probability that he will violate the law, he nevertheless neglects to inform himself of the disposition of the law when he has the opportunity to do so. Thus, one is culpably ignorant of the law, when he realizes that he is in ignorance of the law and is aware that in consequence of his ignorance he may violate the law in the act that he is about to place.[233] As regards the omission of due diligence, *culpa* is present when a person fails to give reasonable consideration to the effects of his actions and in so doing implicitly permits any consequence that derives from his action. As regards the failure to prevent a foreseen criminal effect, *culpa* is present only when a person is bound by law or precept to prevent such effects. Moreover, the omission of an act or the failure to perform some positive duty can be either *dolosum* or *culposum*, depending upon the directness or the indirectness of the intention to violate the law.[234]

c. *The Juridic Element of a Crime.*—The third element of a crime, the juridic element, is the penalty itself which is attached to the violation of the law. As demonstrated above[235] the penalty of the deprivation of the right to accuse marriage is a

[232] Canon 2199; Regatillo, *Institutiones Iuris Canonici,* II, 448; Michiels, *De Delictis et Poenis,* I, 107; Swoboda, *Ignorance in Relation to the Imputability of Delicts,* The Catholic University of America Canon Law Studies, n. 143 (Washington, D. C.: The Catholic University of America Press, 1940), pp. 107-108.

[233] Michiels, *De Delictis et Poenis,* I, 107.

[234] Swoboda, *Ignorance in Relation to the Imputability of Delicts,* pp. 104-105.

[235] Cf. *supra,* p. 109.

vindicative punishment[236] incurred *ipso facto* upon the direct and dolose placing of the act which causes the nullity of or the impediment to the marriage. It has been noted that, according to Canon 19, laws which decree a penalty, or restrict the exercise of one's rights, or establish an exception from the law, must be interpreted in the strict sense. Canon 2219, § 1 confirms this general principle by declaring that in penalties, the milder or the more benign interpretation is to be applied. The *benignior interpretatio* of Canon 2219, § 1 is that which reduces the concepts of the law to their true, yet most literal and narrowest meaning.[237] Clearly, an interpretation that is so narrow as to render the law illusory and meaningless is contrary to the mind of the lawgiver.

Finally, if there is a doubt whether the law binds (*dubium iuris*) in a particular case[238] or if there is a doubt whether the facts and circumstances truly point (*dubium facti*)[239] to a *causa et directa et dolosa,* the natural and juridic right of the parties prevails.[240] It is to be expected that in the context of Canon 1971, § 1, 1°, doubts of fact arise most frequently. It is often difficult to determine in a particular case whether a party was truly the direct and dolose cause of the impediment or of the nullity of marriage. Canon 15 makes a provision for a doubt of fact. In doubts of fact, the Ordinary may dispense from the law provided the law is one from which the Holy See is accustomed to dispense. It is to be wondered whether the Holy See is accustomed to dispense from Canon 1971, § 1, 1°.[241]

236 ". . . ipse conceptus inhabilitatis accusandi, quae rationem poenae vindicativae habet."—S.R.R. *Decisiones,* XXVIII (1936), 78, n. 10; XXXVI (1944), 354, n. 4b.

237 "Odia restringi et favores convenit ampliari; in poenis benignior est interpretatio facienda."—R. J. in VI°, 15, 49.

238 Cf. *supra,* p. 107.

239 Cf. Canon 15.

240 ". . . sufficit dubium absentiae doli in apponendo impedimento, ut aliquis non privetur per legem incertam et quidem humanam ac poenalem, certo suo iure naturali libere agendi in iudicio."—S.R.R. *Decisiones,* XXXIX (1947), n. 3.

241 Cf. Ciprotti, "De Coniuge dubie habili ad matrimonium accusandum," *Apollinaris,* XII (1939), 226.

Let it be supposed, however, that the tribunal knows well the rules for establishing the culpability of a spouse under the provisions of Canon 1971, § 1, 1°, but is in doubt whether, from the evidence, culpability is present in this particular plaintiff. In this case, there is no need to seek a dispensation from the Ordinary according to Canon 15. The tribunal may follow the rule of law: *In dubio melior est conditio possidentis.* A person in possession of the natural and juridic right of accusing marriage should not be deprived of the exercise of this right until it is proved with moral certainty that the exercise of this right has been actually forfeited by his acts in transgression of the law.[242] This principle is in accord with the prescription of Canon 2233, § 1 which states that no penalty can be inflicted unless it is proved with certainty that the offense has been committed.

2. The Concepts of *Dolus* and *Culpa* in Relation to *Voluntarium Secundum Se* and *Voluntarium Secundum Suam Causam*

The canonical concepts of *dolus* and *culpa* are related to the Thomistic concepts of *voluntarium secundum se* (or, *in se*) and *voluntarium secundum suam causam* (or, *in causa*) employed by moral theologians.[243] It will be recalled that *voluntarium in se* is verified if the will directly tends toward some specific object or effect.[244] The object willed may be sought immediately as an end or mediately as a means to a further end. In other words, in order that an effect be willed *secundum se,* it is not necessary that the effect be willed as an end in itself (*propter se*). *Voluntarium secundum causam* is verified if the intention of the will is not immediately directed toward a given object or effect as a means or as an end. Rather, the object or effect is foreseen to follow from an act of commission or omission which is directly willed. In the act which is *voluntarium secundum*

[242] Cf. Canons 87, 1646, 1667, 2219, § 1; Beste, *Introductio in Codicem,* 4. ed., p. 923; Bouscaren, *Canon Law Digest,* III, 642.

[243] St. Thomas Aquinas, *Summa Theologiae,* Ia, IIae, q. 77, a. 7; Merkelbach, *Summa Theologiae Moralis,* I, 10. ed., n. 62; Zalba, *Theologia Moralis Summae,* I, 83; cf. S.R.R. *Decisiones,* XXXVI (1944), 354, n. 4b.

[244] ". . . quod aliquid potest esse voluntarium . . . secundum se, sicut quando voluntas directe in ipsum fertur . . ."—St. Thomas Aquinas, *Summa Theologiae,* Ia, IIae, q. 77, a. 7.

causam, the object or the effect which is not intended or willed is not essentially connected with nor is it necessarily the motive of the act of commission or omission which caused the effect. It is foreseen and known that with an immediately intended act of commission or omission there is also conjoined a simultaneous or consecutive effect. But such an effect, considered in itself, is not intended by the will. Rather, the will merely permits, actively or passively, the effect which is known to be conjoined with the act of commission or omission but without any affection or tendency toward it.[245]

3. The Interpretations of Authors

On the basis of the concept of *dolus* as a source of criminal imputability in general, and of the vindicative character of the *latae sententiae* penalty of the deprivation of right to accuse marriage in particular, the interpretation of the words *causa dolosa impedimenti vel nullitatis matrimonii* will now be assayed. Just as there is a variety of definitions of a *causa directa* presented by authors, so there is an equal variety of definitions of *causa dolosa.*

Beste asserts that a person is said to be the dolose cause of the impediment or of the nullity of marriage if he produces the impediment or the nullity with a will to violate the law. He bases his definition on Canon 2200, § 1 because of the penal character of the deprivation of a right to accuse a marriage.[246]

Vermeersch-Creusen hold that a person is the dolose cause of the nullity of marriage who, knowing that he is acting against the law, nevertheless, freely procures the impediment or the nullity. These authors base their definition on the necessity to interpret the word "dolose" strictly and in opposition to the concept of *culpa iuridica.*[247]

245 ". . . secundum suam causam, quando voluntas fertur in causam et non in effectum . . ."—St. Thomas Aquinas, *Summa Theologiae,* I, IIae, q. 77, a. 7; I, IIae, q. 73, a. 8: cf. Zalba, *Theologia Moralis Summae,* I, 83; Noldin, *Summa Theologiae Moralis,* I, 31. ed., n. 43; Merkelbach, *Summa Theologiae Moralis,* I, 10. ed., n. 62.

246 ". . . dolosa, qui effectum producit cum voluntate violandi legem ad tramitem can. 2200, § 1."—*Introductio in Codicem,* 4. ed., p. 923.

247 "Dolosa causa est nullitatis qui sciens se contra legem agere, nihilo-

Regatillo states simply that he is a dolose cause who contracts an impediment or an invalid marriage morally imputable to himself as a sin.[248]

Reh holds that by the term, dolose cause, the Code Commission intended to indicate "a person who, as the cause of the nullity of the marriage, acted *ex dolo,* that is, knew the malice of his act and intended it." Reh holds that *causa dolosa* must be interpreted according to Canon 2200 because the deprivation of the right to accuse a marriage is a vindicative penalty.[249]

Donnelly declares that "what would make one an *impedimenti causa dolosa* . . . would be his wilful deceit in declaring directly and formally that no impediment existed." [250] He bases his definition on the obligation of each party to a marriage *in facie Ecclesiae* to reveal any impediment which he knows to exist. [251]

Marquardt defines a *causa dolosa* as "an action or omission by virtue of which a person knowingly and willingly had maliciously effected the nullity of the marriage or had maliciously placed a matrimonial impediment." [252]

It may be of interest to note here the observations of Gasparri and Roberti, who wrote some nine years before the Code Commission defined the concept of a *causa culpabilis* as a *causa et directa et dolosa.*

Gasparri held that spouses are be considered culpable causes if, in bad faith, they were the cause of the impediment and consequently of the nullity of the marriage. He based his assertion on the principle of Pope Alexander III that it was not fitting

minus impedimentum vel nullitatem libere procurat."—*Epitome Iuris Canonici,* 6. ed., III, 151.

[248] "Dolosa qui impedimentum vel matrimonium nullum contrahit moraliter imputabile sibi ad peccatum."—*Interpretatio et Iurisprudentia C.I.C.,* p. 537.

[249] "Guilt of the Plaintiff in a Marriage Case," *The Jurist,* III (1943), 405, 409.

[250] "Fraud and the Estoppel of Canon 1971, § 1, 1°," *The Jurist,* VI (1946), 379, 386.

[251] Cf. Canons 1019-1027.

[252] *The Loss of Right to Accuse a Marriage,* p. 94.

that such spouses reap an advantage from their own culpable action.[253] Gasparri added that cases of this kind arise in the impediment of *crimen,* in defect of form, in conditional consents, and in grave fear inflicted by one party so that the other is forced to give consent. Those who caused these impediments (in the wide sense) *in mala fide* were to be deprived of the right to accuse their marriage. On the other hand, Gasparri held that if the spouses knowingly neglected to seek a dispensation from an impediment known to themselves, they were not to be considered to be the cause of the nullity of the marriage and therefore were not to be deprived of the right to accuse. In explanation of this latter conclusion Gasparri merely states that the deprivation of a natural right is a *res odiosa* and is therefore to be restricted.[254]

Roberti is one of the few authors who actually anticipated the reply of the Code Commission nine years before it was issued. Roberti observed that the word *culpabilis* in the response of the Code Commission of July 17, 1933 [255] is to be understood in the sense of *imputabilitas,* that is, *imputabilitas dolosa.*[256] For example, impotence, according to Roberti, takes away the right of acting only if it was procured freely and directly in order that the celebration of the marriage be invalid.[257]

It need scarcely be observed that just as the authors are not in agreement over the fundamental definition of a "direct cause"

[253] "Dedecet enim coniuges, qui mala fide causam fuerunt impedimenti et consquenter nullitatis matrimonii, ex culpabili actione commodum reportare."—*De Matrimonio,* II, n. 1260; cf. Rotal decision published in *Monitor Ecclesiasticus,* LXXV (1950), 73; see also S.R.R. *Decisiones,* XXVII (1935), 453, n. 2.

[254] *Loc. cit.*

[255] "An ad normam eiusdem canonis 1971, § 1, n. 1, habilis sit ad accusandum matrimonium etiam coniux, qui fuerit causa culpabilis sive impedimenti sive nullitatis matrimonii. R. Negative."—*AAS,* XXXV (1933), 345.

[256] "Quae imputabilitas cum ex dictis debeat esse formalis, et ex dicendis afficere debeat impedimentum in ordine ad matrimonium consequitur ut sit intelligenda dolosa."—"De Matrimonii Accusatione," *Apollinaris,* VI (1933), 441.

[257] "Impotentia, tantum directe et libere provocata in ordine ad nullitatem celebrandi matrimonii iure agendi privat."—*Loc. cit.*

so neither are they agreed over the basic concept of a "dolose cause." Because of this lack of concurrence among authors concerning the interpretation of these expressions, especially the meaning of a *causa dolosa*, there is bequeathed to the officials of tribunals a potpourri of inconsistent terminology and annoying uncertainty as to who should be deprived and who should not be deprived of the right to accuse a marriage. Confronted by a welter of conflicting views regarding the juridic withdrawal of the right to accuse a marriage, one looks to Rotal jurisprudence to provide a suitable explanation of the principles involved and the manner in which they are to be applied in particular cases.

4. The Jurisprudence of the S. Roman Rota

Since July 27, 1942, the date on which the Code Commission defined a culpable cause as a cause which is both direct and dolose, five pertinent Rota decisions worthy of note have been published. In general, the Rota treats of the definition of a dolose cause, the effect of ignorance of the law or of the penalty, the effect of fear or mental disturbance on the criminal imputability of an act, the question of whether the impediment or the nullity was intended or merely permitted, and the matter of doubt as to whether the person was truly the dolose cause. The following are the observations of the Rota on each of these topics.

a. *The Definition.*—On May 20, 1944, the Rota (*coram* Canestri) defined a dolose cause in terms of Canon 2200, § 1, that is, the deliberate will to violate the law and to which is opposed on the part of intellect a lack of knowledge and on the part of the will a lack of freedom.[258] *Dolus* is not verified in an act unless the person foresaw the crime and willed the crime (*animus nocendi*).[259] On February 28, 1951, the Rota (*coram* Mattioli)

[258] *Decisiones,* XXXVI (1944), 354, n. 4a

[259] ". . . dolum non censet adesse, nisi cum facinus praevidit et voluit (animus nocendi)."—*Ibid.,* p. 354, n. 4a. Michiels, in his discussion of the various kinds of *dolus* distinguishes between *dolus genericus* and *dolus specificus*. *Dolus genericus* is verified when there is present the anti-juridic will to violate the law which is not attended by determined motives compelling the deliquent to violate the law. *Dolus specificus* is present, when over and above the anti-juridic will to violate the law, there is pres-

stated that *dolus*, in the context of Canon 1971, § 1, 1°, signifies the deliberate evil will of procuring the nullity of the sacrament (of matrimony) through a pact or purpose against the substance of marriage.[260] On August 6, 1952, the Rota (*coram* Pinna) stated that a person is to be considered the direct and dolose cause of the nullity or of the impediment of marriage who knowingly and willingly through a direct act of the will (*causa directa*) placed an action constituting an impediment contrary to the law by intending the nullity of the marriage (*causa dolosa nullitatis*) or at least by intending the impediment of the marriage (*causa dolosa impedimenti*).[261]

b. *The Effect of Ignorance.*—As regards the intellect, the *causa dolosa* of the impediment or of the nullity of marriage must have known that a certain act or fact was defiling marriage and he must have known that the existence of the act or fact in contracting marriage constituted a grave sin.[262] In its decision of May 30, 1949, the Rota (*coram* Jullien) declared that a person cannot be considered the dolose cause of the impediment or nullity who did not know the malice of his action or who was unaware that his action was against the law.[263]

---

ent a specifically determined intention, or motive, or aim which is forbidden by law. Michiels gives as an example, the *animus nocendi.—De Delictis et Poenis*, I, 104.

260 "Dolus, autem, heic est deliberata mala voluntas procurandi nullitatem sacramenti per pactum aut propositum contra substantiam."—*Monitor Ecclesiasticus*, LXXX (1955), 254; cf. Bouscaren, *Canon Law Digest*, IV, 417-418.

261 ". . . directa et dolosa sive nullitatis sive impedimenti, i.e., qui sciens et volens, scil. deliberata voluntate directe, seu per voluntarium directum, (causa directa) actionem posuit legi contrariam, constituentem impedimentum, intendendo (causa dolosa nullitatis) vel minus (causa dolosa impedimenti) matrimonii nullitatem."—*Monitor Ecclesiasticus*, LXXVII (1952), 611.

262 ". . . qui contrahit ideo, nosse debet actum foedantem matrimonium; vel factum: atque horum existentiam in contrahendo constituere grave peccatum."—S.R.R. *Decisiones*, XXXVI (1944), 354, n. 4b.

263 ". . . causa dolosa impedimenti vel nullitatis matrimonii dici nequit qui nesciat malitiam sui actus seu ignoret proprium actum esse contra legem . . ."—*Monitor Ecclesiasticus*, LXXVI (1951), 276, n. 5.

In 1944, the Rota noted that knowledge of the invalidating effect or of the nullity of the contract connected to the delict is not required, and much less is knowledge required of the penalty of the incapacity of accusing the marriage.[264] The Rota cited as the reason for this conclusion Canon 16, § 1 and Canon 2229, § 3, 1°. Canon 16 states that no ignorance of invalidating or incapacitating laws excuses from observing them, unless the law states otherwise.[265] Canon 2229, § 3, 1° states that crass or supine ignorance of the law or of the penalty only does not exempt from any penalty *latae sententiae;* ignorance which is not crass or supine excuses from medicinal penalties but not from vindicative penalities *latae sententiae.* In the decision of May 30, 1949, the Rota stated that a party does not cease to be a dolose cause, and therefore incapable of accusing marriage, who was unaware that the law which he knowingly violated was incapacitating or invalidating in character, and much less if he was ignorant that the law rendered him incapable of accusing. Here again the Rota cited Canon 16, § 1 and Canon 2229, § 3, 1°.[266] The Rota applied the same principles in its decision of August 6, 1952[267] and July 19, 1954.[268]

In this regard, an interesting commentary can be found in the decision of June 16, 1945 (*coram* Canestri) concerning the prescription of Canon 2200, § 2 that *dolus* is presumed in the external forum when there has been an external violation of the

[264] "Non requiritur tamen notitia effectus irritantis seu nullitatis contractus connexi delicto, multoque minus consequentis poenae inhabilitatis ad accusandum postea matrimonium . . ."—S.R.R. *Decisiones,* XXXVI (1944), 354, n. 4b.

[265] Cf. *supra,* p. 107.

[266] ". . . attamen non desinet esse causa dolosa et ideo inhabilis ad accusandum qui violatae scienter legis ignorabat indolem inhabilitantem vel irritantem eoque minus ignorabat solum se ex violata lege fieri inhabilem ad accusandum (cfr. can. 16, § 1 et can. 2229, § 3, n. 1)."—*Monitor Ecclesiasticus,* LXXVI (1951), 276, n. 5.

[267] *Monitor Ecclesiasticus,* LXXVII (1952), 611.

[268] "Ideoque requiritur deliberata voluntas violandi legem, eique opponitur ex parte intellectus ignorantia legis, sed talis ignorantia non efficit si cognoscitur existentia legis, sed ignoratur ipsius natura irritans; hoc enim in casu dolose contra legem agitur."—*Ephemerides Iuris Canonici,* XI (1955), 320, n. 3; cf. S.R.R. *Decisiones,* XXXVII (1945), 394, n. 17.

law. This presumption of law, according to the Rota, does not obtain or, at least, cannot be urged because of an opposite presumption of fact which arises in the ordinary course of human affairs.[269] For example: a man, who for the reason that he has caused pregnancy in a woman, or for the reason that he has abused her in some way, goes through the external observance of the celebration of marriage with her though internally he excludes all intention of sharing a common life. How many persons, the Rota asks, who simulate consent in the circumstances mentioned above, think that in so doing they are gravely disturbing the moral order? The Rota conjectures that under these circumstances many persons not only think they are not sinning, they believe rather that they are contributing to a peaceful and happy solution to the problem.[270] The Rota employs this example to emphasize the attention that must be given by tribunals to the possibility that, in cases of simulation of consent, ignorance and good faith may preclude the existence of a delict.[271] Ignorance, the Rota insists, provides a substantial presumption against *dolus* especially in cases of simulation of consent, since the ignorance in question concerns a matter which is familiar only to enlightened minds and which is entirely removed from the normal intellectual considerations of the average man.[272]

Attention must be given here to a case decided by the Rota on February 28, 1951,[273] in which both parties were co-causes of the nullity of the marriage inasmuch as the plaintiff positively willed to avoid having children and inasmuch as his consort positively concurred in the evil will of the plaintiff. Because of "peculiar circumstances," the judges of the court of

269 ". . . ut per oppositam etiam facti praesumptionem, quae eruitur ex ordinarie contingentibus . . ."—S.R.R. *Decisiones,* XXXVII (1945), 395, n. 20.

270 *Loc. cit.*

271 "Haec evidenter non ad laudem, sed ad factum ignorantiae et bonae fidei comperiendum revocantur."—*Loc. cit.*

272 "Ignorantia ideo iam magnam contra dolum in casu parit praesumptionem, cum agatur de materia superiores excultasque conscientias tantum attingente ac prorsus a communi hominum opinione remota."—*Loc. cit.*

273 *Monitor Ecclesiasticus,* LXXX (1955), 249-263.

first instance admitted the man to accuse his marriage. The sentence of the court was in favor of the *actor*. The court of second instance and the first *turnus* of the Rota held that the actor was incapable of accusing his marriage because it was scarcely possible to predicate faith of the man, that is, that he had not adverted to the violation of the moral law through the agreement or intention of not conceiving children, even to the point of destroying a fetus.[274] The second *turnus* of the Rota to review this case did not accept the view of the preceding *turnus*. The court of fourth instance insisted that the question did not revolve around the good faith that excuses from sin. The question was whether *dolus* was present.[275] But *dolus*, the Rota declared, is the deliberate will of procuring the nullity of the sacrament through an agreement or intention contrary to its substance.[276] In the case under consideration, asserted the Rota, *dolus* was lacking. For in this case, the plaintiff was one who was so plagued with physical and mental distress, that he was described by experts as completely devoid of any moral sense. The Rota concluded that such a man, lacking stability and influenced by the worst kind of advice, was not capable of adverting sufficiently to the abnormality of the crime and, therefore, was not possessed of the moral guilt necessary to incur the penalty of Canon 1971, § 1, 1°.[277]

c. *The Effect of Fear and Mental Disturbance.*—As regards the lack of freedom on the part of the will, the Rota noted in its decision of May 20, 1944 that Canon 2229, § 3, 2° and

[274] "Habilitatem viri ad accusandum quod respicit, edixit Turnus, in hoc cum praecendenti concordans, talem bonam fidem in viro, ut ipse nullatenus adverterit legem moralem violari per pactum, vel per propositum non concipiendi, et, quod summum est, prolem forte conceptam necandi, vix et ne vix quidem admitti posse."—*Ibid.*, p. 254.

[275] "At non de bona fide, quae a peccato excusat, sed de dolo quaestio agitanda est."—*Loc. cit.*

[276] Cf. *supra*, p. 155.

[277] "Quid mirum talem virum, aequilibrio carentem, pessimis consiliis insuper excitatum, potuisse (sic), non sat advertendo abnormalitatem delicti et de prole non concipienda, et de forte concepta enecanda, firmiter cum sponsa pacisci."—*Ibid.*, p. 255.

Canon 2205, § 2 apply. Canon 2229, § 3, 2° states that drunkenness, mental weakness, and heat of passion do not excuse from *latae sententiae* penalties if, notwithstanding the diminution of liability, the action was gravely sinful. Canon 2205, § 2 states that grave fear, even if only relatively grave, necessity and grave inconvenience, as a rule, excuse from all liability, if there is a question of purely ecclesiastical laws.[278]

An observation made by the Rota concerning the influence of fear and mental disturbance on the simulation of consent is worthy of note. In its decision of June 16, 1945,[279] the Rota called attention to cases in which a man will simulate consent because he foresees that he is about to contract marriage with a woman who is possessed of a weak character or an ailing constitution. Or perhaps he foresees the certainty of untoward situations with the relatives of his consort. Flight to simulation of consent, observes the Rota, in such circumstances, although ignoble and hateful, is not, nevertheless, so dolose that it merits the gravest penalty of the deprivation of a right of the natural law of accusing the nullity of his own marriage.[280]

In this regard, note should be made of the decision of August 6, 1952,[281] which ruled that the *libellus* of a woman who had simulated consent must be accepted because of the circumstances in which the woman had found herself at the time when she attempted to contract marriage. The circumstances were psychological depression, illness, poverty, and illicit pregnancy.[282] Here the Rota states that the above circumstances taken singly do not, perhaps, excuse from *dolus*. But taken together, the circumstances seem to excuse from grave theological fault because of the lack of complete advertence.[283] But

278 *Decisiones*, XXXVI (1944), 355, n. 4b; cf. *supra*, p. 124.

279 *Decisiones*, XXXVII (1945), 396, n. 21.

280 *Loc. cit.*

281 *Monitor Ecclesiasticus*, LXXVII (1952), 611.

282 The observations made by the Rota in this case differ somewhat from those made in the decision of June 16, 1945; cf. *supra*, p. 157.

283 "Circumstantiae tamen huius matrimonii . . . licet forsan seiunctim . . . a dolo non excusent, si in suo complexu sumantur . . . quatenus a

in Canon Law, *dolus* supposes the presence of theological fault. Since, under the circumstances, it was doubtful that the woman had actually sinned gravely in simulating a consent she did not intend, the Rota decided that the lower court must accept her *libellus.* In this decision, the Rota held that the necessity of avoiding embarrassment does not itself excuse the eliciting of invalid consent.[284]

d. *Impediments Foreseen—Not Intended.*—The Rota gives particular attention to the question of whether the impediment or the nullity of marriage was intended or merely permitted in its decision of May 20, 1944.[285] It is in this regard that the Rota contributes immensely to the proper understanding of that which constitutes a dolose cause of an impediment or of the nullity of marriage. The general principle to be remembered throughout this discussion is that *dolus* is not present unless the person foresaw the crime and willed the crime (*animus nocendi*).[286] If the person had foreseen but had not willed the crime, and nevertheless the criminal effect followed, according to the law of the Code, *culpa* (not *dolus*) is present.[287] The

culpa theologica gravi, ob semiplenam advertentiam, excusare videntur."—*Ibid.,* p. 12, n. 3.

284 "Sola quidem necessitas legitimandi filios in peccato conceptos vel effugiendi dedecus non excusat ipsum invalide praestantem consensum . . ." —*Ibid.,* p. 613.

285 The Rota undertakes this consideration under its discussion of the concept of a direct cause. It will be recalled that in this decision the Rota held that the *causa directa* corresponded to the Thomistic concept of *voluntarium in se* and that the *causa indirecta* produced an effect which was *voluntarium in causa.* In the Nick-Harrington decision of May 30, 1949 the Rota held that the *causa directa* was better understood in terms of the Thomistic concept of *voluntarium directe,* and that the *causa indirecta* was to be understood in terms of *voluntarium indirecte;* cf. *Decisiones,* XXXVI (1944), 354, n. 4a.

286 ". . . dolum non censet adesse, nisi cum quis facinus praevidit et voluit (*animus nocendi*)."—*Loc. cit.*

287 "Si praeviderit, sed non voluerit, et nihilominus effectus secutus sit iure nostro culpa adest (cfr. can. 2200, § 1 cum can. 2203, § 1)."—*Loc. cit.* Canon 2200, §1 defines *dolus* as the deliberate will to violate the law, to which is opposed on the part of the intellect a lack of knowledge, and on the part of the will a lack of freedom. Canon 2203, § 1, states that if a

Rota noted that in Canon Law, *dolus* is verified only through an act which is *voluntarium directum* (*in se*) as opposed to *voluntarium indirectum* (*in causa*). *Voluntarium in se* is present when the effect is the immediately intended object of the will. *Voluntarium in causa* is present when the effect is not intended immediately but rather is repelled and only permitted, because it is inseparably conjoined with some other effect which is immediately sought after.[288]

According to the principles of moral theology, it is licit to place an act from which follow two effects, one good and the other evil, if the following four conditions are present simultaneously:

a. the act must be good in itself, or at least indifferent;
b. both the good effect and the evil effect must come from the cause with equal immediacy, that is, the good effect cannot come through the evil effect;
c. the evil effect which is foreseen must not be intended, but merely permitted;
d. and there must be a proportionately grave reason for placing the cause and for permitting the evil effect.

Having reviewed these celebrated principles,[289] the Rota then proceeds to illustrate the distinction between a grave theological fault and *dolus*. The following summary of the observations made by the Rota in the decision of May 20, 1944 are not only important but absolutely essential to a proper appreciation of a *causa dolosa* as defined in Canon 2200, § 1.[290]

person violates a law by the omission of proper diligence or care, the liability is diminished to a degree to be determined from the circumstances at the prudent discretion of the judge. If the offender forsaw the violation of the law and nevertheless neglected to use those precautions which any prudent person would have employed, *culpa* is nearly (*proxima*) equivalent to *dolus*.

288 Primum illud est (voluntarium in se), quod in seipso intenditur . . . alterum vero est illud (voluntarium in causa), quod non intenditur immediate sed potius repellitur et solummodo admittitur, quia est inseparabiliter conjuncto cum aliquo alio quod efficaciter appetitur."—*Loc. cit.*

289 See also the Rota decision of May 30, 1949 in *Monitor Ecclesiasticus,* LXXVI (1951), 276, n. 5.

290 Cf. S.R.R. *Decisiones,* XXXVI (1944), 353, n. 4a.

Dolus is the deliberate will (*voluntarium in se seu voluntarium directum*) to violate the law. If a person foresees (act of the intellect) that from a certain act which he is to perform the law will be violated but does not intend (act of the will) the violation, the violation of the law is imputed to the person as a *voluntarium in causa seu indirectum*. Therefore, in cases in which the will does not intend the violation of the law but merely permits the violation, *dolus* is lacking. And if *dolus* is lacking, the penalty of Canon 1971, § 1, 1° does not apply. Moreover, even if the person is able to prevent the violation of the law and fails to do so, he must not be considered the dolose cause of the violation of the law (even though his action in law is the closest thing that can be found to a dolose cause),[291] as long as he did not *intend* the violation of the law.[292] If the violation of the law is grave, a person cannot even permit the violation without a grave and proportionate reason. Otherwise, he is accounted as guilty of grave theological fault. But the fact that the person is guilty of serious sin does not mean that he has been the dolose cause of the sin. The reason must be clearly understood in order to appreciate the significance of a dolose cause. The reason is that the grave theological fault of which the party is guilty is not attributed to the deliberate will to violate the law (*dolus*). Rather, the sinfulness of the act arises from the grave negligence in failing to prevent the violation of the law (*culpa iuridica*). Therefore, it is possible that a person place an act which is only indirectly voluntary (that is, he foresees an effect but does not intend it) and which is illicit because of a lack of a proportionate reason, without giving rise to the delict of Canon 1971, § 1, 1°.[293]

The Rota cites the example of a man who consents to a marriage with a woman whom he knows is placing an intention

[291] ". . . quod si rem praeviderit, et nihilominus cautiones ad eam evitandum omiserit, quas diligens quivis adhibuisset, culpa est proxima dolo."—*Loc. cit.;* cf. canon 2203, § 1.

[292] "Si praeviderit, sed noluerit et nihilominus effectus secutus est, iure nostro culpa adest (cfr. can. 2200, § 1 cum can. 2203, § 1)."—*Loc. cit.*

[293] ". . . patet dari posse voluntarium indirectum illicitum ob defectum causae proportionatae ad illud eliciendum, quin oriatur delictum."—*Loc. cit.*

contra bonum prolis or *contra bonum fidei.* The reason for his marrying the woman is no other than his love for her. In contracting this marriage, he wills, as far as he is able, a true marriage. He is well aware of the bad effects of the infidelity and the acts of onanism that will follow. He even knows that the marriage contract is invalid. But these effects he does not intend. He wants to marry validly. He knows that he will marry invalidly. Certainly, he commits a grave sin in attempting to contract a marriage under these circumstances. The reason is clear. His love for this consort is not proportionate to the gravity of the act of contracting an invalid marriage.[294] According to the Rota, the sin which he commits is not *voluntarium in se;* the sin is *voluntarium in causa.* Because there is lacking the deliberate will to violate the law, *dolus* is not present.[295] Therefore, the man is not to be considered the *causa dolosa* of the nullity of his marriage, and hence does not fall under the penalty of Canon 1971, § 1, 1°.

On August 6, 1952, the Rota stated that a reason for simulation of consent is to be considered grave and proportionate, (though one is not able to call it "just"), if the simulation seems fully justified to the party who exposes the sacrament to nullity, so that he thinks himself to be acting licitly.[296] The ardent love one has for another person, the legitimation of children illegitimately conceived or born, or other similar circumstances are, without a doubt, to be considered proportionately grave reasons for the simulation of matrimonial consent.[297]

[294] "Talis contrahens vult quidem, quantum in se est, verum matrimonium, novit malos effectus infidelitatis aut onanismi consecuturos, invaliditatem ipsam connubii, sed a concursu cum illis suam intentionem excludit, peccat nihilominus, quia causam proportionatam tam gravis actus ponendi non habet, amor in consortem illum non justificat . . ."—*Loc. cit.;* cf. the Rotal decision of August 6, 1952 in *Monitor Ecclesiasticus,* LXXVII (1952), 612, n. 2.

[295] Canon 2200, § 1.

[296] *Monitor Ecclesiasticus,* LXXVII (1952), 612, n. 2.

[297] "Causa vero simulandi considerari quidem poterit gravis, proportionata, nimium tamen esset eam appellare iustam ac si videatur plene iustificatus qui sacramentum exponit nullitati, veluti si licite ageret. Legitimatio prolis illegitime concepta aut natae, vel dedecus effugiendum

e. *Doubtful Cases.*—One final observation should be made concerning an allusion made by the Rota in its decision of May 30, 1949.[298] The Rota noted that it often happens that in the preliminary investigation of a matrimonial cause, the parties exaggerate their own culpability because they believe that, in so doing, the declaration of nullity will be more easily secured. Therefore, all things being equal, if it is not proved with certainty that the party was the direct and dolose cause of the impediment or of the nullity of marriage, he should be considered as capable of accusing marriage.[299]

5. An Opinion Regarding the Requirement of Knowledge of the Invalidating Impediment or of the Nullity of Marriage

Before presenting a summary of the elements necessary to constitute a dolose cause of the impediment or of the nullity of marriage, it is necessary to consider an apparent difficulty that arises from the study of the Rotal decisions presented in the preceding paragraphs. Especially in its decisions of February 28, 1951 and August 6, 1952, the Rota has stated very clearly that for the verification of a dolose cause the party must intend the nullity of the marriage or, at least, must intend the impediment of the marriage.[300] On the other hand, in its decisions of May 20, 1944,[301] May 30, 1949,[302] and August 6, 1952,[303] the Rota has indicated that knowledge of the nullity of the con-

---

ex foedo commercio etc. inter causas proportionate graves accenseri procul dubio potest . . ."—*Loc. cit.*

298 *Monitor Ecclesiasticus,* LXXVI (1951), 276, n. 6.

299 *Loc. cit.;* cf. *supra,* p. 150.

300 "Dolus, autem, heic est deliberata mala voluntas procurandi nullitatem sacramenti per pactum aut per propositum contra substantiam."—*Monitor Ecclesiasticus,* LXXX (1955), 254; " . . . qui sciens et volens . . . (causa directa) actionem posuit legi contrariam, constituentem impedimentum, intendendo (causa dolosa nullitatis) vel minus (causa dolosa impedimenti) matrimonii nullitatem."—*Monitor Ecclesiasticus,* LXXVII (1952), 611.

301 *Decisiones,* XXXVI (1944), 354, n. 4b.

302 *Monitor Ecclesisasticus,* LXXVI (1951), 276, n. 5.

303 *Monitor Ecclesiasticus,* LXXVII (1952), 611.

tract is not required to incur the penalty of Canon 1971, § 1, 1°. To support this position that ignorance of the invalidity of the marriage does not excuse from the penalty of the incapacity to accuse marriage, the Rota cites Canon 16, § 1 which states that ignorance of an invalidating or incapacitating law does not excuse from its observance unless the law explicitly admits ignorance as an excuse; and Canon 2229, § 3, 1° which prescribes that crass or supine ignorance of the law or of the penalty alone does not excuse from a *latae sententiae* penalty; ignorance which is not crass or supine excuses from medicinal but not from vindicative penalties (in cases in which perfect *dolus* is not required).

On the one hand, the Rota seems to declare that in order to incur the penalty of Canon 1971, § 1, 1°, one must be aware of and intend the invalidating impediment or the nullity of the marriage. On the other hand, the Rota asserts that according to Canon 16, § 1 and Canon 2229, § 3, 1° knowledge of the invalidating effect of the matrimonial contract is not necessary for a party to forfeit his right to accuse marriage. It is submitted that the solution to this apparent discrepancy must be sought in the answer to the question, in what does the violation of Canon 1971, § 1, 1° specifically consist? Precisely what must the party know and what must the party intend before he is considered to be the direct and dolose cause of the impediment or of the nullity of marriage? In other words, before a party can be said to have committed a *delictum dolosum* through the deliberate violation of Canon 1971, § 1, 1°, must he know and intend merely the material fact from which the invalidating impediment or the nullity of marriage arises (without knowledge of its operative effect of nullity); or must the party know of the existence of the invalidating impediment or of the nullity as such and intend the impediment as such or the nullity as such?

In this regard, it is submitted that Canon 16, § 1 has application to Canon 1971, § 1, 1° only in respect to the absence of knowledge of the penalty alone precisely because the incapacitating character of the provision of Canon 1971, § 1, 1° is specified by a vindicative penal nature. Translated in terms of Canon 1971, § 1, 1°, Canon 16, § 1 determines that a party, who, *de facto*, is the direct and dolose cause of the impediment or of the nullity of marriage, incurs the penalty of being rendered juridically incapable of accusing his marriage even though he was unaware of this penalty. Similarly, it is further submitted that Canon 2229, § 3, 1° has application to Canon 1971, § 1, 1° only to the extent that if a person alleges that he was not aware of a law that forbids the attempting of an invalid marriage or that he was not aware of the penalty of the juridic withdrawal of the right to accuse his marriage which he directly and dolosely caused to be invalid, he, nevertheless, incurs the vindicative *latae sententiae* penalty of Canon 1971, § 1, 1°. It is suggested that Canon 2229, § 3, 1° cannot be cited as applying to Canon 1971, § 1, 1° to the extent that knowledge of the invalidating effect of the marriage contract is not necessary, because Canon 2229, § 3, 1° treats only of ignorance of the law (or of the penalty alone) as the law itself is written. The law in question is that a person is forbidden to enter an invalid marriage in a manner which is both direct and dolose. The penalty is the juridic incapacity to accuse the marriage of invalidity. Care must be taken here to distinguish between ignorance of the law and ignorance of the fact. In other words, Canon 2229, § 3, 1°, in no manner, determines the elements that constitute the law in respect to the knowledge that is necessary to verify that which must be considered as the direct and dolose cause of an impediment or of the nullity of marriage. One must look to Canon 1971, § 1, 1° not to Canon 2229, § 3, 1° to determine precisely what the party as a dolose cause must know and intend before the vindicative penalty of the incapacity of accusing marriage is incurred. It is submitted that Canon 1971, § 1, 1° is to be interpreted in the sense that the party must know of and intend the impediment as such or the nullity as such in order to incur the penalty of the deprivation of the right to accuse his marriage.[304] This opinion is based on the following considerations.

The strict interpretation of Canon 1971, § 1, 1°, demanded by Canon 19, restricts the meaning of the words "impediment"

[304] Cf. Pendola, "De Iure Accusandi Matrimonium," *Periodica,* XXXVIII (1949), 164-165; 248-250.

and "nullity" to their most literal and narrowest signification in relation to the knowledge and intention required to constitute them as effects of a direct and dolose cause. It is one thing to know and to intend the violation of the moral law. It is another thing to know and intend the violation of the moral law in order to cause an invalidating impediment to marriage.[305] To incur the penalty of Canon 1971, § 1, 1°, it would seem that the object of the intellect and the object of the will is not merely the violation of the moral law, but the violation of the moral law precisely insofar as the intellect recognizes this violation as giving rise to an invalidating impediment or the nullity of marriage and insofar as the will freely intends the invalidating impediment or the nullity of marriage. The strict interpretation of Canon 1971, § 1, 1° appears not to warrant an extention of the meaning of the words, direct and dolose cause of the impediment or of the nullity of marirage, so as to include merely the fact out of which the impediment or the nullity arises.

Thus, for example, Paul marries a woman to whom he knows that he is related by blood. What he does not know is that she is related to him by a degree of consanguinity which invalidates a marriage. Certainly Paul cannot reasonably be said to have deliberately (with knowledge and free will) caused the nullity of his marriage. Therefore, he cannot be said to have been the dolose cause of the nullity of the marriage. Again, Paul and Anna commit adultery and grievously sin thereby. Moreover, Paul and Anna mutually promise to marry and thereby incur the impediment of crime. If these parties were not aware that the impediment of crime was incurred, they can scarcely be said to have knowingly and willingly caused the impediment of crime. Similarly, a person whose consent is invalidated by a condition *contra bonum prolis* cannot be said to be the knowing and willing cause of the nullity of marriage if he was not aware that consent conditioned rendered the marriage invalid.[306]

Not only is this opinion in accord with the strict interpretation demanded by Canon 19, it is also in harmony with the

[305] *Ibid.*, p. 234.

[306] *Ibid.*, p. 243.

fundamental norm of interpretation prescribed in Canon 18,[307] which states that ecclesiastical laws are to be understood according to the proper significance of the words in their text and context. Moreover, this opinion is further supported by Canon 2219, § 1 which prescribes that, in penal matters, the more benign interpretation is to be used.[308]

Finally, this opinion is also in keeping with the purpose of Canon 1971, § 1, 1°, the fundamental revelation of which is found in pre-Code law. The purpose of Canon 1971, § 1, 1° is found in the principle of Pope Alexander III who decreed the penalty of the deprivation of the right to accuse marriage in order to punish a party who, bound by the impediment of *ligamen,* took to himself a second wife.[309] In the course of time, the first wife of the man died. The man, intent on leaving his second consort, sued for a separation from her. Pope Alexander III declared that it was not fitting that this man who knowingly contravened the law of the Church should thereby profit from his own guilt.[310] Otherwise, the man would be benefitting by his own crime.[311] In this case, the party knowingly contravened the canons of the Church not by placing the act out of which the impediment arose (his first marriage), but rather by knowing that the law of the Church forbids second marriages during the time a valid consort is still alive, and by freely willing to break this law in entering a second marriage. But, a person who unknowingly incurs the impediment of *crimen* cannot be said to have known the law of the Church concerning the impediment of *crimen* and therefore cannot be said to have knowingly contravened the law of the Church in this regard.[312]

307 *Loc. cit.;* Marquardt, *The Loss of Right To Accuse a Marriage,* p. 101.

308 Cf. Marquardt, *loc. cit.*

309 C. 1, X, *de eo, qui duxit in matrimonium quam polluit per adulterium,* IV, 7.

310 " . . . nec dignum est, ut praedictus vir, qui scienter contra canones venerat, lucrum de suo dolo reportet . . ."—*Loc. cit.*

311 " . . . ex suo dolo delicto videretur commodum reportare . . ."—*Loc. cit.*

312 Cf. Marquardt, *The Loss of Right to Accuse a Marriage,* p. 102;

Though it is true that the purpose of Canon 1971, § 1, 1° is to prevent spouses from profiting from a fraudulent action, care must be taken to understand the nature of the fraud which the law intends to prevent. The fraudulent action which Canon 1971, § 1, 1° intends to punish is not simply the violation of the moral law but rather the action of entering sacrilegiously into a marriage which a party knows to be invalid and which the party intends with a criminal will.[313] In other words, the fraudulent action or the crime that Canon 1971, § 1, 1° intends to prevent is the criminal will to enter an invalid marriage.[314] Thus, though Paul and Anna may fully realize the moral sinfulness of their act of adultery, and though they may also be aware of the mortal sinfulness of their mutual promise to marry, they should not be classified as the direct and dolose cause of the impediment of *crimen* unless they deliberately intended to incur this impediment or to enter a marriage which they knew to be invalid.

This opinion is held by Roberti,[315] Vermeersch-Creusen,[316]

Pendola, "De Iure Accusandi Matrimonium," *Periodica,* XXXVIII (1949), 159.

[313] S.R.R. *Decisiones,* XXXVI (1944), 353, n. 4a; *Monitor Ecclesiasticus,* LXXVII (1952), 611, n. 1; LXXX (1955), 254.

[314] Pendola, "De Iure Accusandi Matrimonium," *Periodica,* XXXVIII (1949), 159, 164-165, 236-237, 248.

[315] ". . . imputabilitas . . . debeat esse formalis, et . . . afficere debeat impedimentum in ordine ad matrimonium consequitur ut sit intelligenda dolosa. . . . Hic autem adhuc quaeri potest utrum ad auferendam actionem nullitatis necesse sit quis causa fuerit impedimenti cum intentione matrimonium nullum celebrandi. Cum Codex et responsa Pont. Commissionis constanter loquantur de causa impedimenti et non de facto ex quo oritur impedimentum, videtur etiam intentio requiri. Quare non sufficit ut quis actionem illicitam fecerit sed necesse est ut fecerit in ordine ad matrimonium."—"De Matrimonii Accusatione," *Apollinaris,* VI (1933), 443; cf. Roberti, "De Iure Accusandi Matrimonium," *Apollinaris,* III (1930), 57. It should be observed here that Roberti quite accurately anticipated the response of the Code Commission of July 27, 1942; cf. Pendola, "De Iure Accusandi Matrimonium," *Periodica,* XXXVIII (1949), 158.

[316] "Dolosa causa est nullitatis qui sciens se contra legem agere, nihilominus impedimentum vel nullitatem libere procurat. . . . Quare iure accusandi non privabitur qui etiam libere consensum matrimonialem praestat dum scit ob compartis impedimentum absolutum aut defectum

Regatillo,[317] Marquardt,[318] and Pendola.[319] This opinion has also been represented by the Rota especially in its decisions of February 28, 1951[320] and August 6, 1952.[321]

6. An Outline of the Concept of a Dolose Cause

The concept of a dolose cause of the impediment or of the nullity of marriage may be outlined in the following manner.

As regards the intellect:

1. the party must know that by his act he is committing a grave sin; that is, he must understand the gravity of the malice of his action.[322]

---

consensus matrimonium fore nullum."—*Epitome Iuris Canonici,* 6. ed., III, 151. Vermeersch-Creusen base their opinion on the strict interpretation of Canon 1971, § 1, 1°. Cf. Sipos, *Enchiridion Iuris Canonici,* 6. ed., p. 786.

317 "Causa directa et culpablis impedimenti, ut mihi videtur, est qui ponit factum illicitum ex quo surgit impedimentum, et quidem scienter et in ordine vel cum intentione contrahendi matrimonium nullum. Hinc non esset inhabilis ad accusandum, qui commisit crimen adulterii cum promissione matrimonii (c. 1075, n. 1) ignorans inde impedimentum exsurgere."—*Interpretatio et Iurisprudentia C.I.C.,* pp. 536-537.

318 "It is not sufficient that a party merely cause the material fact from which an impediment springs. He must, if he is to incur the punishment place the fact knowing and intending the impediment or the nullity."—*The Loss of Right to Accuse a Marriage,* p. 101. Marquardt holds that this interpretation is necessitated by the strict interpretation of Canon 1971, § 1, 1°; cf. Conway, "Right to Bring Action of Nullity of Marriage" *Irish Ecclesiastical Record,* LXXXVI (1955), 420-423.

319 As Promoter of Justice of the Sacred Roman Rota, Pendola wrote at length on this topic in 1942; cf. "De Iure Accusandi Matrimonium," *Periodica,* XXXVIII (1949), 140-165, 235-251.

320 ". . . directa et dolosa sive nullitatis sive impedimenti, i.e., qui sciens et volens, scil. deliberata voluntate directe, seu per voluntarium directum, (causa directa) actionem posuit legi contrariam, constituentem impedimentum, intendendo (causa dolosa nullitatis) vel minus (causa dolosa impedimenti) matrimonii nullitatem."—*Monitor Ecclesiaticus,* LXXVII (1952), 611.

321 "Dolus, autem, heic est deliberata mala voluntas procurandi nullitatem sacramenti per pactum aut propositum contra substantiam."—*Monitor Ecclesiasticus,* LXXX (1955), 254.

322 S.R.R. *Decisiones,* XXXVI (1944), 353, n. 4a; 354, n. 4b; XXXVII

2. the party must understand that his action is not only against the law, but also that it constitutes an impediment to marriage or invalidates marriage.[323]
3. the party must not be so ignorant or so disturbed in mind that his act is no longer imputed to him as gravely evil.[324]
4. the party need not know that by his act he renders himself subject to the penalty of being incapable of accusing marriage.[325]

As regards the will:

1. the party must deliberately intend to defile the substance of marriage; that is, he must intend the nullity of the marriage or, at least, he must intend the impediment as a cause of the nullity of marriage.[326]
2. the party must not merely permit or fail to prevent the the impediment or the nullity of the marriage. He must directly intend the impediment or the nullity.[327]
3. the party must not be coerced into marriage by grave fear, necessity, or grave inconvenience.[328]

To illustrate the differences between a direct and an indirect cause and a dolose and a non-dolose cause of the impediment or of the nullity of marriage, the following examples are presented.

(1945), 394, n. 17; *Monitor Ecclesiasticus,* LXXVI (1951), 276, n. 5; cf. Canon 2229, § 3, 2°.

323 Canon 1971, § 1, 1°; Canons 18, 19; Comm. Pont. 4 Januarii, 1946, *AAS,* XXXVIII (1946), 162; S.R.R. *Decisiones,* XXXVI (1944), 354, n. 4b; *Monitor Ecclesiasticus,* LXXVII (1952), 611, n. 1; LXXX (1955), 254.

324 Canon 2202, § 1; 2201, 2206, 2229, § 3, 2°; S.R.R. *Decisiones,* XXXVI (1944), 355, n. 4b; *Monitor Ecclesiasticus,* LXXVII (1952), 611, n. 1.

325 Canons 16, 2229, § 3, 1°; *Monitor Ecclesiasticus,* LXXVII (1952), 611, n. 1.

326 S.R.R. *Decisiones,* XXXVI (1944), 353, n. 4a; *Monitor Ecclesiasticus,* LXXVII (1952), 611, n. 1; LXXX (1955), 254.

327 S.R.R. *Decisiones,* XXXVI (1944), 353, n. 4a; *Monitor Ecclesiasticus,* LXXVII (1952), 611, n. 1; cf. Canons 2199, 2203, § 1.

328 Comm. Pont., 17 Julii, 1933, *AAS,* XXV (1933), 345; cf. Canon 2205, § 2.

D. *Examples of Direct and Dolose Causes of the Impediment or of the Nullity of Marriage*

In the cases below, the impediment or the nullity of the marriage is an effect of a positive act of the will (*causa directa*) of Paul. The direct object of the will of Paul is the violation of the law by deliberately contracting a marriage which he knows to be seriously sinful and wills to be invalid (*causa dolosa*).

a) Paul, aware of both the gravely sinful and invalidating character of his act, positively concurs with the intention of Anna who is placing a condition against the substance of marriage.
b) Paul, harboring the intention of contracting an invalid marriage, and realizing the gravity of the evil of his act, attempts marriage with Anna whom he knows to be disqualified by the impediment of impotence.
c) Paul deliberately procures the nullity of his marriage with Anna by placing an intention *contra bonum prolis*, aware of the grave wrongfulness of his act but unaware that he renders himself thereby incapable of accusing marriage.

E. *Examples of Direct and Non-Dolose Causes of the Impediment or of the Nullity of Marriage*

In these cases, the impediment or the nullity of marriage is an effect directly produced by a positive act of the will (*causa directa*) of Anna. The impediment or the nullity of marriage is not, however, the effect of Anna's deliberately evil intention to violate the law because of either a lack of sufficient knowledge on the part of her intellect, or a lack of freedom on the part of her will. Therefore, Anna is not to be considered the *causa dolosa* of the impediment or of the nullity of marriage.

a) Anna, moved by an unreasonable fear, places a condition *contra bonum sacramenti*, aware that such a condition invalidates her marriage but invincibly ignorant of the sinfulness of her act.
b) Anna, realizing that her marriage will be invalid, simu-

lates consent under the influence of relatively grave, unjust, external fear.

c) Anna, aware that her marriage will be invalid, simulates consent merely to give a name to a child born out of wedlock, which action Anna performs without adverting to the grave sinfulness of the simulation of a sacrament.

F. *Examples of Indirect and Dolose Causes of the Impediment of Marriage, and of Direct and Dolose Causes of the Nullity of Marriage*

In respect to the cases that follow, a preliminary observation is in order; namely, that they are purely theoretical in the sense that if Anna wished to invalidate the marriage, she herself could have placed a condition contrary to the substance of marriage. For the sake of illustrating a point, however, Anna, in the cases below, is the indirect cause of the impediment to the extent that she was able to prohibit the impediment but did not. Anna is the dolose cause of the impediment inasmuch as she intended the impediment as a means to an invalid marriage.

a) Anna knows that Paul is placing an intention *contra bonum prolis*. Though she is able to do so, she does nothing to prevent it, in order to contract an invalid marriage which she knows to be gravely sinful.
b) Anna knows that Paul is similating consent under the influence of relatively grave, unjust, external fear from a third person. Though she is able to do so, she does nothing to prevent it in order to contract an invalid marriage which she realizes to be gravely sinful.
c) Anna knows that Paul is marrying her merely to overcome her embarrassment of being an unwed mother. Though she is able to do so she does nothing to prevent his simulation of consent in order to contract an invalid marriage which she knows to be gravely sinful.

Concerning these examples, it may be observed that on the grounds that Anna is not both the direct and dolose cause of the impediment of marriage, she does not incur the penalty of Canon 1971, § 1, 1°. On the other hand, it is of paramount importance to note that on the grounds that Anna is both the direct and dolose cause of the nullity of marriage, she is thereby rendered incapable of accusing her marriage according to Canon 1971, § 1, 1°. Difficulties in this regard are easily resolved if it is recalled that the actual attempt to contract an invalid marriage, with the knowledge of its invalidity, is an effect of the will inasmuch as the will has acted (*causa directa*). Therefore, the three cases listed above are examples of indirect and dolose causes of the impediment of marriage but direct and dolose causes of the nullity of marriage.

G. *Examples of Indirect and Non-Dolose Causes of the Impediment of Marriage, and Direct and Non-Dolose Causes of the Nullity of Marriage*

In these cases, the impediment to the marriage is only indirectly willed by Anna to the extent that she can prevent the impediment but she does not. Moreover, the impediment is not an effect of *dolus* on the part of Anna because she does not concur with the intention of Paul deliberately to violate the law through the simulation of matrimonial consent. Because she foresees the simulation by Paul and because she has no proportionate reason for exposing the Sacrament of Matrimony to defamation, she commits a grave sin of sacrilege. But the impediment and the invalidity of the marriage are *voluntarium in causa,* not *voluntarium in se* in respect to the will of Anna. Therefore, the impediment and the invalidity of the marriage are not effects of *dolus* but of *culpa iuridica* on the part of Anna.

a) Anna knows that Paul is placing a condition *contra bonum prolis*. She is aware that this condition invalidates marriage. Though she is able to do so, she does nothing to prevent it because of her extreme embarrassment of being labeled by the community as an unwed mother. She does not concur with the intention of Paul, but moved by grave internal fears, she enters marriage with Paul permitting its invalidity.
b) Anna knows that Paul is placing a condition *contra bonum prolis*. She is a aware this condition invalidates

marriage. Though she is able to do so, she does nothing to prevent it because of her passionate infatuation with him. She does not concur with the intention of Paul, but moved by passion, she enters the marriage permitting its invalidity.

c) Immediately prior to her marriage with Paul, Anna discovers that Paul is placing an intention *contra bonum sacramenti.* She is conscious that such an intention renders marriage null. Though she is able to do so, she does not prevent it because of her infatuation for him and because of her suspicion that she may have been made pregnant by Paul. She does not concur with the intention of Paul but enters the marriage permitting its nullity.

Here again, it should be noted that it is impossible to speak of the indirect cause of the nullity of marriage, since the actual contracting of a marriage which is known to be invalid is an effect of a positive act of the will (*voluntarium directe*).

H. *Conclusions*

The application of the principles that determine a direct and dolose cause of each of the impediments prescribed in Canon Law, understood in both their strict and wide signification, and also of the nullity of marriage, indicates the following conclusions.[329]

Age [330]

A. Neither Paul nor Anna can be considered the direct and dolose cause of the impediment of age, since this impediment is not dependent on the free will of either party.

B. Paul is the direct and dolose cause of the nullity of marriage

 a) if he knows that he is under the age required by Canon Law to marry validly and if he procures the nullity of his marriage by attempting to contract mar-

[329] For conclusions that differ in some respects from those of the writer, see Marquardt, *The Loss of Right to Accuse a Marriage*, pp. 105-110. In regard to the examples that follow, it is to be remembered that if there is any element in the case such as ignorance, fear, or mental disturbance which excuses from grave fault, the penalty of Canon 1971, § 1, 1° is not incurred.

[330] Canon 1067.

riage without the necessary dispensation (indirect cause of the impediment of age but direct cause of the nullity).

b) if he knows that Anna is under the age required by Canon Law to marry validly and if he procures the nullity of the marriage by attempting marriage without a dispensation.[331]

Impotence [332]

A. Paul is the direct and dolose cause of the impediment of impotence if he freely submits to an operation causing the canonical impediment of impotence with the intention of entering in the future an invalid marriage.

B. Anna is the direct and dolose cause of the nullity of the marriage if she marries Paul realizing that his impotence causes the marriage to be invalid and intending the invalidity of the marriage.

Ligamen [333]

A. Neither Paul nor Anna can be normally considered the direct and dolose cause of the impediment of ligamen since this impediment is founded in a good act.

B. Paul is the direct and dolose cause of the nullity of the marriage

a) if he knowingly and willingly procures the nullity of the marriage aware that a previous spouse of his own is still living.

b) if he knowingly and willingly procures the nullity of the marriage aware that a previous spouse of Anna is still living.

Disparity of Cult [334]

A. Neither Paul nor Anna, as a general rule, can be considered as the direct and dolose cause of the impediment

[331] According to Canon 2230, children who have not yet attained the age of puberty are excused from *latae sententiae* penalties and therefore are excused from the penalty of Canon 1971, § 1, 1°.

[332] Canon 1068.

[333] Canon 1069.

[334] Canon 1070.

of disparity of cult because of the nature of this impediment.

B. Paul, a baptized Catholic, is the direct and dolose cause of the nullity of the marriage if he procures the nullity of the marriage by marrying Anna, unbaptized, without a dispensation, realizing that an invalidating impediment exists between them.

Major Orders—Solemn Vows [335]

A. Neither Paul nor Anna can be considered as the dolose cause of the impediments of major orders or solemn vows or those simple vows which have by the special law of the Holy See the power to annul marriage since these impediments are founded in good acts.

B. Paul is the direct and dolose cause of the nullity of the marriage if he procures the nullity of the marriage by marrying Anna, without a dispensation, realizing the existence of the invalidating impediment of major orders in himself or of solemn vows in his consort.

Abduction [336]

A. Paul is the direct and dolose cause of the impediment of abduction if he deliberately procures the impediment by abducting or detaining Anna against her will with the purpose of marrying her, aware that by his action an invalidating impediment arises between himself and Anna.

B. Anna is the direct and dolose cause of the nullity of the marriage if she, still in the power of Paul, deliberately procures the nullity of the marriage by marrying Paul, realizing that her consent under these conditions is invalid.

Crime [337]

A. Paul is the direct and dolose cause of the impediment of crime in any of its three forms if he realizes that his action constitutes an invalidating impediment to marriage and intends it as such.

[335] Canons 1072-1073.

[336] Canon 1074.

[337] Canon 1075.

B. Anna is the direct and dolose cause of the nullity of the marriage even though at the time those acts are performed which constitute the impediment of crime, she is unaware of the invalidating impediment involved, provided she later discovers that as a result of these acts an invalidating impediment has arisen, and she nevertheless deliberately procures the nullity of the marriage by marrying Paul without a dispensation.

Consanguinity—Affinity [338]

A. Neither Paul nor Anna can be considered the direct and dolose cause of the impediment of consanguinity or affinity since the former is independent of the will of the parties, and the latter depends from a good act of a previous marriage.

B. Paul is the direct and dolose cause of the nullity of marriage if he procures the nullity by marrying Anna without a dispensation, realizing that an invalidating impediment exists between them.

Public Propriety [339]

A. Paul is the direct and dolose cause of the impediment of the marriage if he lives with Anna in an invalid union or in public or notorious concubinage in order to procure an invalidating impediment between himself and her mother or grandmother, deliberately intending thereby to invalidate a marriage between himself and Anna's mother or grandmother.

B. Anna is the direct and dolose cause of the nullity of marriage if she procures the nullity by marrying, without a dispensation, the father or grandfather of Paul with whom she has lived in an invalid union or in public or notorious concubinage, realizing that such a union gives rise to an invalidating impediment between them and her.

Spiritual-Legal Relationship [340]

A. Paul is the direct and dolose cause of the impediment of spiritual or legal relationship if he knowingly and will-

[338] Canons 1076–1077.

[339] Canon 1078.

[340] Canons 1079–1080.

ingly contracts the impediment of spiritual or legal relationship with Anna intending thereby to invalidate his forthcoming marriage with her.

B. Anna is the direct and dolose cause of the nullity of the marriage if she realizes that she has contracted the impediment of spiritual or legal relationship with Paul and if she attempts marriage with Paul, without a dispensation, intending thereby to invalidate the marriage.

Substantial Error [341]

A. Paul is the direct and dolose cause of the impediment of substantial error if he willingly causes his consort to be in error knowing that the marriage will be invalid.

B. Paul is the direct and dolose cause of the nullity of the marriage if he procures the nullity of the marriage by marrying Anna knowing and intending her consent to be invalid because of substantial error.

Simulated Consent [342]

A. Paul is the direct and dolose cause of the impediment if, by a positive act of the will, he deliberately excludes marriage itself, or all right to the conjugal act, or any of the essential qualities of marriage, realizing that such intentions are not only gravely illicit but also render the marriage invalid.

B. Anna is the direct and dolose cause of the nullity of the marriage if, realizing that he has placed an intention contrary to the substance of marriage and that such an intention renders the marriage invalid, she nevertheless marries Paul with the deliberate intention to invalidate the marriage.

Force and Fear [343]

A. Paul is the direct and dolose cause of the impediment if he deliberately causes Anna to elicit consent under the influence of fear which invalidates a marriage contract (the agent under Canon 1087), and if he realizes and intends that the consent of Anna be invalid.

[341] Canon 1083.

[342] Canon 1086.

[343] Canon 1087.

B. Anna is the direct and dolose cause of the nullity of marriage, if she deliberately attempts marriage with Paul, who is under the influence of fear from a third party, the invalidating effect of which Anna realizes and intends.

Marriage by Proxy[344]

A. Paul is the direct and dolose cause of the impediment if realizing that the non-fulfillment of the conditions necessary for the validity of a marriage by proxy renders the marriage invalid, he procures the impediment by deliberately conspiring to avoid the fulfillment of these conditions.

B. Anna is the direct and dolose cause of the nullity of the marriage if she is aware that Paul has deliberately failed to comply with the conditions necessary for the validity of a marriage by proxy and concurs in the intention of Paul to render the marriage invalid.

Conditional Consent[345]

A. Paul is the direct and dolose cause of the impediment of marriage if he deliberately places an invalidating condition against the marriage contract realizing that such a condition is not only gravely illicit but also renders the marriage invalid.

B. Anna is the direct and dolose cause of the nullity of marriage
   a) if she is aware that the condition that Paul has placed is both gravely illicit and invalidating, and if she deliberately concurs with the intention of Paul to invalidate the marriage.
   b) if she deliberately fails to fulfill a future condition made by herself or by Paul with the intention of causing the nullity of marriage.

Lack of Form[346]

A. Paul is the direct and dolose cause of the impediment if he deliberately violates the law of the Church regarding

[344] Canons 1088-1089.

[345] Canon 1092.

[346] Canon 1094.

the form of marriage realizing and intending the nullity of the marriage.

B. Anna is the direct and dolose cause of the nullity of the marriage if, realizing that Paul has completed arrangements to violate the law of the form of marriage, she concurs with the intention of Paul to invalidate the marriage.

Section IV. The Penalty of the Juridic Withdrawal of the Right to Accuse Marriage and the Excepted Cases of Canon 1990

A question that must be answered here is whether the penalty of the juridic withdrawal of the right to accuse marriage is restricted in its application to causes adjudicated according to formal judicial procedure, or whether this penalty is also to be extended in its application to cases which are to be adjudicated according to summary judicial procedure prescribed in Canon 1990. Beste unequivocally asserts that the penalty of Canon 1971, § 1, 1° is to be restricted in its application exclusively to causes which are tried according to the norms of formal procedure.[347] Beste gives no specific reason to support his position. Against the opinion of Beste it may be argued that whether a matrimonial cause is to be adjudicated in a formal or a summary manner seems to have no essential relation to the clear intention of the legislator to forestall parties from deliberately entering marriages which they know to be invalid. If the reason is the same, the disposition of the law should be the same, regardless of the manner in which the tribunal takes cognizance of the case. On the other hand, the opinion of Beste appears to be supported by two sound juridic considerations. First, the strict interpretation demanded by Canon 1971, § 1, 1° would seem to indicate that the penalty of the juridic deprivation of the right to accuse marriage should not be extended in its application to cases which are explicitly described by the Code as "excepted cases" under the title "*De casibus exceptis a regulis hucusque traditis.*"[348] Second, Canon 2219, § 3 states

[347] *Introductio in Codicem,* 4. ed., p. 923.

[348] C.I.C., Liber IV, titulus xx, caput vii.

that penalties are not to be extended from person to person or from one case to another even if there is a same or greater reason for holding the person guilty. It would seem that there is present here a genuine doubt of law. Therefore, according to Canon 15, the opinion that the penalty of Canon 1971, § 1, 1° does not apply to Canon 1990 cases may be safely followed until the Code Commission determines otherwise.[349]

Section V. The Dispensation of the Penalty of the Juridic Withdrawal of the Right to Accuse a Marriage

There is no prescription in Canon Law that prevents a party who was the direct and dolose cause of the impediment or of the nullity of marriage to seek a dispensation from the penalty of the juridic withdrawal of the right to accuse his marriage. According to Canon 36, § 1, rescripts of the Holy See may be freely petitioned by all who are not explicitly forbidden to do so by law.[350] Canon 2236, § 1 declares that the remission of any penalty may be granted by the authority who has inflicted the penalty. Since the penalty of Canon 1971, § 1, 1° is determined by the common law, the only authority empowered to dispense from this penalty is that of the Holy See. The vindicative penalty of Canon 1971, § 1, 1° is remitted in the manner of a dispensation [351] by the Sacred Congregation for the Discipline of the Sacraments in cases in which both parties are Catholics; [352] and by the Supreme Congregation of the Holy Office in cases in which one of the parties is a non-Catholic,[353] and by the Sacred Congregation for the Oriental Church in cases in which one of the parties is a member of an Oriental Rite.[354]

Only under the prescriptions of Canon 81 and Canon 84, § 1 does the local Ordinary have the power to dispense from the penalty of Canon 1971, § 1, 1°. Canon 81 states that Ordinar-

[349] Cf. Bevilacqua, "Competence of the Ordinary in the Documentary Process of Canons 1990-1992," *The Jurist,* XXII (1961), 251-252.

[350] Cf. Canons 2265, § 2; 2275, 3°.

[351] Canon 2236, § 1.

[352] Canon 249, § 3; Instr. *Provida,* Art. 3, § 4.

[353] Canon 247, § 3; Instr. *Provida,* Art. 12.

[354] Canon 257, §§ 1, 2.

ies other than the Roman Pontiff cannot dispense from the general laws of the Church, even in a particular case, unless this power has been conceded to them explicitly or implicitly or unless recourse to the Holy See is difficult, and there is danger of grave harm in delay, and the case is one in which the Holy See usually dispenses. Canon 84, § 1 states that no dispensation should be granted from an ecclesiastical law without a just and reasonable cause which should be proportionate to the gravity of the law from which the dispensation is given; otherwise, a dispensation granted by an inferior is both illicit and invalid.

Section VI. The Appeal or Recourse Against a Sentence by Spouses Juridically Lacking the Right to Accuse a Marriage

Article 1. Cases Envisioned by the Response of the Code Commission of May 3, 1945

On May 3, 1945, the Commission for the Authentic Interpretation of the Code declared that spouses incapable of accusing marriage according to Canon 1971, § 1, 1° do not enjoy the right of appealing or of recourse against a sentence upholding the validity of a marriage except through a manner of recourse which is extrajudicial.[355]

This response is subject to four possible interpretations[356] which are exemplified in the following cases.

a) If a party who was the culpable cause of the impediment or of the nullity of the marriage is admitted as an accuser in the court of first instance after a dispensation from the Holy See has been obtained, he does not enjoy the right of appealing or of recourse except through extrajudicial means.

b) If a party who was the culpable cause of the impediment or of the nullity of marriage is admitted as an accuser in

[355] "An coniugi, inhabili ad accusandum matrimonium ad normam canonis 1971, § 1, n. 1, competat ius appellandi vel recurrendi adversus sententiam in favorem matrimonii latam. R. Negative, salvis extraiudicialibus recursibus."—*AAS,* XXXVII (1945), 149.

[356] Cf. Regatillo, *Interpretatio et Iurisprudentia C.I.C.*, p. 537.

the court of first instance, because of his own deceit or because of an oversight of the tribunal, without a dispensation from the Holy See from the penalty of Canon 1971, § 1, 1°, he does not enjoy the right of appealing or of recourse except through extrajudicial means.

c) If the accuser in the court of first instance was not the culpable party but rather the promoter of justice, the culpable party does not have the right of appealing or of recourse against the sentence except through extrajudicial means.

d) If the accuser in the court of first instance was not the culpable party but rather the *"coniux habilis,"* the culpable party does not have the right to appeal or of recourse against the sentence except through extrajudicial means.

It is the mind of Regatillo that the response of the Code Commission of May 3, 1945 envisions only the latter two cases.[357] Aguirre seems to restrict the significance of the response to a case in which the promoter of justice has accused the marriage (case "c").[358] The writer suggests that the response of the Code Commission was intended to include all of the cases listed above except the first. This opinion is based on the following reasons.

In the first supposition mentioned above, that is, in the case in which a *"rescriptum restitutionis"* has been obtained by the culpable party, the right of judicial appeal by the culpable party, against a sentence upholding the validity of marriage, prevails. The reason is that the papal rescript, in which the right to accuse is juridically restored to the culpable spouse, may be reasonably understood to include the right to pursue judicially the cause of nullity until a definitive sentence has been executed.[359]

In the case in which the culpable spouse has been admitted as an accuser without a dispensation from the Holy See and a sentence has been handed down by the court of first instance,

[357] *Loc. cit.*

[358] "Annotationes," *Periodica,* XXXIV (1945), 286.

[359] Cf. Canon 1987; Instr. *Provida,* Art. 224; Regatillo, *Interpretatio et Iurisprudentia C.I.C.*, p. 537.

the culpable spouse does not have the right of appeal except through extrajudicial means. This opinion is based on an observation made in a decision of the Rota given on July 19, 1954 (*coram* Bonnet).[360] In this decision, the Rota noted that before the issuance of the response of the Code Commission of January 4, 1946[361] (in which the Code Commission declared that the inability of a spouse to accuse a marriage according to Canon 1971, § 1, 1° did not imply the incapacity to stand in judgment according to Canon 1892, 2° so that the sentence was not thereby irremediably null), it was incumbent on the court of appeal not only to consider the cause which had been decided by an inferior court but also the capacity of the parties to stand in judgment. The Rota continued that since January 4, 1946, however, if the defender of the bond appeals against the sentence of the court of first instance in a case in which the *actor* was incapable of accusing, the appeal court should not spend its time in adjudicating the capacity of the *actor* to accuse the marriage. For the appeal made by the defender of the bond is made not in favor of but in opposition to the parties. In this sense, the appeal is presented by the defender of the bond so that the action (contained in his appeal) may possibly be sustained in the court of appeal. The Rota then makes a pertinent observation. The Rota states that if the sentence of the court of second instance is in favor of the bond of marriage (that is, if the appeal of the defender of the bond is sustained), the party who is capable of accusing marriage does not have the right of appeal or of recourse except through means which are extrajudicial, according to the response of the Code Commission of May 3, 1945.[362]

[360] *Ephemerides Iuris Canonici,* XI (1955), 320, n. 3.

[361] Cf. *supra,* p. 67.

[362] "Cum autem, iuxta responsionem memoratae Pontificiae Commissionis diei 4 ianuarii 1946 . . . si a sententia aliqua primi gradus, cuius actor forsan inhabilis fuit, appellavit vinculi tutor non est ratio cur tribunal appellationis tempus terat in dijudicanda capacitate actoris, appellante enim ex officio vinculi defensore appellatio interposita prodest etiam partibus. Attamen hoc sensu praedicta appellatio prodest quod actio sustinetur in processu appellationis; sententia vero secundi gradus, si esset in favorem vinculi non competit coniugi inhabili ad accusandum matri-

In the case in which the promoter of justice is the accuser and the petitioner is the culpable cause of the impediment, the culpable party does not have the right to appeal a sentence upholding the validity of the marriage except through means which are extrajudicial. Having been deprived of the right to introduce judicially a cause of the nullity of marriage in a court of first instance, the culpable spouse is, *a pari,* deprived of the right to appeal judicially an unfavorable sentence. On November 27, 1937, the Rota (*coram* Jullien) declared that parties who depend on the promoter of justice to accuse their marriage because they themselves have been deprived of this right, lack the right to appeal an unfavorable sentence.[363] The Rota observed that the law which denies to denouncing parties an action or right of accusing would certainly contradict itself, if it conceded to them, even under the title of "intervention of third parties," the right of appealing or of accusing marriage in a new instance.[364]

Creusen,[365] on the other hand, calls attention to the response of the Code Commission of January 4, 1946 and suggests that the negative reply of the Commission to the question whether the inability to accuse a marriage implies the incapacity to stand in judgment so that the sentence is irremediably null, supports the opinion that the inability to accuse a marriage does not imply the absolute incapacity to stand in judgment as an actor in a case which has been properly introduced by the promoter of justice. Therefore, though a party is incapable of

---

monium, ad normam canonis 1971, § 1, 1°, jus appellandi vel recurrendi, salvis extraiudicialibus recursibus, prout declaravit eadem Pontificia Commissio die 3 maii 1945."—*Ephemerides Iuris Canonici,* XI (1955), 320, n. 3.

363 ". . . absque igitur iure accusandi nullitatem matrimonii, carent iure appellandi adversus sententiam illam."—XXIX (1937), 721, n. 8; cf. XXVIII (1936), 77, n. 9.

364 "Lex enim denuntiantibus denegat actionem seu jus accusandi, non parum sibi contradiceret, si iisdem concederet, etiam titulo oppositionis tertiorum, jus appellandi seu jus accusandi matrimonium in nova instantia."—XXIX (1937), 721, n. 8.

365 "Iure Accusandi Matrimonium," *Nouvelle Revue Theologique,* LXVIII (1946), 345; cf. Jemolo, *Il Matrimonio nel Diritto Canonico,* nn. 221, 222.

accusing marriage, he nevertheless retains the right to appeal an unfavorable sentence or to demand that a cause, abandoned by the promoter of justice, be prosecuted.[366]

It is submitted that the response of the Code Commission of January 4, 1946 cannot be cited as the juridic foundation of the right of a spouse, incapable of accusing marriage according to Canon 1971, § 1, 1°, to appeal judicially a sentence upholding the validity of marriage. To argue otherwise is to place one's self in the relatively indefensible position of asserting that the Code Commission has issued two contradictory responses on the same topic within a period of six months.[367] It is true that the response of the Code Commission of January 4, 1946 indicated that the inability to accuse a marriage does not imply the incapacity to stand in judgment to place all other procedural acts which culminate in a judicial sentence. But this response does not necessarily affirm that a spouse, juridically incapable of accusing a marriage, can make a demand based on the right of action that his cause be adjudicated and that a declaration of nullity be granted. In short, the provision of the response of the Code Commission of January 4, 1946 declares that the juridic inability of a spouse to accuse a marriage does not invalidate the sentence of a tribunal; it does not thereby recognize the right of parties who are culpable causes of the impediment or of the nullity of marriage to make a demand on a tribunal, based on the right of action, to adjudicate a cause of nullity and to grant an official declaration of the same. By the same token, and according to the response of the Code Commission of 1945, a spouse, who is incapable of accusing marriage according to Canon 1971, § 1, 1°, can claim no right to appeal judicially the sentence of a tribunal in a cause duly prosecuted by the promoter of justice.

Attention is called to a decision of the Rota (*coram* Staffa) handed down on August 5, 1949 (three years after the disputed response of the Code Commission of January 4, 1946) in which a man was not permitted to accuse his marriage in the court of

[366] *Loc. cit.*

[367] Comm. Pont. 3 Maii, 1945, *AAS,* XXXVII (1945), 149; Comm. Pont. 4 Januarii, 1946, *AAS,* XXXVIII (1946), 162.

first instance because he was considered to have been the direct and dolose cause of the alleged nullity of his marriage. To the promoter of justice of Tribunal X he denounced his marriage according to Canon 1972, § 2. The promoter of justice of Tribunal X constructed the process and the sentence was rendered in favor of the validity of the marriage. The man then appealed the sentence to Metropolitan Tribunal Z. The admission by Tribunal Z of the appeal of the denouncing party evoked from the Rota an observation which clearly indicates that the response of the Code Commission of January 4, 1946 in no manner derogates from the response of the same Commission on May 3, 1945. The Rota declared that Metropolitan Tribunal Z erred in admitting the appeal of the denouncer in the light of the reply of the Code Commission of May 3, 1945.[368]

Finally, if the accuser in the court of first instance was the "*coniux habilis*," the "*coniux inhabilis*" does not have the right to appeal a sentence upholding the validity of the marriage except through extrajudicial means of recourse. This conclusion is derived from the clear language of the response of the Code Commission of May 3, 1945.

Article 2. Extrajudicial Means of Recourse

There are two extrajudicial means of recourse available to a party who does not have the right of judicial appeal against a sentence upholding the validity of marriage.[369] The first is

[368] "His in genere praemissis, animadvertimus in casu praesenti coniugem inhabilem ad accusandum matrimonium, iuxta responsum Pontificiae Commissionis . . . diei 3 Maii, 1945, ius non habere appellandi contra sententiam in favorem matrimonii latam. Erravit igitur Tribunal Z appellationem admittendo denunciantis."—XLI (1949), 465, n. 11.

This decision of the Rota of August 5, 1949 lends support to the conclusion of the writer that a party who is deprived of the right to accuse a marriage is thereby deprived of the right to stand in judgment to accuse a marriage in any court of any instance (*supra*, p. 87). But just as a sentence is not irremediably void if the accuser in the court of first instance does not have the right to stand in judgment, so the sentence of the appellate court is not invalid if the plaintiff who is incapable of accusing marriage is erroneously admitted by the appeal court. Cf. A Rotal decision published in *Monitor Eccleiasticus*, LXXX (1955), 426; Bouscaren, *Canon Law Digest*, IV, 406-408.

[369] Regatillo, *Interpretatio et Iurisprudentia C.I.C.*, p. 538.

that of recourse to the Sacred Congregation for the Discipline of the Sacraments[370] or to the Sacred Congregation that is competent to handle the case depending on whether non-Catholics or Orientals are involved or whether the case arises in mission lands.[371] The recourse in this case would have for its purpose the obtaining of a dispensation from the vindicative penalty of Canon 1971, § 1, 1°. Having obtained the necessary rescript, the culpable party may introduce his appeal to the court of second instance.[372] The second extrajudicial means available to the party who was the culpable cause of the impediment or of the nullity of marriage is through the promoter of justice.[373] If the promoter of justice and not the culpable party was the *actor* in the court of first instance, the promoter of justice has the right to appeal the case.[374] If the culpable party was admitted as an *actor* in the court of first instance because of deceit or an oversight, he may present his cause to the Ordinary of the court of first instance who, in turn, should refer the case to the promoter of justice.[375] The promoter of justice may then, in a proper case, initiate proceedings to institute the appeal in the court of second instance.[376] In this latter case, the provisions of Articles 35, § 2, 38 and 39 of the Instruction *Provida* apply in the light of Canon 20.[377] These articles, in particular, and the right of the promoter of justice, in general, are discussed in Chapter VI.

370 Canon 249, § 3; Instr. *Provida,* Art. 2, § 4.

371 Canon 247, § 3; Instr. *Provida,* Art. 12; Canon 257, § 1; 252, § 1.

372 Canon 1879; Instr. *Provida,* Art. 212, § 1; cf. Canons 1971, § 1, 1°; 2236.

373 Aguirre, "Annotationes," *Periodica,* XXXIV (1945), 287; Regatillo, *Interpretatio et Iurisprudentia C.I.C.,* p. 538.

374 Canon 1879; Instr. *Provida,* Art. 212, § 1.

375 Instr. *Provida,* Art. 40.

376 Cf. Canon 1879; Instr. *Provida,* Art. 212, § 1.

377 Canon 20 states that if there is no explicit provision concerning some affair either in the general or in the particular law, a norm of action is to be taken from the law in similar cases.

CHAPTER VI

THE RIGHT OF THE PROMOTER OF JUSTICE TO ACCUSE A MARRIAGE

SECTION I. PRELIMINARY OBSERVATIONS CONCERNING THE ROLE OF THE PROMOTER OF JUSTICE IN MARRIAGE CAUSES

By divine institution, Bishops, as successors of the Apostles, are placed over individual Churches which they govern with ordinary power under the authority of the Roman Pontiff.[1] Not least among the grave obligations of Bishops is that of protecting from abuse the ecclesiastical discipline of his diocese.[2] To this end, the bishop is obliged to appoint to the ecclesiastical tribunal of his diocese a promoter of justice, that is, a priest who is renowned for his integrity, gifted with prudence, and skilled in Canon Law,[3] whose office, according to Canon 1586, is precisely the prosecution of justice in criminal trials, and in all other trials in which the Bishop believes that the public welfare of his diocese is in jeopardy. It is important to keep in mind throughout this discussion, that Canon 1586 establishes the fundamental juridic basis of all of the rights and duties of the promoter of justice. The principal right and primary duty of the promoter of justice is the protection of the common good.[4] All further determinations of the office of the promoter of justice, whether specified by the common law of the Code, the authentic interpretations of the Pontifical Code Commission, the instructions and decrees of the Sacred Congregations, or the jurisprudence of the Sacred Roman Rota must be interpreted as explanations and applications of the juridic principle contained in Canon 1586.[5]

[1] Canon 329, § 1.

[2] Canon 336, § 2.

[3] Canon 1589, § 1.

[4] Cf. Instr. *Provida,* Art. 16; Wernz-Vidal, *Ius Canonicum,* 3. ed., V, 902.

[5] Cf. Fair, "The Promoter of Justice and His Duty to Impugn the

The office of the promoter of justice in matrimonial causes, according to the Rota, is very similar to his office in criminal cases.[6] In a criminal cause in which the crime is notorious and altogether certain, the promoter of justice, *ex officio*, immediately makes a formal accusation to the judge against the guilty party.[7] In cases in which the crime is neither notorious nor altogether certain, the promoter of justice, before he accuses, must await a public report or denunciation of the crime. The denunciation having been made, a special inquisition must be conducted under the authority of the Ordinary to determine how far the incrimination is justified before the promoter of justice can place the formal accusation.[8] Similarly, in matrimonial causes, if the impediment involved is public of its nature, the promoter of justice acts *ex officio* and immediately accuses the marriage.[9] If the impediment is not public of its nature, the promoter of justice must await a denunciation and a subsequent inquisition authorized by the Ordinary before making an accusation.[10]

Validity of a Marriage," *The Jurist*, VII (1947), 378 (hereafter cited "The Promoter of Justice").

[6] "Munus igitur promotoris iustitiae in re matrimoniali valde simile est ejusdem muneri in re criminali."—*Decisiones*, XXIX (1937), 721, n. 8; cf. Gasparri, *De Matrimonio*, ed. nova, n. 1257.

[7] ". . . in causa criminali . . . promotor justitiae ex officio, i.e. si agitur de crimine notorio et omnino certo, ipse statim accusationem formalem facit . . ."—*Loc. cit.;* cf. Canon 1934; Noval, *De Judiciis*, p. 491; Stitt, *De Promotore Justitiae* (Romae: Ed. Scientifica Internazionale, 1939), pp. 184, 189.

[8] "In ceteris autem casibus . . . accepta denunciatione criminis promotor justitiae ante omnia instantiam facit Ordinario ad inquisitionem instituendam, et postea, inquisitione peracta, si casus ferat, ad accusationem formalem procedit."—S.R.R. *Decisiones*, XXIX (1937), 721, n. 8; cf. Canons 1939, 1940.

[9] "Eodem modo in re matrimoniali, si agitur de impedimento natura sua publico, promotor justitiae ex efficio agit et matrimonium statim accusat."—*Loc. cit.;* Canon 1971, § 1, 2°; Instr. *Provida*, Art. 35, § 1, 2°.

[10] "In ceteris autem casibus denuntiationem expectat, qua accepta instantiam facit Ordinario ad inquisitionem instituendam."—*Loc. cit.;* Canon 1971, § 2; Instr. *Provida*, Art. 35, § 1, 2°; § 2; Art. 38, 39, 40.

Throughout the discussion that follows, it is always to be remembered that the principal and ultimate "promoter of justice" in any diocese is the Ordinary himself.[11] The promotion of the public good or the removal of a public evil in the diocese pertains to the ordinary power of the Bishop by divine institution. It is through the ordinary power of the Bishop that the office of the promoter of justice is derived.[12] Hence, the exercise of the rights and duties of the promoter of justice to safeguard the public good is subject to and not independent of the prudent judgment of the Ordinary.[13] This principle has its application to accusations against the validity of marriage made by the promoter of justice whether the impediment involved is or is not public of its nature.[14] It is true that the Rota (*coram* Jullien) in its decision of November 27, 1937[15] stated that in matrimonial causes, if the impediment involved is public of its nature, the promoter of justice, *ex officio*, immediately accuses the marriage.[16] However, the immediacy of the accusation of the promoter of justice in cases involving impediments which are public of their nature must be correctly understood. The accusation of the promoter of justice is immediate in the sense that he need not await a denunciation of the marriage by another. The accusation of the promoter of justice is not so immediate that it precedes the knowledge and consent of the Ordinary. This opinion is supported by a decision of the Rota (*coram* Teodori) handed down on June 8, 1943[17] in which the Rota discussed the role of the promoter of justice in criminal

[11] Wernz-Vidal, *Ius Canonicum,* 2. ed., VI, 102; Noval, *De Judiciis,* p. 519; Coronata, *Institutiones Iuris Canonici,* 2. ed., III, n. 1465.

[12] Cf. S.R.R. *Decisiones,* XXIX (1937), 721, n. 8.

[13] Cf. Bartoccetti, "De iure et officio promotoris iustitiae accusandi matrimonium," *Apollinaris,* X (1937), 578.

[14] Cf. Wolter, "The Promoter of Justice and the Common Good in Matrimonial Causes," *The Jurist,* XI (1951), 221.

[15] *Decisiones,* XXIX (1937), 721, n. 8.

[16] *Supra,* p. 191.

[17] *Decisiones,* XXXV (1943), 410, n. 4.

cases.[18] Since the Rota has observed that the office of the promoter of justice in matrimonial causes is to be compared to his office in criminal cases, the remarks of the Rota in this decision are apropos. The Rota declared that in criminal cases the promoter of justice institutes criminal actions under the guidance and rule of the Ordinary.[19] The Rota continued that before the criminal action is instituted, it is clear that the promoter of justice, in no manner, is able to institute or exercise an action or an accusation, unless the Ordinary has consented.[20]

Again, though the office of the promoter of justice in marriage cases may be likened to his office in criminal cases, it is to be observed that, *de facto*, marriage causes are contentious causes as understood in Canon 1552, § 2, 1°, that is, causes in which the prosecution or vindication of the rights of individuals are involved.[21] But according to Canon 1586, the promoter of justice may not enter such cases unless the Ordinary has first determined that the public good requires protection. As will be seen, the fact that an impediment is public of its nature is not, in itself, a guarantee that an accusation against the validity of the marriage in which this impediment is present will contribute to the public good. Therefore, even in cases in which the impediment is public of its nature, the promoter of justice, before instituting an action, must seek the advice and consent of the Ordinary.[22]

18 Can. 1934.—Actio seu accusatio criminalis uni promotori iustitiae, veteris omnibus exclusis, reservatur.

19 "Verum Promotor iustitiae habet exercitium actionis criminalis sub ductu et regimine Ordinarii . . ."

20 " . . . antequam processus criminalis instituatur . . . patet Promotorem iustitiae nullo modo valere actionem vel accusationem antea promovere et postea exercere nisi Ordinarius consenserit."—*Loc. cit.*

21 "In causis contentiosis Ponentis est ferre judicium de eo utrum bonum publicum in discrimen vocari possit necne, nisi interventus promotoris iustitiae ex natura rei evidenter necessarius dicendus est, ut in causis impedimenti ad matrimonium contrahendum . . ."—*Normae Sacrae Romanae Rotae Tribunalis,* 29 iunii, 1934, Art. 27, § 1—*AAS,* XXVI (1934), 457.

22 Cf. Fair, "The Promoter of Justice," *The Jurist,* VII (1947), 381, 383.

Finally, in the course of this study, when the promoter of justice is described as acting by virtue of his office (*ex officio, vi muneris sui*),[23] or in his own right (*jure proprio*) as opposed to the right of any other party,[24] it is not to be concluded that his activity is independent of the Ordinary, but rather that his rights and duties derive from the obligations of the office that the Ordinary has committed to him.[25] Whether the cause is criminal or contentious, or whether it specifically concerns the invalidity of the marriage bond or it does not, the fundamental consideration which bids the promoter of justice to intervene in a trial is the safeguarding of the public ecclesiastical good in general and the law of judicial procedure in particular.[26] As the public prosecutor of justice in a diocese, it is his office to safeguard the interests of law and justice, to promote the public ecclesiastical good and to remove or to forestall whatever is or will be detrimental to the spiritual welfare of the faithful of the diocese.[27]

Thus, the difference between a matrimonial cause which is introduced into court by the promoter of justice and a matrimo-

[23] Comm. Pont. 17 Julii, 1933, *AAS*, XXV (1933), 345; Instr. *Provida*, Art. 41, § 3.

[24] Instr. *Provida*, Art. 35, § 1, 2°.

[25] Cf. Wolter, "The Promoter of Justice and the Common Good in Matrimonial Causes," *The Jurist*, XI (1951), 221.

[26] Canon 1586; Instr. *Provida*, Art. 16; cf. Wernz-Vidal *Ius Canonicum*, 3. ed., V, 902.

"In causis criminalibus et in iis quae natura sua ordinem et bonum publicum respiciunt, tribunal primae instantiae, quoad ordinem stricte iudicialem, nequit repraesentari a procuratore aut advocato proprio, sed ordinem et bonum publicum defendet Promoter iustitiae apud S. Rotae tribunal."—*Regulae servandae in iudiciis apud Sacrae Romanae Rotae Tribunal*, 4 aug., 1910, § 39, 1—*AAS*, II (1910), 798.

"Promotor justitiae in causis contentiosis in bonum publicum tuetur. Itaque, quoad fieri potest, salva rei veritate, defendit e re nata iura matrimonii . . ."—*Normae S. Romanae Rotae Tribunalis*, 1 sept., 1934, Art. 28, § 1—*AAS*, XXVI (1934), 457.

[27] Canon 1586; Instr. *Provida*, Art. 16; cf. Lega (ed. Bart.), *Iudicia Ecclesiastica*, II, 153-154; III, 152-153; Noval, *De Iudiciis*, pp. 77, 568; Blat, *Commentarium Textus Codicis Iuris Canonici*, (5 vols., Romae, 1921-1927), IV, 503.

nial cause which is brought to trial by the parties themselves becomes apparent. The essential disparity between a matrimonial cause in which the promoter of justice is the *actor* and one in which the spouses themselves are parties to the action lies principally in the nature of the action itself which, in turn, is determined by its end. The end pursued by the promoter of justice who accuses a marriage of invalidity is and must be, in every case, the public good. The end which is ordinarily intended in matrimonial causes in which the spouses themselves are the accusers is the removal of the inconveniences that have arisen from a present, invalid marriage.[28] The good derived from a declaration of nullity sought by the promoter of justice is intended to affect principally the community at large. The good derived from a declaration of nullity petitioned by the parties themselves usually is intended to affect only the petitioners.

In this regard, it should be understood, that every matrimonial cause is, in some manner, pertinent to the public good because of its intimate relationship with the salvation of souls and with the substratum of society itself.[29] Moreover, viewed in relation to the doctrine of the Mystical Body of Christ, the spiritual welfare of an individual soul or a particular marital couple has a direct influence on the whole Christian community.[30] Hence, when a juridic distinction is made between an action that is brought against the bond of matrimony by the promoter of justice in behalf of the public good and an action which is brought against marriage by the parties themselves for their own private good, the distinction is based on peculiar circumstances which surround the invalidity of the marriage.[31] On the one hand, the circumstances may be so occult and so private in nature that the invalidity of the marriage is not, at

[28] Bartoccetti, "De iure et officio Promotoris iustitiae accusandi matrimonium," *Apollinaris*, X (1937), 570.

[29] Pius XI, litt. encyc. "Casti Conubii," Dec. 31, 1930—*AAS*, XXII (1930), 540.

[30] Pius XII, litt. encyc. "Mystici Corporis," June 23, 1943—*AAS*, XXXV (1943), 193-248 *passim*.

[31] Cf. Bartoccetti, "art. cit.," *Apollinaris*, X (1937), 571.

least, an external occasion of the spiritual ruination of the other members of the community. To this extent, it may be said that the invalidity of the marriage affects only the consorts themselves, and in this sense, affects only the private good. On the other hand, the circumstances attaching to the invalidity of the marriage may be so manifest and apparent to the eyes and ears of the community that the spiritual welfare of the community at large is endangered. To this extent, at least in the juridical order, the invalidity of the marriage is said to affect the public good. It is in terms of this distinction that the concepts of the private good of the parties and of the public good of the community will be employed in the study that follows. It is only in terms of this distinction that the role of the promoter of justice in marriage cases may be properly evaluated.[32]

Section II. The Right of the Promoter of Justice to Accuse a Marriage Without a Previous Denunciation

Article 1. Introduction

According to the Code of Canon Law, the right to accuse the validity of a marriage is not reserved exclusively to the spouses themselves. Canon 1971, § 1, 2° states that the promoter of justice is capable of accusing a marriage in cases in which the impediments involved are public of their nature.[33] On July 17, 1933, the Commission for the Authentic Interpretation of the Code declared that the promoter of justice takes part in a trial *vi muneris sui,* by virtue of Canon 1971, § 2.[34] Article 35, § 1, 2° makes explicit reference to the reply of the Code Commission of July 17, 1933 and states that the promoter of justice, in his own right, and without any previous denunciation (is capable of accusing a marriage) in cases involving impediments public of their nature.[35]

[32] Cf. Noval, *De Judiciis,* pp. 569-570.

[33] "... Promotor iustitiae in impedimentis natura sua publicis."

[34] "An, vi canonis 1971, § 2, promotor iustitiae vi muneris sui agat in iudicio. R. Affirmative."—*AAS,* XXV (1933), 345, ad IV.

[35] "Promotor iustitiae, in impedimentis natura sua publicis, iure proprio (Comm. Pont. 17 Iulii, 1933 ad IV) et absque praevia denuntiatione. ..."

Insofar as the right to accuse marriage is not restricted to the spouses themselves, the new law of the Code does not differ from the pre-Code legislation. According to the law of the Decretals, the Bishop, *ex officio*, was empowered to accuse a marriage, even though the spouses themselves were unwilling, in cases in which there were no accusers and in which the impediment was manifest or public.[36] According to the law of the Austrian Instruction of 1855, the ecclesiastical tribunal, *ex officio,* had the duty and the right to accuse a marriage when the fact of the impediment was notorious, or when denunciations had been made against the marriage, or when, in some other way, a sufficient reason was afforded for the tribunal to act.[37] This right of the ecclesiastical tribunal was restricted, however, only to those cases in which the accusation of the impediment was not reserved to the spouses. The accusation of the impediments of occult impotence, substantial error, force or fear, and servile condition was limited to the spouses themselves.[38] But if, for example, the impediment of impotence was notorious, the ecclesiastical tribunal, *ex officio,* had the right to accuse the marriage.[39] On the other hand, insofar as the right to accuse marriage was possessed also by any trustworthy Catholic in cases in which the impediment was not restricted to the spouses,[40] the present law of the Church does differ from the ecclesiastical legislation in existence before the Code. According to the current Code of Canon Law, only the promoter of justice shares cumulatively with the spouses the right to accuse the validity of a marriage without the necessity of any previous denunciation in cases in which the impediment is public of its nature.[41]

[36] C. 3, X, *de divortiis,* IV, 19; cf. Gonzalez-Tellez, Lib. IV, tit. 19, n. 2; Reiffenstuel, Lib. IV, tit. 19, n. 19.

[37] *Instr. Austr.,* § 122.

[38] *Instr. Austr.,* § 122; cf. §§ 115-121.

[39] *Instr. Austr.,* § 118.

[40] *Instr. Austr.,* § 115.

[41] Canon 1971, § 1, 2°; Instr. *Provida,* Art. 35, § 1, 2°.

Article 2. The Concept of Impediments Public of Their Nature

A. *Interpretations of the Authors*

The Code of Canon Law, the Commission for the Authentic Interpretation of the Code, and the Instruction *Provida* provide no definition of an impediment public of its nature. The Code does employ the word "public" in many canons and attributes to it different definitions depending upon the context.[42] No definition, however, accompanies the expression, *in impedimentis natura sua publicis,* found in Canon 1971, § 1, 2°. Authors offer many and varied opinions of the concept of an impediment which is, of its very nature, public. In general, their interpretations are reducible to three general categories.

In the first category are those[43] who hold that an impediment is public of its nature if it is normally provable in the external forum.[44] In the second category are those[45] who hold that an impediment is public of its nature not only if it is normally provable in the external forum, but also if the impediment is occult of its nature and public in fact, that is, already known or in danger of becoming known by the community.[46] To grasp more fully the significance of the first two interpretations, it is

[42] Cf. Canon 1813; 1188, § 2; 2197; 1037.

[43] Blat, *Commentarium Textus Codicis Iuris Canonici* IV, n. 526; Gasparri, *De Matrimonio,* ed. nova, n. 1260; Vermeersch-Creusen, *Epitome Iuris Canonici,* 6. ed., III, 152; De Smet, *De Sponsalibus et Matrimonio,* n. 465; Cocchi, *Commentarium in Codicem Iuris Canonici* (Taurinarum Augustae, 1925), IV, n. 294; Coronata, *Institutiones Iuris Canonici,* III, n. 1486. Beste, *Introductio in Codicem,* 4. ed., p. 924; Haring, "De Iure Accusandi Matrimonium," *Apollinaris,* VI (1933), 244.

[44] Cf. Canons 1037, 1791, 1816, 1827, 1829.

[45] Cappello, *De Matrimonio,* 5. ed., n. 200; Regatillo, *Interpretatio et Iurisprudentia C.I.C.,* p. 539; Noval, *De Judiciis,* pp. 569-570; De Becker, *De Matrimonio* (ed. nova, Louvain, 1931), 275-276; Triebs, "De Promotore Justitiae in Causis Nullitatis Matrimonii," *Apollinaris,* X (1937), 396; Stitt, *De Promotore Justitiae,* pp. 183-189; Roberti, "De Iure Denuntiandi Nullitatem Matrimonii," *Apollinaris,* III (1930), 250; ——, "De Matrimonii Accusatione," *Apollinaris,* VI (1933), 442.

[46] Cf. Canon 2197, 1°.

necessary to review briefly the pre-Code legislation regarding public and occult impediments.

According to the old law, impediments, *ratione notitiae,* were divided into public impediments and occult impediments. Public impediments were so called for a two-fold reason, namely, because they were considered public of their nature or because they were public in fact.[47] Those impediments were called public in nature which, for the most part, were easily provable in the external forum.[48] The readiness of such impediments to proof in the external forum was due to the fact that they were based on *facto de se publico.*[49] The impediments which were considered *publica natura sua* were consanguinity, affinity, spiritual and legal relationship, disparity of cult, major orders, solemn vows and public decency.[50] Those impediments were considered public in fact if the fact out of which the impediments arose was already known, or if the fact was known in such a way that its divulgation was very likely and therefore possible of proof in the external forum.[51] An impediment which was public *de facto* was considered *famosum* if the rumor of the fact of the impediment had been spread throughout the greater part of the community, even though no one had certain knowledge of the impediment, and even if the author of the rumor was uncertain.[52] An impediment was considered *manifestum* if certain knowledge of the impediment was had by just a few people through whom the impediment was likely to be divulged to the rest of the community.[53] An impediment was considered *notorium* if certain knowledge of the fact out of which the impediment arose was had by the greater part of the community

47 DeBecker, *De Sponsalibus et Matrimonio* (2. ed., Lovanii, 1903-1913), p. 48.

48 *Loc. cit.;* cf. Wernz-Vidal, *Ius Canonicum,* 3. ed., V, n. 147, p. 178, ad V.

49 *Loc. cit.*

50 Wernz, *Jus Decretalium,* IV, n. 216, note 9.

51 Gasparri, *De Matrimonio* (ed. 1891), n. 251.

52 DeBecker, *De Sponsalibus et Matrimonio,* p. 49.

53 *Loc. cit.;* cf. Gasparri, *De Matrimonio* (ed. 1891), n. 251.

through a judicial sentence or because of circumstances which could not be concealed.[54] In contradistinction to impediments which were public of their nature were impediments which were occult of their nature. Such impediments were so-called because they were not, as a rule, observed by witnesses or recorded by public documents.[55] For this reason, they were not normally capable of proof in the external forum. Impediments which were considered *occulta natura sua* were *crimen,* occult impotence, simulation of consent, and conditioned consent.[56] Impediments were considered occult in nature but public in fact if they could, nevertheless, be proved in the external forum. Impediments were considered public of their nature but occult in fact if they were unable to be proved in the external forum because of the lack of witnesses or evidential records. Impediments were also considered public of their nature but occult in fact even if they were capable of demonstration in the external forum, but because of the discretion of the witnesses there was no danger of divulgation of the fact to the community.[57]

Applying these principles to the extent of the right of the promoter of justice to accuse a marriage, the first category of authors mentioned above hold that the expression "public of its nature" used in Canon 1971, § 1, 2°, is to be interpreted according to its strict meaning of the same expression which was used in the old law. Therefore, according to Canon 1971, § 1, 2°, an impediment public of its nature is an impediment which is based on a fact that is *de se* public, that is, normally provable in the external forum. Therefore, according to the first category of authors, the promoter of justice in his own right and by virtue of his office, may accuse a marriage of invalidity, without a previous denunciation, in cases in which the impediments are not, for example, occult impotence, *crimen,* simulation, or conditioned consent. Moreover, even if

[54] *Loc. cit.*

[55] Aichner, *Compendium Iuris Ecclesiastici,* p. 569; Feije, *De Impedimentis,* n. 584.

[56] DeBecker, *De Sponsalibus et Matrimonio,* p. 49; cf. Wernz-Vidal, *Ius Canonicum,* 3. ed., V, n. 147, p. 179, ad V.

[57] DeBecker, *op. cit.,* pp. 49-50.

the impediment is occult of its nature but public in fact, the promoter of justice is not empowered to accuse the marriage in his own right according to Canon 1971, § 1, 2°. Vermeersch-Creusen state that the reason for this restriction of the right of the promoter of justice is found in the clear language of Canon 1971, § 1, 2°.[58]

The second group of authors mentioned above hold that the promoter of justice, according to Canon 1971, § 1, 2°, by virtue of his office and independently of any denunciation by a third party, may accuse a marriage of invalidity not only in cases in which the impediment is *de se* public, but also in cases in which the impediment is, *ex communiter contingentibus,* occult, but *de facto* public. The reason given for this opinion is presented in concise manner by Noval.[59] According to Noval, the promoter of justice has a right and a duty to accuse a marriage invalid because of an impediment which of its nature is normally occult, such as the impediment of impotence or force and fear, when by reason of some accidental circumstance the impediment becomes manifest, in the sense that it is capable of proof in the external forum. The reason that Noval offers to support his opinion is that the knowledge of the impediment which is already divulged, or which, in the normal course of human affairs will be related to the community, will give rise to scandal, and hence will be prejudicial to the public ecclesiastical good. By way of objection to the opinion of Noval, it has been stated that "Noval simply dispenses with all consideration of the pre-Code legislation on the nature of an impediment by its nature public and defines such impediments to his own satisfaction."[60] This observation appears to be unduly severe. As will be demonstrated in the article that follows, the only permissible interpretation of the expression, "impediments public of their nature" is that which is in conformity

[58] *Epitome Iuris Canonici,* 6. ed., III, 152; cf. Haring, "De Iure Matrimonium Accusandi," *Apollinaris,* VI (1933), 244.

[59] *De Judiciis,* p. 569.

[60] Glynn, *The Promoter of Justice,* The Catholic University of America Canon Law Studies, n. 101 (Washington, D. C.: The Catholic University of America, 1936), p. 159.

with the office of the promoter of justice. The opinion of Noval is, at least, in its general outline, in harmony with this requirement. Moreover, the suggestion of Noval is also in accord with the law of the decretals, which asserted that the Bishop, *ex officio,* had the right and duty to impugn a marriage the invalidity of which was caused by an impediment "*manifesta seu publica existente.*"[61]

In the third category are those[62] who believe that the expression, *in impedimentis natura sua publicis,* should be interpreted according to the pre-Code distinction, *ratione iuris accusandi matrimonium,* between impediments that are related directly to the public interest and impediments that are concerned principally but not exclusively with the parties themselves. This distinction is discussed in the paragraphs that follow.

B. *An Interpretation Adopted by the Sacred Roman Rota*

On August 11, 1928, the Sacred Roman Rota (*coram* Wynen),[63] in an effort to determine the mind of the legislator concerning the concept of an impediment of its nature public, called attention to the pre-Code division of matrimonial impediments, *ratione iuris accusandi matrimonium.*[64] According to this distinction (which is not to be confused with the pre-Code distinction between public and occult impediments men-

[61] C. 3, X, *de divortiis,* IV, 19. It may be noted here that the division of impediments, drawn in pre-Code legislation *ratione notitiae,* was made with a view toward the extent of the power of the Ordinary to dispense. The distinction between public and occult impediments in the old law was in no manner related to the right of the parties or of the promoter of justice to accuse a marriage; cf. DeBecker, *De Sponsalibus et Matrimonio,* p. 49. The opinion of Noval was explicitly acknowledged and confirmed by the Sacred Roman Rota (*coram* Heard) on June 20, 1936; cf. *Decisiones,* XXVIII (1936), 398, n. 7.

[62] Wernz-Vidal, *Ius Canonicum,* 3. ed., V, n. 147, p. 181, ad VIII; Doheny, *Canonical Procedure,* 2. ed., pp. 107-113; Fallon, "Meaning of Public Impediment in the Code," *The Irish Ecclesiastical Record,* LIX (1942), 273; Glynn, *The Promoter of Justice,* pp. 165-166; Fair, "The Promoter of Justice," *The Jurist,* VII (1947), 379-380.

[63] *Decisiones,* XX (1928), 406, n. 8.

[64] Cf. Feije, *De Impedimentis,* 3. ed., nn. 85, 584.

tioned above), matrimonial impediments were divided into those which were considered of public right and those which were considered of private right. Impediments of public right were those which directly affected the public interest. Impediments of private right were those which principally, but not exclusively, affected the parties themselves.[65] Impediments of public right had as their purpose the safeguarding of the sanctity of the Sacrament of Matrimony, the purity of Christian marriage, and the preservation of the common good.[66] According to pre-Code authors, impediments of public right were *impubertas, defectus aptitudinis ad consentiendum, disparitatis cultus, ligamen, ordo sacer et votum solemne, crimen, raptus, cognatio naturalis et spiritualis et legalis, et publica honestas.*[67] Of private right were *impedimenta erroris substantialis personae, vel conditionis servilis, vis et metus, defectus conditionis appositae et impotentiae occultae.*[68] Marriages that were contracted invalidly by virtue of the existence of an impediment of public right were subject to accusation not only by the spouses themselves but also by the ecclesiastical judge or the *promotor fiscalis, ex officio,* or by any Catholic who was not forbidden by law to accuse marriage.[69] Marriages that were contracted invalidly by force of an impediment of private right could be accused, as a rule, only at the instance of the contracting parties themselves.[70] Nor could the *promotor fiscalis, ex officio,* accuse a marriage invalid because of an impediment of private right unless the knowledge of the impediment was manifest or notorious.[71]

[65] Feije, *De Impedimentis,* n. 85; cf. Wernz-Vidal, *Ius Canonicum,* 3. ed., V, n. 147, p. 181, ad VIII.

[66] *Loc. cit.*

[67] Aichner, *Compendium Iuris Ecclesiastici,* pp. 570-578; Feije, *De Impedimentis,* n. 85; Wernz, *Jus Decretalium,* IV, n. 216.

[68] Aichner, *op. cit.,* p. 569; Feije, *op. cit.,* n. 85; Wernz, *op. cit.,* V, n. 216.

[69] *Instr. Austr.,* §§ 115, 122; S. C. Prop. de Fide, instr., *"Causae Matrimoniales,"* a. 1883—*Fontes,* VII, n. 4901, § 3.

[70] *Loc. cit.*

[71] C. 3, X, *de divortiis,* IV, 19; *Instr. Austr.,* § 118; Wernz-Vidal, *Ius Canonicum,* 3. ed., V, n. 698, p. 906, note 43.

According to the Rota, all those impediments which affect directly the common good (*impedimenta iuris publici*), and which were enumerated in pre-Code legislation under the division of impediments *ratione iuris accusandi matrimonium,* are embraced under the concept of "impediments public of their nature" employed in Canon 1971, § 1, 2°.[72] It will be recognized immediately that the impediments that were considered public of their nature under the pre-Code division of impediments made *ratione notitiae,* and the impediments that were considered of public right under the pre-Code division of impediments made *ratione iuris accusandi* are practically identical with two notable exceptions. The impediments of *ligamen* and *crimen* were included under the latter category but were not listed in the former. The Rota has insisted that in cases involving the matrimonial impediment of crime,[73] the promoter of justice has the right, *ex officio,* to accuse the marriage without any previous denunciation. The reason lies in the fact that the impediment of crime was instituted to protect "*publicam matrimonii honestatem et sanctitatem*" and, therefore, must be included among the impediments which are public of their nature.[74]

To summarize, the Rota in its decision of August 11, 1928, interpreted Canon 1971, § 1, 2° in terms of the pre-Code distinction *ratione iuris accusandi matrimonium* between impediments of public right and impediments of private right. According to this interpretation, the expression, *in impedimentis natura publicis,* is to be understood as embracing all those impediments which pertain principally to the public ecclesiastical good. In this category the Rota placed all impediments except those of "*conditionis servilis, vis et metus, impotentiae occultae.*" [75] It should be noted here, however, that

[72] *Decisiones,* XX (1928), 404, n. 4; XXVI (1934), 106, n. 4; XXVII (1935), 263, n. 7; XXVIII (1936), 74, n. 6; 398, n. 7; XXX (1938), 707, n. 4.

[73] Canon 1075.

[74] S.R.R. *Decisiones,* XXVI (1934), 106, n. 4; cf. *Decisiones,* XX (1928), 404, n. 4; XXX (1938), 707, n. 4.

[75] *Decisiones,* XX (1928), 406, n. 8.

Wernz, whom the Rota cited as its principal authority, included the impediments "*erroris substantialis personae,*" and "*defectus conditionis appositae*" in the class of "private right." [76]

C. *An Evaluation of the Interpretations*

The first opinion of the authors, which is based on the strict interpretation of an impediment public of its nature as understood in the old law, is not completely in accord with the office, rights, and duties of the promoter of justice. The promoter of justice has the right and duty to intervene in cases in which, in the judgment of the Ordinary, the public ecclesiastical good is at stake.[77] According to this interpretation, however, the promoter of justice, without a previous denunciation, could not accuse a marriage invalid because of an impediment which is *de se* occult and yet *de facto* public, even if the ecclesiastical good was endangered. This conclusion seems to render illusory the prescription of Canon 1586 and the intendment of Canon 1971, § 1, 2°.

The second opinion of authors which is based on an interpretation of an impediment public in fact as understood in the old law is basically but not completely in harmony with the office of the promoter of justice to the extent that an impediment may be a matter of public knowledge and yet may not necessarily constitute a source of public scandal or a danger to the common good.[78]

The opinion of the Rota, expressed in its decision of August 11, 1928, seems to be the preferred opinion, because of its intimate alliance with the pre-Code rules governing the right to accuse marriage.[79] This opinion, however, does not, at least

[76] Cf. *Jus Decretalium,* V, n. 216; Wernz-Vidal, *Ius Canonicum,* 3. ed., V, n. 698; Doheny, *Canonical Procedure,* 2. ed., pp. 107-113; Glynn, *The Promoter of Justice,* pp. 165-166; Fallon, "Meaning of Public Impediment in the Code," *Irish Ecclesiastical Record,* LIX (1942), 273.

[77] Canon 1586.

[78] Cf. Instr. *Provida,* Art. 38, § 2; 39; S.R.R. *Decisiones,* XX (1928), 404, n. 2.

[79] Cf. Canon 6, 2°

explicitly, take into consideration an impediment which is of private right (e.g., force and fear) but which is, *de facto*, divulged in such a way that it is known by the community or is in danger of becoming apparent to the public. Moreover, the opinion adopted by the Rota in 1928 does not explicitly take into consideration the right of the promoter of justice in cases in which the impediment is public of its nature but *de facto* occult. It is submitted that the answer to these questions must be resolved not so much through a minute and analytic study of the pre-Code concepts of an impediment public of its nature (*ratione notitiae*) or of an impediment of public right (*ratione iuris accusandi*), but rather through a study of that which the current Code has legislated on the nature of the office, rights, and duties of the promoter of justice.[80]

D. *Impediments Public of Their Nature and the Office of the Promoter of Justice*

It has been determined that the right of the promoter of justice, *vi muneris sui*, to accuse a marriage without a previous denunciation according to Canon 1971, § 1, 2°, must be understood in the light of Canon 1586. In Canon 1586 there is established the juridical basis and the fundamental scope of the rights and duties of the promoter of justice. According to Canon 1586, the sufficient juridical reason for any exercise of rights on the part of the promoter of justice is the common good. The scope of the rights of the promoter of justice extends not only to criminal cases[81] but to any contentious cause[82] concerning which, in the judgment of the Ordinary, the public good may be compromised. A matrimonial cause is a contentious cause.[83] In a cause of matrimonial nullity, the prosecution or the vindication of the rights of spouses is most certainly verified. Therefore, according to Canon 1586, once the Ordinary determines that the trial and decision of a matrimonial cause constitutes matter in which the public welfare is

[80] Cf. Lega (ed. Bart.), *Iudicia Ecclesiastica*, III, 88*.

[81] Cf. Canons 1933-1959.

[82] Cf. Canon 1552, § 2, 1°.

[83] Cf. *supra*, p. 193, note 21; Wernz-Vidal, *Ius Canonicum*, 3. ed., V, n. 697.

involved, the promoter of justice has the right and duty to intervene by virtue of his office and without any previous denunciation. This principle obtains regardless of whether the impediment is public by its nature (*impedimentum iuris publici*) or occult by its nature (*impedimentum iuris privati*).[84] Thus, for example, if the Ordinary determines that the public welfare is endangered because of certain knowledge by the greater part of a parish of the fact that a parishioner elicited consent under the influence of grave fear (impediment of private right), *ceteris paribus*, the promoter of justice *vi muneris sui*, has the right to accuse the marriage without any previous denunciation.[85]

On the other hand, what is to be said of the case, unusual though it may be, in which the impediment is public of its nature, according to Canon 1971, § 1, 2°, and *de facto* occult? May the promoter of justice, without any previous denunciation, accuse a marriage invalid because of an impediment which is public by its nature but concerning which the public actually has no knowledge? For example, a displaced married couple with their family arrive in the United States from eastern Europe. They are totally unknown by the American community of which they become members. Also unknown is the fact that their marriage is invalid because of the impediment of consanguinity (*impedimentum iuris publici*). The fact of the impediment is discovered accidentally by an observant curate who privately reveals the case to the promoter of justice. Does the promoter of justice, by virtue of his office, have the obligation to accuse this marriage according to Canon 1971, § 1, 2°?

[84] "Ubi eadem legis ratio, ibi eadem legis dispositio."—Triebs, "De Promotore Iustitiae in Causis Nullitatis Matrimonii," *Apollinaris*, X (1937), 396; S.R.R. *Decisiones*, XXVIII (1936), 398, n. 7; Noval, *De Iudiciis*, pp. 569-570; Wernz-Vidal, *Ius Canonicum*, 3. ed., V, 906, note 43; Cappello, *De Matrimonio*, 5. ed., nn. 878, 881; Torre, *Processus Matrimonialis*, 3. ed., p. 75; Regatillo, *Interpretatio et Iurisprudentia C.I.C.*, p. 539; Stitt, *De Promotore Justitiae*, p. 187; Roberti, "De Iure Denuntiandi Nullitatem Matrimonii," *Apollinaris*, III (1930), 250 and "De Matrimonii Accusatione," *Apollinaris*, VI (1933), 442.

[85] Cf. Instr. *Provida*, Art. 38, § 1, b.

This question is not discussed by the generality of authors. Cappello[86] and Stitt[87] hold that if the impediment is able to be proved in the external forum according to Canon 1037, the promoter of justice has the right and the duty to accuse the marriage of invalidity. If, on the other hand, the impediment cannot be proved in the external forum, the promoter of justice has no such obligation because his accusation would be altogether fruitless. Torre[88] asserts that the answer of those who hold that the promoter of justice must accuse the marriage, under the aspect of purging the profanation of the Sacrament of Matrimony, cannot always be sustained if the invalid union has not given rise to scandal in the community. It is the opinion of Torre that no accusation should be made by the promoter of justice until the impediment ceases to be occult. He adds that though it is true that an obligation exists on the part of the promoter of justice to accuse the marriage, *vi muneris sui*, because the impediment is by its nature public, nevertheless, the tranquillity of the lives of the spouses and the occult character of the impediment are sufficient reasons to warrant abstinence of action by the promoter of justice.[89]

It is submitted that the answer to the question whether or not the promoter of justice has the duty, by virtue of his office, to accuse a marriage that is invalid because of an impediment which is of its nature public but *de facto* occult, must be answered, once again, in the light of Canon 1586. By virtue of his office, the promoter of justice is committed to the protection and promotion of the public ecclesiastical welfare. In contentious causes, such as causes of matrimonial nullity, the activity of the promoter of justice is subject to the authority and surveillance and the decisions of the Ordinary. Canon 1586 is clear in this matter. Canon 1971, § 1, 2° represents an application of the prescription of Canon 1586 in relation to matrimonial causes. It is suggested that it is in the light of Canon 1586 that Canon 1971, § 1, 2° must be interpreted. Under the application of these principles to the case mentioned above,

86 *De Matrimonio,* 5. ed., p. 883.

87 *De Promotore Justitiae,* p. 189.

88 *Processus Matrimonialis,* 3. ed., p. 79.

89 *Loc. cit.*

let it be supposed that according to the judgment of the Ordinary, the parties involved would not accept the decision of the tribunal because of circumstances peculiar to their present union (e.g., six children). Let it be similarly supposed that the Ordinary judges that the present union is in no manner a danger to the spiritual welfare of the community because of the hidden character of the impediment involved. It would seem that under these circumstances, the promoter of justice not only should not but cannot licitly accuse the marriage of invalidity because of the impediment of consanguinity. A public accusation in this case would seem to promote rather than to prevent a public scandal in the community.

Briefly, it may be stated that *per se,* under the provisions of Canon 1586 [90] the promoter of justice has the right and duty to accuse marriages which are invalid because of an impediment of public right according to Canon 1971, § 1, 2°. Canon 1586, establishes the character and scope of the office, rights, and duties of the promoter of justice, especially in contentious causes. A matrimonial cause is a contentious cause. It follows that the interpretation of Canon 1971, § 1, 2° must be made in the light of Canon 1586. If, therefore, an impediment of public right is unknown to the community, and if the public accusation of the marriage would result in nothing more than a refusal of the parties to separate, the purpose of the public good is not served; and hence, there is no basis for the obligation and right of the promoter of justice to accuse the marriage. The foundation or the source of his obligation to accuse the marriage, namely, the common good, is not present.[91]

Cappello and Stitt believe that the promoter of justice would be obliged to accuse a marriage if the impediment was of public right but *de facto* occult, if the impediment is provable in the external forum.[92] An objection may be raised against this opinion. May it not be questioned, to what avail is proof in the external forum if the parties will not or humanly cannot but

[90] Triebs, "De Promotore Justitiae in Causis Nullitatis Matrimonii," *Apollinaris,* X (1937), 395.

[91] Cf. Glynn, *The Promoter of Justice,* pp. 161, 167.

[92] Cf. Cappello, *De Matrimonio,* 5. ed., p. 883; Stitt, *De Promotore Justitiae,* p. 189.

persist in the invalid union? The public accusation made by the promoter of justice and the subsequent judicial sentence has one purpose, the preservation or promotion of the public ecclesiastical good. But if the impediment is *de facto* occult and the parties will not or cannot separate, one may rightly conclude that, under the circumstances, scandal or its real danger would be created rather than prevented by the intervention of the promoter of justice. The writer submits that though it is true that a sinful matrimonial union is matter for the internal forum, such a union does not become subject to the external forum until the juridic social order of the Church is endangered.[93] The protection and preservation of the latter constitutes the only juridic basis and reason for the right and duty of the promoter of justice to accuse a marriage.[94] The sinfulness of the union, considered as such, is of no direct, juridic concern whatsoever to the external forum and to the promoter of justice. His judicial activity is based on and determined by one consideration, the public good, which is necessarily realized only in the external forum.

Section III. The Right of the Promoter of Justice to Accuse a Marriage Previously Denounced

Article 1. The Concept of a Denunciation

A. *The Definition*

A denunciation of marriage is an extrajudicial manifestation of the nullity of a marriage madė to the Ordinary or to the promoter of justice, so that it may be determined whether the action of the nullity of marriage should be introduced into an ecclesiastical court by the promoter of justice.[95]

[93] "Nobis datum est de manifestis tantummodo iudicare."—C. 34, X, *De simonia,* V, 3. "Ecclesia de internis non iudicat."—Ottaviani, *Institutiones Iuris Publici Ecclesiastici* (2. ed., 2 vols., Romae: Typis Polyglottis Vaticanis, 1935), I, 231; cf. Kuttner, "Ecclesia De Occultis Non Judicat," *Jus Pontificium,* XVII (1937), 13-28.

[94] Cf. Canon 1586, 1971, § 1, 2°.

[95] Roberti, "De Iure Denuntiandi Nullitatem Matrimonium," *Apollinaris,* III (1930), 249; Vermeersch-Creusen, *Epitome Iuris Canonici,* 6. ed., III,

B. *The Distinction between a Denunciation and an Accusation*

The significance of a denunciation of marriage is more readily grasped when it is related to the concept of an accusation of marriage. A juridic denunciation of marriage and a legal accusation differ by reason of their purpose, their nature, and their effects.[96]

The end or the purpose of the law in recognizing in the spouses the right of accusation is primarily the private good of the spouses themselves and indirectly the good of society itself.[97] The end or purpose of the law in recognizing the right of any reliable person (even the spouse who was the culpable cause of the impediment or of the nullity of marriage) to denounce a marriage is solely the preservation or the promotion of the public good.[98] Because the exclusive object of a denunciation is the common good of ecclesiastical society, the denunciation is to be directed, not to the tribunal, but to the Ordinary or to the promoter of justice.[99] From the purpose of a denunciation there can be derived the practical conclusion that the tribunal which takes the attitude that Canon 1971, § 2 simply provides a convenient juridic escape or legal remedy for those parties who have been deprived of the right to accuse a marriage, according to Canon 1971, § 1, 1°, is contravening the law of the Church.[100] The intervention of the promoter of justice following a denunciation is not made principally for the spiritual welfare of the parties but for the spiritual good of the community at large. A denunciation of a marriage is of interest to the promoter of justice only if and when the Ordinary determines that the public good is endangered.[101]

150; Cappello, *De Matrimonio,* 5. ed., 881; Regatillo, *Institutiones Iuris Canonici,* II, n. 750; Lega (ed. Bart.), *Iudicia Ecclesiastica,* III, 73*.

96 Toso, "De Matrimonio Accusando vel Denuntiando," *Jus Pontificium,* XVII (1937), 6.

97 Wernz-Vidal, *Ius Canonicum,* 3. ed., V, 905.

98 *Loc. cit.;* cf. *infra,* p. 231.

99 Canon 1971, § 2.

100 Cf. Bartoccetti, "De iure et officio promotoris justitiae accusandi matrimonium," *Apollinaris,* X (1937), 573-575.

101 Wernz-Vidal, *Ius Canonicum,* 3. ed., V, 902; Triebs, "De Promotore Justitiae in Causis Nullitatis Matrimonii," *Apollinaris,* X (1937), 406.

Clearly, a party who denounces a marriage may certainly benefit by an action instituted by the promoter of justice. But the action which is instituted by the promoter of justice must be determined directly by the interests of the public good. Indirectly, the preservation of the public good may redound to the interests of the parties themselves.[102]

An accusation of marriage and a denunciation of marriage differ also in their nature. The right to accuse a marriage is both personal and judicial. The right of accusation is personal, because it is recognized by law only in the parties whose rights are affected, namely, the spouses themselves.[103] The right of accusation is a judicial right because the accusation itself supposes that the accuser has a right to stand in judgment to introduce the action of invalidity of the marriage.[104] The right of denunciation, on the other hand, is not considered as a personal right, that is, it is not restricted to the spouses only. The right of denunciation is considered rather as a public right which may be exercised according to law by any responsible member of the community.[105] The right of denunciation is an extrajudicial right because the denouncer does not stand in judgment to introduce an action but merely makes manifest the invalidity of a marriage to the Ordinary or to the promoter of justice.[106] Moreover, the denunciation of a marriage is made not in order to vindicate a private right but in order to safeguard the public ecclesiastical welfare.[107]

An accusation of marriage and a denunciation of marriage differ also in their effects. An accusation, made according to

[102] Toso, "De Matrimonio Accusando vel Denuntiando," *Jus Pontificium,* XVII (1937), 8.

[103] Canon 1971, § 1, 1°; cf. Toso, "art. cit.," *Jus Pontificium,* XVII (1937), 7.

[104] Canons 1646, 1667, 1679, 1709, § 1; cf. Roberti, "De Iure Denuntiandi Nullitatem Matrimonium," *Apollinaris,* III (1930), 249; Cappello, "Annotationes," *Periodica,* XXXV (1946), 195; Beste, *Introductio in Codicem,* 4. ed., p. 922; *supra,* p. 76.

[105] Canon 1971, § 2.

[106] Coronata, *Institutiones Iuris Canonici,* 2. ed., II, n. 1485; Lega (ed. Bart.), *Iudicia Ecclesiastica,* III, 73*.

[107] De Smet, *De Sponsalibus et Matrimonio,* 4. ed., p. 603.

law, necessarily gives rise to a judicial process in which the spouses themselves prosecute their rights. A denunciation, on the other hand, merely occasions a judicial process which is initiated by a public accusation of the promoter of justice only if the public good requires it, and provided the conditions stipulated in the Instruction *Provida* are fulfilled. These conditions are examined in detail in Article 3 of this section.

Article 2. Persons Capable of Denouncing a Marriage

It has been determined that the right to accuse a marriage, that is, the right to introduce into an ecclesiastical court an action relating to the nullity of marriage, is reserved to:

a) the spouses themselves, regardless of the nature of the impediment, provided that they themselves were not the direct and dolose cause of the impediment or of the nullity of the marriage;
b) the promoter of justice, by virtue of his office and without any previous denunciation, in cases in which the impediment is public of its nature.[108]

All other persons, including the blood relatives of the spouses, can claim no right to accuse marriages of invalidity.[109]

Though the existence of an invalid marriage may not affect the private substantive rights of individuals, it may well constitute a danger to the tranquillity of the community, or to the authority of the Church as the guardian of faith and morals.[110] In the interest of the public ecclesiastical welfare, therefore, Canon 1971, § 2 recognizes the right of anyone, who does not have the right to accuse marriage, to call attention of the invalidity of a marriage to the Ordinary or to the promoter of justice.[111] The term "*omnes reliqui*" employed in Canon 1971, § 2 may be understood as embracing:

108 Canon 1971, § 1, 1°, 2°; Instr. *Provida,* Art. 35, § 1, 1°, 2°.

109 Canon 1971, § 2.—"Reliqui omnes, etsi consanguinei, non habent ius matrimonia accusandi . . ."

110 Cf. Canon 1935; *infra,* p. 235.

111 "Reliqui omnes, etiam consanguinei, non habent ius matrimonia accusandi, sed tantummodo nullitatem matrimonii Ordinario vel promotori iustitiae denuntiandi."

a) any responsible person other than the spouses themselves [112]
b) any spouse who was the direct and dolose cause of the impediment or of the nullity of the marriage [113]
c) the non-Catholic spouse who is forbidden to be a plaintiff in a matrimonial cause, according to the law of the Code, especially Canon 87.[114]

In the article that follows, attention is given to the norms governing the right of the promoter of justice to accuse a marriage denounced by Catholics other than the spouses, spouses who have been deprived of the right to accuse marriage by force of the provision of Canon 1971, § 1, 1°, and persons who are non-Catholic.

Article 3. Norms Governing the Right of the Promoter of Justice to Accuse a Marriage Previously Denounced

A. *Introduction*

Fundamental norms governing the right of the promoter of justice to accuse a marriage that has been previously denounced are presented in Article 41 of the Instruction *Provida.* The first paragraph of this article provides for written denunciations whose authors cannot be questioned personally.[115] As a general rule, written denunciations whose authors cannot be questioned personally are to be considered, *per se,* as insufficient cause for instituting judicial proceedings. Exceptions to this rule are to be made only if the Ordinary determines that special circumstances attach to the denunciation and only after proper and efficient investigations have been made concerning the truth of

[112] Cf. Instr. *Provida,* Art. 41, §§ 1, 2, 3.

[113] Cf. Comm. Pont. 17 Februarii, 1930, *AAS,* XXII (1930), 196; Instr. *Provida* Art. 37, § 4; 38, 39.

[114] Cf. S.C.S. Officii, 27, Januarii, 1928, *AAS,* XX (1928), 75; Instr. *Provida,* Art. 35, § 3; S.C.S. Officii, 22 Martii, 1939, *AAS,* XXXI (1939), 131.

[115] "Denunciationes scripto exhibitae, quarum auctores personaliter interrogari nequeant, ut sufficiens causa instituendi processus, in peculiaribus tantum rerum adiunctis, Ordinario iudicio, haberi possunt; praehibitis tamen opportunis aptisque investigationibus."

the allegations of the denouncer. It would seem that the Ordinary would be under no obligation even to investigate the assertions of the denouncer unless the evidence he produced was of such a character as to make reasonable an inquisition into the matter. Clearly, prudence and caution are to be exercised in a preeminent manner in such cases.[116]

Article 41, § 2 declares that no account is to be given to anonymous denunciations unless they indicate positive and grave proofs of fact.[117] In the light of Article 165 of the *Provida*, it would seem that positive and grave proofs of fact may be interpreted as referring to facts that are most readily capable of corroboration.[118] Doheny wisely observes that any court official of extended experience can usually distinguish between truthful expositions of cases and libellous notes and letters.[119]

Allegations against the validity of a marriage made by persons who cannot be questioned personally, or whose identity is unknown, are not the only kinds of denunciations that normally are to be rejected by the Ordinary or the promoter of justice. Article 41, § 2 also prescribes that no attention is to be given to denunciations which are not anonymous when the consorts themselves have the right to accuse the marriage and when the impediment is not public by its nature.[120] Doheny asserts that the reason that a denunciation is not to be considered, when the spouses have the right to accuse the marriage, is that the parties themselves will accuse the marriage in due time.[121] If the supposition of Doheny does not transpire, it would seem that the

116 Cf. Doheny, *Canonical Procedure*, 2. ed., I, 145.

117 "Nulla ratio habenda est tum denunciationum anonymarum, nisi positivas et graves facti probationes indicent . . ."

118 "Litterae, quas vocant anonymas, aliaque cuiuscumque generis anonyma documenta per se ne tamquam indicium quidem haberi possunt; nisi facta referant quae et quatenus aliunde comprobari possint." Cf. Canons 1645, § 4; 1942, § 2.

119 *Op. cit.*, I, 146.

120 "Nulla ratio habenda est . . . denuntiationum non anonymarum, quando jus accusandi coniugibus competit, neque de impedimentis agitur natura sua publicis (cfr. art. 35, § 1, n. 2).

121 *Canonical Procedure*, 2. ed., I, 146.

denunciation is to be considered in the light of Canon 1586 and, by way of analogy, Article 41, § 3. Thus, if the parties have not been the direct and dolose cause of the impediment or the nullity of marriage, the promoter of justice has the right to accuse the marriage only after it is determined by the Ordinary that the denunciation contains positive facts pointing to the nullity of marriage, and that there is no possibility to convalidate the marriage, and that the public good may be in jeopardy. In the absence of any one of these conditions, action by the promoter of justice, in the case under consideration, has no basis in law.

B. *Denunciations by Third Parties*

Article 41, § 3 of the *Provida* considers specifically denunciations made by third parties of the invalidity of marriages which cannot be accused by the spouses themselves because of the penalty of Canon 1971, § 1, 1°. Article 41, § 3 states that if any denunciation made by other parties contains facts from which the nullity of the marriage appears probable, it is the duty of the Ordinary or the promoter of justice to investigate, by cautiously and secretly questioning the denunciators whether there is a case for an accusation *ex officio*, in accordance with the provisions of Articles 38 and 39, or for a dispensation to convalidate the marriage.[122]

It is clear that denunciations may be made by persons of the Catholic Faith[123] of the invalidity of a marriage between two other Catholics or of the nullity of a marriage between a Catholic and a non-Catholic, whether baptized or unbaptized.[124] The question to be asked here is whether a person of the Catholic Faith has the right to denounce the invalidity of a marriage between two non-Catholics, so that the promoter

[122] Si qua denunciatio ab aliis facta probationes contineat, ex quibus matrimonii nullitas probabilis appareat, Ordinarii vel promotoris iustitiae erit investigare, interrogatis caute et secreto denunciatoribus, utrum locus sit accusationi ex officio, ad normam art. 38 et 39, an vero dispensationi ad matrimonium revalidandum.

[123] The rules governing the denunciations by non-Catholics are treated under sub-title "D" of this article.

[124] Cf. Instr. *Provida,* Art. 12.

of justice may institute proceedings without the authorization of the Holy Office.

Schaaf,[125] writing in 1934, answered that if the case is one that can be handled according to the procedure provided in Canon 1990, the declaration of nullity of the marriage between two non-Catholics can be given by the Ordinary. But if the case must be instituted formally or remanded to formal procedure, the marriage between two non-Catholics cannot be investigated by the diocesan matrimonial tribunal without recourse to the Holy Office by virtue of the response of the Holy Office of 1928 which forbids the admission of a non-Catholic as a plaintiff according to Canon 87. Schaaf continued that the cause cannot be considered *ratione connexionis* according to Canon 1567 [126] because of the expressed prohibition of the Holy Office decree of 1928. Moreover, the promoter of justice cannot accept a denunciation by the Catholic party, according to Schaaf, "because his power is intended exclusively for the direct benefit of Catholics." Schaff admitted that there are cases in which the Church claims and exercises jurisdiction over matters pertaining to non-Catholics. But in such matters as marriage, the cases are always those in which the Church is directly and immediately concerned with the Catholic and only indirectly with the non-Catholic, that is, because of the relation of the non-Catholic with the Catholic. According to Schaaf, in the case under discussion, it is not the case of the Catholic that is to be immediately and directly examined. Rather it is the case in which the non-Catholics alone are concerned, and in which the Catholic in question has no direct interest. Therefore, the Church does not permit the case to be brought to the diocesan tribunal according to the response of the Holy Office of 1928.

Schaaf concluded that two rescripts issued to the Bishop of Berlin settle the question with finality. He refers to the letter of the Sacred Congregation for the Discipline of the Sacraments of November 3, 1931 in which the Congregation declared

125 "Diocesan Tribunal Lacks Competence over Marriages between Non-Catholics," *The American Ecclesiastical Review,* XCI (1934), 79-80.

126 "Ratione connexionis seu continentiae ab eodemque iudice cognoscendae sunt causae inter se connexae nisi legis praescriptum obstet."

that subsequent to a denunciation by a person who is incapable of accusing marriage, the Ordinary or the promoter of justice may institute proceedings without consulting the Holy See unless there is a question of cases which are reserved to the Holy Office according to the Decree of January 27, 1928.[127] Schaaf also refers to a reply of the Holy Office of November 30, 1931 in which the Holy Office declared that a denunciation by a Catholic party of the invalidity of a marriage between non-Catholics may not be acted upon by the Ordinary or the promoter of justice without recourse to the Holy Office in each case.[128]

Certainly, it must be conceded that the opinion of Schaaf appears to be soundly probable. The writer submits, on the other hand, that the reasoning of Schaaf is not so cogent as to preclude all arguments to the contrary. The following observations are made to support this contention.

On June 23, 1903, the Holy Office decreed that the Ordinary of a Catholic person who intends to marry a baptized non-Catholic who, in turn, has been civilly divorced from another baptized non-Catholic is competent to judge the validity of the marriage between the two baptized non-Catholics.[129] It will be observed that this decree relates to the competence of the Ordinary and not to the right of a non-Catholic to stand in judgment. The decree of the Holy Office of January 18, 1928, ad I,[130] however, refers not to the competence of the Ordinary

[127] Cf. Bouscaren, *Canon Law Digest,* II, 542.

[128] *Ibid.,* p. 543.

[129] "Standum Instructioni pro Statibus Foederatis Americae anno 1883 editae . . . Quando vero agitur de matrimonio mixto contrahendo cum haeretico separato per divortii sententiam tribunalis civilis ab haeretica, erit Episcopus domicilii partis catholicae, ad quem spectat iudicare an contrahentes gaudeant status libertate."—*AAS,* XXXVI (1903-1904), 165-166; *Fontes,* IV, n. 1266; cf. *Fontes,* VII. n. 4901, n. 2.

[130] "I. Utrum in causis matrimonialibus acatholicus sive baptizatus, sive non baptizatus, actoris partes gerere possit. Resp. Negative seu standum est Codici I. C., praesertim can. 87. Siquidem autem speciales occurrant rationes ad admittendos acatholicos ut actores in huiusmodi causis, recurrendum ad Supremam Sacram Congregationem Sancti Officii in singulis casibus."—*AAS,* XX (1928), 75; cf. Bouscaren, *Canon Law Digest,* I, 762-763.

but to the right of the non-Catholic to act as plaintiff. Therefore, the decree of the Holy Office of 1928, ad I, does not affect, much less does it abrogate, the decree of the Holy Office of 1903. Similarly, the decree of the Holy Office of 1928 ad II does not contradict the declaration of the Holy Office of 1903, because the former states only that the Holy Office has exclusive competence in all matrimonial causes between a Catholic and non-Catholic party, whether baptized or unbaptized, which are in any way brought before the Holy See.[131]

Hence, the writer submits that at least in cases in which the conditions mentioned in the decree of the Holy Office of June 23, 1903 are verified, namely, in cases which concern the contracting of a mixed marriage between a Catholic and a baptized non-Catholic (heretic) civilly divorced from another baptized non-Catholic (heretic), the diocesan tribunal of the Ordinary of the Catholic party is competent to decide and to issue a declaration of the invalidity of the marriage between the two baptized non-Catholics.[132] The promoter of justice of the mentioned tribunal, on the other hand, may institute a public accusation of a marriage between two baptized non-Catholics only if his intervention is warranted by the circumstances surrounding the case.[133] Depending on the nature of the case, these circumstances are determined in Articles 38 and 39 of the *Provida*. Clearly, such cases will occur rarely. If there is doubt as to the verification of the conditions of the response of the Holy Office of June 23, 1903 or of the existence of the circumstances of articles 38 and 39 of the *Provida*, recourse should be made to the Sacred Congregation of the Holy Office.

Concerning the private response of the Sacred Congregation of the Sacraments of November 3, 1931 and the private reply

[131] "II. Utrum in quibuslibet causis matrimonialibus inter partem catholicam et partem acatholicam, sive baptizatam sive non baptizatam, quocumque modo ad Sanctem Sedem delatis, Suprema Sacra Congregatio Sancti Officii exclusivam habeat compententiam." "R. Ad II. Affirmative, habita praesertim ratione can. 247, § 3, et salvo praescripto can. 1557, §1, 1°."—*AAS*, XX (1928), 75; Bouscaren, *Canon Law Digest*, I, 762-763.

[132] Cf. Canon 1567.

[133] Ayrinhac, *Marriage Legislation in the Code of Canon Law*, 1952 ed., 368.

of the Supreme Congregation of the Holy Office of November 30, 1931,[134] the following observations may be made. First, it is clear that these responses do not have the force of a general law.[135] Second, these replies are not even remotely alluded to in the detailed Instruction *Provida* of 1936.[136] Third, it is submitted that the private replies of the Sacred Congregations of the Sacraments and of the Holy Office to the Bishop of Berlin are of a most generic character, particularly with respect to the baptismal status of the non-Catholic parties, and that they cannot be construed as abrogating the specifically detailed decree of the Holy Office issued for the universal Church at an earlier date. Finally, it would seem that Canon 6, 4° is applicable in this case at least *a stylo et praxi Curiae Romanae*.[137] Canon 6, 4° provides that in case of doubt whether the law of the Code differs from the old law, the prescriptions of the old law prevail. Thus, the decree of the Holy Office of 1903 [138] is law at the present time.

Whether the invalidity of a marriage is denounced by a third party, or whether it is denounced by the culpable spouses themselves, the rules that govern the exercise of the right of the promoter of justice to accuse marriage are the same. To avoid needless repetition, therefore, consideration of these norms is given in the following sub-title which treats of denunciations by spouses who were the direct and dolose causes of the impediment or of the nullity of marriage.

C. *Denunciations by Spouses Who Were the Direct and Dolose Causes of the Impediment or of the Nullity of Marriage*

It will be recalled that in the cases in which the impediment to a marriage is public by its nature, the exercise of the right

[134] See also the private response of the Holy Office of April 8, 1925 to the Archbishop of Friburg. This response is published in Bouscaren, *Canon Law Digest*, I, 763.

[135] Cf. Canons 17, § 3; 49.

[136] Cf. Triebs, "De Promotoris Justitiae in Causis Nullitatis Matrimonii," *Apollinaris*, X (1937), 399.

[137] Cf. Canon 20.

[138] *Fontes*, IV, n. 1266; cf. *supra*, p. 218, note 129.

of the promoter of justice to accuse the marriage of invalidity is not dependent upon the denunciation of the nullity of the marriage by the spouses or by any other person.[139] To be considered here is the right of the promoter of justice to accuse a marriage in cases in which the impediment is not public by its nature, and in which the consorts have been deprived of the right to accuse their marriage according to Canon 1971, § 1, 1°.

Article 35, § 1, 2° of the *Provida* states that in the case of impediments other than those public by their nature, the promoter of justice may accuse the marriage when a denunciation has been made by a spouse who has been deprived of the right to institute an action to obtain a declaration of nullity of marriage.[140] It is most important to note, however, that this right of the promoter of justice as represented in Article 35, § 1, 2° and also in Article 41, § 3 of the *Provida* is most severely conditioned by a concluding clause, "*salvo tamen praescripto art. 38 et 39.*"[141] Because of the importance of Articles 38 and 39

[139] Canon 1971, § 1, 2°; Instr. *Provida,* Art. 35, § 1, 2°; cf. *supra,* p. 198.

[140] Promotor iustitiae . . . praevia autem denunciatione in aliis impedimentis, si iure actionem instituendi ob obtinendam declarationem nullitatis sui matrimonii denuncians careat, salvo tamen praescripto art. 38 et 39. This article represents a condensation of the reply of the Code Commission of February 17, 1930, which stated that the consorts who, according to Canon 1971, § 1, 1°, and the interpretation of March 12, 1929, are incapable of accusing their marriage have at least the right to apprise the *Ordinary* or the promoter of justice of the nullity of the marriage in virtue of the second paragraph of the same canon.

"An coniuges qui, iuxta canonem 1971, § 1, n. 1 et interpretationem diei 12 Martii 1929, habiles non sunt ad accusandum matrimonium, vi eiusdem canonis § 2 ius saltem habeant nullitatem matrimonii Ordinario vel promotori iustitiae denuntiandi." "R. Affirmative."—*AAS,* XXII (1930), 196. On March 12, 1929, the Code Commission interpreted the word, *impedimentum* of Canon 1971, § 1, 1° in the wide sense of the term; cf. *AAS,* XXI (1929), 171; *supra,* p. 113.

[141] It may be well to call attention to the fact that whether the promoter of justice accuses a marriage of invalidity without a previous denunciation, or whether he accuses a marriage the invalidity of which has been previously denounced, the promoter of justice acts by virtue of his office. The wording of Article 35, § 1, 2° appears, at first sight, to indicate that only in cases involving impediments public by their nature does the promoter of justice act in his own right, that is, by virtue of his office:

of the *Provida*,[142] and because of the frequent reference that will be made to them during the discussion that follows, their texts are presented here in full.

1. The Texts of Articles 38 and 39 of the Instruction *Provida*

Art. 38—§ 1. Ubi agitur de denuntiatione nullitatis a coniuge vel coniugibus facta, quia alteruter vel ambo

a) positivo voluntatis actu excluserunt matrimonium ipsum, aut omne ius ad coniugalem actum, aut essentialem aliquam matrimonii proprietatem; vel

b) conditionem apposuere contra matrimonii substantiam, promotor iustitiae matrimonium ne accuset, sed coniugem vel coniuges pro viribus moneat suae conscientiae consulant, et, si fieri possit, causam impedimenti auferant, e. g. per novum consenum rite praestandum.

§ 2. Si tamen matrimonii adserta nullitas publica evaserit et scandalum revera adsit, denuncians autem resipiscentiae signa, Ordinarii iudicio, revera dederit; itemque denunciata nullitatis causa argumentis nitatur, sive in facto sive in iure, ita certis et validis, ut probabilis omnino sit ipsius matrimonii nullitas, tunc

---

"Promotor iustitiae, in impedimentis natura sua publicis, iure proprio (Comm. Pont. 17 Iulii 1933 ad IV) et absque praevia denuntiatione; praevia autem denuntiatione in aliis impedimentis, si iure actionem instituendi ad obtinendam declarationem nullitatis sui matrimonii denuncians careat, salvo tamen praescripto art. 38 et 39." On the other hand, the reply of the Code Commission of July 17, 1933 is clear. This response states that a promoter of justice takes part in a trial, *vi muneris sui*, by virtue of Canon 1971, § 2 (*AAS*, XXV [1933] 345). The second paragraph of Canon 1971, however, treats specifically of marriages which are previously denounced to the Ordinary or to the promoter of justice. Moreover, Article 41, § 3 of the *Provida* unequivocally refers to accusations made by the promoter of justice in accordance with Articles 38 and 39 (which consider marriages previously denounced) as accusations which are made *ex officio:* ". . . utrum locus sit accusationi ex officio, ad normam art. 38 et 39. . . ." Cf. Wernz-Vidal, *Ius Canonicum*, 3. ed., V, 901; Triebs, "De Promotoris Justitiae in Causis Nullitatis Matrimonii," *Apollinaris*, X (1937), 405; Fair, "The Promoter of Justice," *The Jurist*, VII (1947), 386.

142 Attention is called to a Rotal decision of April 10, 1940 (*coram* Pecorari) in which a certain promoter of justice was scolded by the Rota for his most lax attitude toward the provisions of Article 38, § 2 in particular. —*Decisiones*, XXXII (1940), 262-263, n. 9.

promotori iustitiae ius et officium est denunciatum matrimonium rite accusandi.

Art. 39—Si vero matrimonii nullitas a coniuge vel a coniugibus denunciatur, qui causa culpabilis fuerint sive impedimenti sive nullitatis matrimonii, exceptis casibus de quibus in art. praecedenti, promotor iustitiae accusationem ne instituat, nisi haec tria concurrant:

a) de impedimento agatur quod publicum evaserit, quodque argumentis nitatur, sive in facto sive in iure, ita certis et validis, ut de eiusdem impedimenti existentia et vi serio dubitari non possit;

b) bonum publicum, scandali nempe amotio, Ordinarii iudicio, id revera postulet;

c) fieri nequeat ut, cessato impedimento, matrimonium rite ineatur.

2. The Differences between the Cases Considered in Articles 38 and 39

A cursory reading of these two articles may not reveal a difference between them which may be considered particularly significant. A closer examination of these articles indicates that the Sacred Congregation of the Sacraments wishes to call the attention of the promoter of justice to two clearly distinct cases.

Article 38 provides for cases in which the denunciation is made by one or both of the spouses who have been deprived of the right to accuse their marriage because either or both of the spouses directly and dolosely caused their marriage to be invalid:

a) by excluding marriage itself (*simulatio totalis*), or all right to the conjugal act (*exclusio boni prolis*), or some essential property of marriage (*exclusio boni sacramenti vel boni fidei*) by a positive act of the will [143]

b) by placing a condition contrary to the substance of marriage.[144]

143 Canon 1086, § 2.

144 Canon 1092.

Article 39, on the other hand, looks to cases in which the denunciation is made by spouses who have been deprived of the right to accuse their marriage because either or both of the spouses directly and dolosely caused their marriage to be null because of the impediments of age, impotence, ligamen, disparity of cult, major orders, solemn vows, abduction, crimen, consanguinity, affinity, public decency, spiritual and legal relationship, substantial error, force and fear, invalid proxy, and lack of form.

It will be noted that the impediments mentioned in Article 38 are more directly and intimately related to the nullity of a marriage than the impediments found in Article 39.[145] Moreover, the nullity of marriage is caused more frequently and more easily by the simulation of consent or by a condition against the substance of marriage than by other impediments to marriage.[146] Again, the impediments of Article 38 are removed by a renewal of consent by the spouses. The impediments of Article 39 are normally set aside by a dispensation. Finally, the spouses who directly and dolosely cause the nullity of a marriage by placing an intention or condition against the substance of marriage more frequently reveal a perverseness of will and hardness of conscience than those spouses who deliberately contract marriage which is invalid because of the impediment, for example, of consanguinity or affinity.[147]

3. The Differences between the Conditions Contained in Articles 38 and 39

Articles 38 and 39 differ not only by reason of the nature of the impediments because of which the nullity of marriage is denounced, but also by reason of the conditions that must be fulfilled before the promoter of justice can act upon the denunciation.

Article 38 states that the promoter of justice has the right

[145] Toso, "De Matrimonio Accusando vel Denuntiando," *Jus Pontificium,* XVII (1937), 11.

[146] *Loc. cit.;* Lega (ed. Bart.), *Iudicia Ecclesiastica,* III, 96*.

[147] Doheny, *Canonical Procedure,* 2. ed., I, 141; Toso, "De Matrimonio Accusando vel Denuntiando," *Jus Pontificium,* XVII (1937), 11.

and the duty duly to accuse the marriage which has been denounced only if the following conditions are verified:

a) the culpable party or parties must be exhorted by the promoter of justice, to the best of his ability, to examine their consciences, and if possible to remove the cause of the impediment, for example, by a renewal of proper consent.

b) if the efforts of the promoter of justice are fruitless, it must then be determined by the Ordinary whether:
   1. the nullity of the marriage has become public;
   2. the nullity of the marriage has given rise to scandal;
   3. the alleged cause of the nullity is supported by arguments so certain and valid in fact or in law that the nullity of the marriage is altogether probable;
   4. the denouncing spouse has given true signs of repentance.

Article 39, it may be observed, presents the same conditions, albeit with slight changes of expression, as are found in Article 38 with one notable exception. This exception emphasizes the formal difference between the two articles. Article 38 which treats of marriages invalid because of simulated consent or because of a condition placed against the substance of marriage, demands that true signs of repentance be given by the culpable spouse or spouses. Article 39 does not stipulate any such requirement. The reason for the presence of the requirement of repentance in Article 38, and the omission of this requirement in Article 39 seems to indicate the concern of the Sacred Congregation for the Discipline of the Sacraments over the increasing number of marriages impugned because of total or partial defect of consent.[148] A second reason is that the Congregation of the Sacraments feels that, in general, there is a greater evidence of perverseness of will in cases in which the spouses directly and maliciously simulate consent in order to produce the nullity of marriage than in cases visualized under Article 39. In other words, there is a danger that a party who had a mind to simu-

[148] Lega (ed. Bart.), *Iudicia Ecclesiastica,* III, 95*; Doheny, *Canonical Procedure,* 2. ed., I, 141.

late consent on one occasion may well do so again. But there is not as great a danger that a party who has married invalidly because of the existence of the impediment of consanguinity will again deliberately make the same mistake.

Article 38 prescribes that the responsibility rests with the Ordinary to determine whether the party who was the culpable cause of the nullity of the marriage has given evidence of repentance for his sacrilegious conduct. Clearly, the most efficacious sign of repentance is the will to rectify the vitiated consent.[149] If this cannot be done, the sincerity and truthfulness of the spouse who affirms that he will never again expose the Sacrament of Matrimony to defilement is left to the judgment of the Ordinary.[150] The repentant attitude, demanded by Article 38, of the spouse who was the culpable cause of the impediment or of the nullity of marriage is in no way to be taken lightly. In the past, the Rota has not hesitated to append to its sentences prohibitory clauses forbidding the guilty consort to contract another marriage until the consort evidenced convincing proof of amendent and sincere acceptation of the noble ideals of Christian marriage.[151]

Apart from the necessity of repentance mentioned in Article 38, the conditions included in Articles 38 and 39 are essentially identical. It is necessary now to examine these remaining requirements. In the course of this analysis, mention will be made of the incidential variations of expression which are found in the texts of the two articles.

4. The Conditions Common to Articles 38 and 39

a. *Exhortation of the Convalidation of the Invalid Marriage.* —Whether the marriage is denounced as invalid by either or both spouses because of the simulation of consent or because of the existence of any other impediment, it is necessary that an effort be made to remove, if possible, the cause of the impediment

149 Bartoccetti, "De iure et officio promtoris justitiae accusandi matrimonium," *Apollinaris,* X (1937), 568.

150 Instr. *Provida,* Art. 38, § 2; cf. Doheny, *Canonical Procedure,* 2. ed., I, 140.

151 S.R.R. *Decisiones,* XXIV (1932), 392, n. 14; XXV (1933), 350, n. 12.

in order that the marriage may be validly contracted.[152] This effort must be made by the promoter of justice according to Article 38, 1, b. If the consort consents to the convalidation of the marriage, the Ordinary, according to Article 65, § 2, is to grant whatever dispensation is necessary, if he is empowered to do so, or he is to obtain the dispensation from the Holy See, employing every means to effect the convalidation without any scandal or gossip. Only if the convalidation of the marriage is impossible because the impediment is such that it cannot be dispensed, or because the spouses are adamant in their refusal to renew consent, or because it is morally impossible for the spouses to renew consent, does the promoter of justice have the right and duty to make a public accusation of the marriage.

Not infrequently, the denunciation of a marriage is made by a spouse who is already separated from the consort and there exists between the couple a deep-rooted animosity or attitudes that are totally irreconcilable, at least in respect to their marriage. In these cases, though an investigation must be made to determine whether the convalidation of the marriage is possible, the efforts to achieve this end must be guided by the principles of prudence and good sense. If, however, such circumstances do not present such a formidable obstacle to the renewal of consent, and especially if there are children born of the invalid union, every conceivable effort should be employed to bring about the convalidation of the marriage in order to preserve the family unit and to insure the spiritual and temporal welfare of the children.

b. *Solid Probability of the Impediment or of the Nullity of the Marriage.*—Article 38, § 2 states that the promoter of justice has the right and duty of impugning the invalidity of a marriage previously denounced by a spouse or spouses who placed an intention or condition against the substance of marriage only if the alleged cause of the nullity of the marriage is supported by arguments so certain and valid, either in fact or in law, that the nullity of the marriage appears altogether probable. Article 39 suggests that the nullity of the marriage is altogether probable if there is no serious doubt of the existence of the impedi-

[152] Instr. *Provida,* Art. 38, § 1, b; 39, c: cf. Canon 1965; Instr. *Provida,* Art. 65.

ment. Bartoccetti,[153] Torre,[154] Doheny,[155] Triebs [156] and Wernz-Vidal [157] agree that the duty to examine whether the nullity of the denounced marriage is "altogether probable" is that of the promoter of justice. In this regard, certain observations should be made.

At first sight, the condition that the evidence of nullity must be so certain and valid as to preclude any serious doubt of the validity of the marriage poses no difficulty. In practise, however, it is no small task for a judge to arrive at a decision in cases involving the simulation of consent or a condition against the substance of marriage even after all of the evidence has been presented. Article 38 seems to require, nevertheless, that even before the evidence of nullity is weighed and evaluated by the tribunal, a decision must be reached, based on arguments that are certain and valid, either in fact or in law, that it is altogether probable that the marriage is null. The impediments embraced under Article 39 are, generally speaking, more susceptible to proof in the external forum. They also lend themselves more readily to a pre-judicial judgment concerning the probable invalidity of the marriage. But, in either case, it must be understood that the promoter of justice is not a judge. It is clearly not within the office of the promoter of justice to decide the merits of a matrimonial cause. The Instruction *Provida* is not demanding of the promoter of justice to determine, even before the parties, witnesses, documents, presumptions, and other sources of evidence are presented to the ecclesiastical tribunal, to make a definitive judgment concerning the certainty and validity of the facts of the case that may or may not point to the nullity of marriage. Article 57, § 3 states that it is neither necessary nor expedient that the *libellus* contain an exact and detailed expo-

[153] Lega (ed. Bart.), *Iudicia Ecclesiastica,* III, 96*.

[154] *Processus Matrimonialis,* 3. ed., p. 122.

[155] *Canonical Procedure,* 2. ed., I, 140.

[156] "De Promotoris Justitiae in Causis Nullitatis," *Apollinaris,* X (1937), 399.

[157] *Jus Canonicum,* 3. ed., V, 902.

sition of the evidence, for this belongs to the subsequent stages of the proof and defense of the case. It suffices to indicate that the petition has not been presented temerariously.

It would seem that Article 38, § 2 and Article 39 of the Instruction *Provida* demand that before the promoter of justice introduces the cause of the parties in behalf of the common good, he must make a close scrutiny of the allegations of the spouses. If the investigation of the assertions of the denouncer reveals certain and valid *prima facie* evidence of simulated or conditioned consent, or any other invalidating impediment which gives rise to a serious doubt concerning the validity of the marriage, the condition of Articles 38 and 39 concerning the probability of the nullity of the marriage would seem to be fulfilled.[158] Therefore, the promoter of justice must call on his experience and sound judgment in striking a balance between the avoidance of the usurpation of the prerogatives of the tribunal in judging the merits of the cause and the introduction of a cause into the tribunal which lacks foundation. It may be finally observed that if, after the investigations of the allegations of the denouncing parties, it is found that the existence of the impediment can be proved from certain and authentic documents which cannot be contradicted or objected to, and if it can be proved that no dispensation from the impediment has been granted, the case may then be tried according to the summary procedure prescribed in Canon 1990, in causes there stated.

c. *Publicity of the Impediment or of the Nullity of the Marriage.*—Before the promoter of justice can act upon the denunciation of a spouse deprived of the right to accuse marriage, it must be ascertained that the impediment or the nullity of the marriage is public. Whether or not the impediment or the nullity is considered public is left to the judgment of the Ordinary.[159] Authors are agreed that the word "public" in this context

[158] Cf. Torre, *Processus Matrimonialis,* 3. ed., p. 122.

[159] Instr. *Provida,* Art. 38, § 2; 39, a; cf. Lega (ed. Bart.), *Iudicia Ecclesiastica,* III, 96*; Torre, *Processus Matrimonialis,* 3. ed., p. 122; Canon 1586. In Article 38, § 2, the condition is expressed: "If the alleged nullity of the marriage has become public" (*Si tamen matrimonii adserta nullitas*

is to be interpreted according to Canon 2197, 1°.[160] Therefore, the fact of the impediment or the nullity of the denounced marriage must be either already known by the community or must be attended by such circumstances that its divulgation to the community is easily possible.[161]

To what extent must the fact or the impediment be known by the community? It is difficult to establish a specific norm of publicity because of the myriad variations of circumstances that can be visualized, for example, place, time, the type of people involved, the nature of the facts, etc. It can be said, however, that it is not necessary that the majority of the community be aware of the impediment or of the nullity. It suffices that a notable part of the community has the knowledge or will easily come to the knowledge.[162] Moreover, the community in which the fact of the impediment or of the nullity is present need only be that of a certain neighborhood, or parish, or college campus, or fraternal organization.[163]

Lessons learned from experience have their application here. It is not unreasonable to presume, for example, that the fact of an attempted marriage by a divorced Catholic, however privately it may have been performed, will generally come to the knowledge of a notable part of the community and, therefore, may be considered public according to Canon 2197, 1°. Finally, it may even be suggested that if the nullity of the marriage is certain, and if it is known by four or five persons outside of the

publica evaserit). In Article 39, the condition is phrased: "if it is a question of an impediment that has become public" (*nisi . . . de impedimento agatur quod publicum evaserit*).

[160] Lega (ed. Bart.), *Iudicia Ecclesiastica,* III, 96*-97*; Doheny, *Canonical Procedure,* 2. ed., I, 138-139; Torre, *Processus Matrimonialis,* 3. ed., p. 122; Toso, "De Matrimonio Accusando vel Denuntiando," *Jus Pontificium,* XVII (1937), 12; Triebs, "De Promotore Justitiae in Causis Nullitatis Matrimonii," *Apollinaris,* X (1937), 404.

[161] Can 2179, § 1. Publicum, si iam divulgatum est aut talibus contigit seu versatur in adiunctis ut prudenter iudicari possit et debeat facile divulgatum iri.

[162] Reiffensteul, Lib. V, tit. 1, *De Accusationibus Inquisitionibus et Denuntiationibus,* nn. 249, 250; cf. Canon 6, § 2.

[163] *Ibid.,* nn. 250-251.

consort's family circle, *ex communiter contingentibus*, it may prudently be presumed that the nullity of the marriage will become a matter of public knowledge in a remarkably brief period of time.

d. *Detriment to the Public Good.*—The final condition, and the condition which is most directly related to the office of the promoter of justice, is that the nullity of the denounced marriage must be detrimental to the public good. Article 38, § 2 expresses this condition by stating that scandal must actually be present (*scandalum revera adsit*). Article 39, b declares that the promoter of justice shall impugn a marriage only if the public good demands this (*bonum publicum scandali nempe . . . id revera postulet*). Article 39, b adds that the Ordinary is to make the decision whether a declaration of nullity is necessary in order to remove the *publicum malum* of scandal from the community.

What norm is to be used to determine when an evil act is detrimental to the public good? What principle is to be employed to distinguish between a *malum privatum* and a *malum publicum?* Bartoccetti confesses that these questions simply cannot be answered by means of a fast and facile formula.[164] The standard that should be employed to decide whether a certain evil is a danger to the public good is more akin to a rough country signpost than to an apothecary scale.

Terms such as the "public good," the "common good," the "welfare of the community," are essentially synonymous. A distinction is recognized, however, between the "public good" and the "public order." Public order is defined as "a pattern of conduct prescribed by law and found to be essential to the security of society in that it is indispensible for the protection of the necessary public good."[165] Public order or the public pattern of conduct prescribed by law varies according to the circumstances of time, place and the needs of a particular community. Authors

[164] Lega (ed. Bart.), *Iudicia Ecclesiastica*, III, 97*; cf. Toso, "De Matrimonio Accusando vel Denuntiando," *Jus Pontificium*, XVII (1937), 12.

[165] Hackett, *The Concept of Public Order*, The Catholic University of America Canon Law Studies, n. 399 (Washington, D. C. : The Catholic University of America Press, 1959), 53; Le Picard, "Bien Public, Bien Privé," *Dictionnaire de Droit Canonique*, II (1937), col. 829.

dispute the nature of the formal element which distinguishes public order from public good.[166] The preferable opinion, which is confirmed in some measure by a comparison of the rules to be observed by the Sacred Roman Rota published in 1910[167] and 1934,[168] is that the laws that secure the public order are legislated as means which are essential to the preservation or the promotion of the public good.[169] The concept of the public good, therefore differs from that of the public order only as the end differs from the means which are necessary to attain it.

The public good of the Church is determined by the end of the Church. The ultimate end of the Church is the eternal salvation of man in heaven. The proximate end of the Church is the sanctification of man on earth.[170] All of the means necessary to achieve the sanctification and eternal salvation of her members have been entrusted to the Church by her Divine Founder, Jesus Christ.[171] Through the power of orders, the Church confects and administers sacraments and sacramentals in order that the members may receive and exercise the theological and moral virtues.[172] Through the power of jurisdiction, the Church as a hierarchic society, governs and directs her members both in the truths they

[166] Cf. Le Picard, "Le Notion d'Ordre Public en Droit Canonique," *Nouvelle Revue Theologique*, LV (1928), 366-376; Van Hove, *Commentarium Lovaniense*, Vol. I, Tom. II, *De Legibus Ecclesiasticis* (Romae: Dessain, 1930), p. 223.

[167] In causis criminalibus et in iis quae natura sua ordinem et bonum publicum respiciunt, tribunal primae instantiae, quoad ordinem stricte iudicialem, nequit repraesentari a procuratore aut advocato proprio, sed ordinem et bonum publicum defendet Promotor iustitiae apud S. Rotae tribunal."—*Regulae servandae in iudiciis apud Sacrae Romanae Rotae Tribunal*, 4 aug. 1910, § 39, 1, *AAS*, II (1910), 198.

[168] "Promotor iustitiae intervenire debet in omnibus causis criminalibus, itemque in contentiosis in quibus bonum publicum in discrimen vocari potest, iis exceptis quae ad vinculi Defensorem spectant."—*Normae Sacrae Romanae Rotae Tribunalis*, 29 iunii 1934, art. 24, § 1, *AAS*, XXVI (1934), 456.

[169] Cf. Hackett, *The Concept of Public Order*, p. 48.

[170] Ottaviani, *Institutiones Iuris Publici Ecclesiastici*, I, nn. 90, 98.

[171] *Loc. cit.*

[172] *Ibid.*, n. 112.

are to believe and the acts they are to perform.[173] Every exercise of the power of jurisdiction or the power of orders contributes directly or indirectly to the common good of the Church, that is, the sanctification and salvation of her members. Therefore, whatever assists in rendering these means more effective promotes the common good of the Church. Conversely, whatever tends to oppose or to weaken or to lessen or to disturb the effectiveness of the Church's power of jurisdiction or power of orders may be said to be harmful to the public good of the Church.[174]

Theological scandal is the principal, but not the only, means through which the public good of the Church is jeopardized. The strict theological definition of scandal is a word or act of commission or omission, evil in itself or having the appearance of evil, that constitutes for others an occasion of sin.[175] For scandal to be present, it is not necessary that the evil act actually lead another person to sin. It is sufficient that the wrong-doing be such as to afford the average man an excuse to commit the same sin.[176] Moralists, as may be expected, consider at length the aspects of scandal relative to the commission of sin on the part of the agent or on the part of him who suffers the scandal.[177]

173 *Loc. cit.;* cf. Canons 1322-1324.

174 Cf. Wolter, "The Promoter of Justice and the Common Good in Matrimonial Causes," *The Jurist,* XI (1951), 214.

175 Cf. St. Thomas Aquinas, *Summa Theologiae,* IIa, IIae, q. 43, a. 1; Aertnys-Damen, *Theologia Moralis* (14. ed., 2 vols., Taurinorum Augustae: Marietti, 1944), I, n. 376; Noldin, *Summa Theologiae Moralis,* 31. ed., II, n. 102.

176 Noldin, *op. cit.,* 31. ed., II, n. 102, d.

177 Moralists distinguish between active scandal and passive scandal. Considered actively, scandal consists in the placing of an act which occasions the spiritual ruin of another. Scandal is called direct when the spiritual ruin of another is intended either from diabolical motives or as a means of gaining some personal advantage. Scandal is called indirect when the spiritual damage done to another is not intended but merely foreseen. Considered passively, scandal is the sin to commit which occasion is given by the evil word or act. If the scandal results from the malice of the person scandalized, it is called pharisaical. If the scandal results from the ignorance of the person scandalized, it is called pusillanimous. Clearly, the moral imputability of a scandalous act will vary accord-

Canonists, on the other hand, understand scandal not so much according to its relation to moral imputability as to the effect which scandal causes on the peace and tranquillity on the juridic social order of the Church.[178] Hence, scandal may be viewed not only in a strictly theological context but also in a broad or juridic sense.

In its juridical sense, the evil act in question does not necessarily provide an occasion or excuse for the commission of the same act by another. Scandal in its juridical sense is present when the evil act (the contracting of an invalid marriage) evokes wonderment or gossip in the community that is tantamount to a lessening of public confidence in ecclesiastical authority.[179] Thus, Article 65, § 1 states that if the consort (who accuses the invalidity of marriage) yields to exhortations to convalidate the marriage by a renewal of consent, the Ordinary shall employ every means to effect the convalidation without any scandal or gossip.[180] Gossip, in this context, is what authors understand as scandal in the wide or juridical sense of the term. The juridic social order of the Church demands that the external actions of the faithful be in accord with the sanctification of each member of the community and thereby promote the spiritual welfare of the community as a whole.[181]

Therefore, if, in the judgment of the Ordinary, the fact of the invalidity of the marriage is such that it provides now or will provide in the future:

a) an occasion or excuse for others in the community to commit the same act and thereby impede the Church's mission of the sanctification of souls (power of orders), or

---

ing to the kind of scandal present. Cf. Noldin, *Summa Theologiae Moralis,* 31. ed., II, n. 103; Zalba, *Theologiae Moralis Summa,* II, n. 492.

[178] Wernz-Vidal, *Ius Canonicum*, VII, n. 29; Michiels, *De Delictis et Poenis*, I, 69; Bartoccetti, "De iure et officio promotoris iustitiae accusandi matrimonium," *Appollinaris,* X (1937), 581.

[179] Cf. Michiels, *De Delictis et Poenis,* I, 69; Noldin, *op. cit.*, n. 102; Vermeersch, *Theologiae Moralis Principia, Responsa, Consilia* (2. ed., 4 vols., Brugis: Beyaert, 1926-1928), II, n. 120; Le Picard, "Bien Public, Bien Privé," *Dictionnaire de Droit Canonique,* II (1937), col. 831.

[180] " . . . remoto omni scandalo aut rumore."

[181] Ottaviani, *Institutiones Iuris Publici Ecclesiastici,* 2. ed., I, 343–344.

b) an occasion or excuse for others in the community to disturb the peace and tranquillity of the community through gossip or rumor, or

c) an occasion or excuse for others in the community to express wonder over the lack of concern of the Church and thereby lessen in the minds of the members of the community the position of the Church as the teacher and protector of faith and morals (power of jurisdiction),

then, and then only, does the promoter of justice have the right, *vi muneris sui,* of placing before the tribunal a public accusation of a marriage denounced by one or both parties who were the culpable cause of the impediment or of the nullity of marriage. It may happen that, in certain communities, the existence of an invalid marriage would not cause concern in the minds of the members of the community. The invalidity of the marriage may be generally looked upon with complete indifference. It is submitted that, this fact, in itself, constitutes a scandalous situation and, therefore, merits the intervention of the promoter of justice.

The problem of the determination of the existence of scandal in a particular case is, indeed, a delicate one. Baroccetti, for example, presents a situation in which Titius and Caius contract marriage on the same day.[182] Both Titius and Caius simulate consent by a positive act of the will. Both marriages result in unhappiness. Titius, on the one hand, divorces his wife and enters a civil union with another woman and thereby gives scandal to the parish. Caius, on the other hand, separates from his consort and lives quietly and innocently alone and gives no scandal to the parish. According to the prescription of Article 38, the promoter of justice, *ceteris paribus,* is not only able but must accuse the invalidity of the marriage of Titius. The promoter cannot, however, accuse the nullity of the marriage of Caius because scandal is not present. Titius is actually in a better condition than Caius precisely because he sinned twice, namely, by deliberately simulating consent with his first consort and by living in concubinage with a second woman. According to Bartoccetti, an accusation by the promoter of justice of the invalidity of the marriage of Titius would constitute an invitation to the faithful not only to deceive the Church in contracting marriage

[182] Lega (ed. Bart.), *Iudicia Ecclesiastica,* III, 98*.

invalidly but also to enter an invalid union with another person, so that they will be in a position to have their first marriage accused by the promoter of justice. In other words, there is a danger that the members of the community will look upon the simulation of the first marriage and a civil attempt at a second marriage as that which truly has its advantages, especially when an official of the Church is ready to assist them in resolving the matter in a manner far more expeditious than if they themselves accused the marriage.[183]

According to Bartoccetti, the greatest cause of scandal in a community is not so much the knowledge of the invalidity of a marriage but rather the knowledge that he who violated the law is benefitting from his crime. Thus, before the promoter of justice may be permitted to accuse a marriage which is invalid especially because of simulation of consent, the Ordinary must choose between the spiritual good of two or four souls and the spiritual welfare of the entire Christian community. The good of the few must cede to the good of the community. The decision to be made is, at times, a most difficult one. It is not always easy to decide whether more good will accrue to the community by declaring a marriage invalid than by refusing to do so. It is the mind of Bartoccetti that the Ordinary should keep in mind that a severe attitude rather than an approach based on indulgence is frequently more conducive to lead culpable spouses to true repentance and the eternal salvation. It is not the lenient but the demanding physician who more often than not restores his sick patients to health.[184]

In the final analysis, nevertheless, even Bartoccetti admits that the circumstances of each case are so diverse that it is almost impossible to state a principle or to present an attitude that will always and everywhere be valid in the determination of whether scandal will be either purged or promoted by a public accusation of the invalidity of the marriage.[185] One thing is clear, however.

[183] *Loc. cit.;* Bartoccetti, "De iure et officio promotoris iustitiae accusandi matrimonium," *Apollinaris,* X (1937), 582.

[184] Bartoccetti, "art. cit.," *ibid.*, p. 585; Conway, "Right to Bring an Action of Nullity of Marriage," *IER,* LXXXIV (1955), 422.

[185] *Ibid.*, p. 584.

The prudent judgment of the Ordinary is paramount in this consideration.

5. Observations Concerning the Interpretation of Articles 38 and 39

It would seem that two extreme attitudes should be avoided concerning the right of the promoter of justice to accuse publicly a marriage that has been denounced by a party or parties incapable of accusing marriage according to Canon 1971, § 1, 1°.

On the one hand, the provision of Canon 1971, § 2, which recognizes the right of spouses, who have culpably caused the invalidity of their marriage, to denounce their marriage, is not to be viewed simply as an all-merciful gesture of the Church in behalf of souls who are presently living in the state of sin. The right granted in Canon 1971, § 2 is not to be considered a juridic device whereby the tribunal may relieve the present burdens, spiritual or otherwise, of any couple who have married invalidly. Otherwise, the vindicative penalty which attaches to Canon 1971, § 1, 1° is completely nugatory. It must be constantly borne in mind that Canon 1971, § 2 and its corresponding explanatory articles in the *Provida* are not to be interpreted in terms of the private good of the culpable spouses but rather in the light of the higher good of the community.[186] In this regard, it is well to recall some of the observations which the Sacred Congregation of the Sacraments directed the Apostolic Delegate to address to the Ordinaries of the United States in the handling of marriage cases.

On September 23, 1938, the following comments were made by the Apostolic Delegate of the United States:

> It is only right that the tribunals examine with benevolent kindness the cases presented by the laity and assist them in their difficulties of married life. But it would be a mistake to consider the ecclesiastical tribunal as a kind of clinic for unhappy marriages where the judges are bound to adjust unfortunate situations at all costs, or at least with exaggerated leniency. Such an erroneous attitude would wound

[186] Cf. Canon 1586. De Guise, *Le Promoteur de La Justice dans Les Causes Matrimoniales* (Universitas Catholica Ottaviensis, Series Canonica, n. 8, Ottawa, Ontario: Les Editions de l'Université d'Ottawa, 1944), p. 178.

> the sacred bond of marriage, and harm the very solidity of the family and society. . . .
>
> As is well known, the Holy See has been constrained to recall to mind, not without good results, first through the Commission for the Interpretation of the Code, and again in the Instruction of August 5, 1936, the inability of consorts to impugn a marriage whose nullity was caused by their own culpability or vitiated consent. To permit such persons to prove their guilt and so be liberated from a burdensome bond, would be to reward the guilty party. Such procedure, by encouraging violations of the law, would be tantamount to its abrogation.
>
> Hence the case in which the Promoter of Justice can impugn the marriage, when the consorts are disqualified, is very rare indeed, not to say exceptional. The reason is that the Promoter of Justice, under the authority and guidance of the Bishop, can act solely to foster the public good. And the public good demands precisely that the culpable parties should not acquire freedom, as if in reward for their fault, but rather, *digna factis recipiant,* that they receive what is due their evil doing, and in this way serve as a warning to the rest of the faithful not to defile the celebration of Christian marriage with the exclusion of the *bona matrimonii* or with the simulations of consent.[187]

On the other hand, the restrictions of Articles 38 and 39 of the *Provida* relative to the right of the promoter of justice to accuse marriages denounced by culpable spouses are not to be considered so severe as to render completely implausible cases visualized under the mentioned Articles. It is true that the denunciation of marriages involving simulated or conditioned consent will call for the intervention of the promoter of justice more rarely than the denunciation of marriages which are invalid because of impediments strictly so-called. But it is also true that the articles of the *Provida* were established to assist ecclesiastical tribunals in the more practical aspects of matrimonial trials. It would seem, therefore, that the Congregation of the Sacraments would not have provided such detailed in-

[187] Excerpted from a letter from the Apostolic Delegation of the United States and published in Bouscaren, *Canon Law Digest,* II, 532-533; cf. Conway, "Right of Instituting Nullity Proceedings," *IER,* LXVII (1946), 53.

structions for cases which were almost impossible to verify. A view adopted by Toso is not entirely out of harmony with the letter of the Apostolic Delegate to the Ordinaries of the United States.

According to Toso, Articles 38 and 39 allow ample latitude for the prudent discretion and wise judgment of the Ordinary.[188] The Ordinary is the final judge of whether or not the impediment is public, or whether the signs of true repentance are present, or whether the public welfare of the community is endangered. In cases of doubt or where the issues are obscure, the interests of the common good should prevail as the guiding norm according to which the Ordinary bases his decision. If it is the judgment of the Ordinary that the public accusation of marriage by the promoter of justice will do nothing more than aggravate and promote scandal or lessen the faith of his people in ecclesiastical discipline, then obviously the accusation by the promoter of justice should never be made.[189] If, on the other hand, the Ordinary determines that good will accrue to the community by a public declaration of the nullity of the marriage, then the accusation of the marriage by the promoter of justice is most certainly warranted, provided that the remaining conditions of Articles 38 or 39 are fulfilled.[190]

D. *Denunciations by Non-Catholics*

It has been determined that those to whom the Code grants the right to denounce the invalidity of a marriage are, on the one hand, persons other than the spouses themselves according to Canon 1971, § 2 [191] and, on the other hand, the spouses who are deprived of the right to accuse their marriage by force of Canon

188 "De Matrimonio Accusando vel Denuntiando," *Jus Pontificium,* XVII (1937), 12; cf. Triebs, "De Promotore Justitiae in Causis Nullitatis Matrimonii," *Apollinaris,* X (1937), 407.

189 Lega (ed. Bart.), *Iudicia Ecclesiastica,* III, 97*-99*; Bartoccetti, "De iure et officio promotoris iustitiae accusandi matrimonium," *Apollinaris,* X (1937), 582.

190 Toso, "art. cit.," *Jus Pontificium,* XVII (1937), 12; cf. Triebs, "art. cit.," *Apollinaris,* X (1937), 407.

191 Cf. Instr. *Provida,* Arts. 35, § 2; 41, § 3.

1971, § 1, 1°.[192] Certainly included in the first group are those persons who were baptized or who were converted to the Catholic Faith. The question to be answered here is whether a non-Catholic,[193] as a third party, may also denounce a marriage so that the promoter of justice may accuse without previous authorization from the Holy Office. It will be noted that the response of the Holy Office of March 22, 1939, which permits the promoter of justice to accuse a marriage without authorization from the Holy Office, provided the Ordinary determines that the public good is at stake, refers to denunciations made by non-Catholic spouses.[194] Canon 1971, § 2 which asserts that "reliqui omnes" have the right to denounce a marriage makes no distinction between Catholics and non-Catholics.[195] Hence, it may be argued, *ex analogia,* from the response of the Holy Office of March 22, 1939, that a non-Catholic as a third party has a right to denounce a marriage.[196] Triebs would forbid an unbaptized person from denouncing a marriage because the unbaptized person is incapable of placing in the Church any act with juridic effect.[197] The position of Triebs is juridically correct but apparently unrealistic. Article 41, § 2 of the Provida allows the Ordinary or the promoter of justice to accept an anonymous denunciation (which contingency could, as easily as not, emanate from an unbaptized person), provided positive and grave proofs of fact are present. The natural law would seem to dictate that the latter norm be adopted by the tribunal in the determination of the admissibility of a denunciation made by an unbaptized person.

The right of the promoter of justice to accuse a marriage denounced by a non-Catholic spouse without previous authoriza-

[192] Cf. Instr. *Provida,* Art. 35, § 1, 1°; Art. 37, § 4; Comm. Pont. 17 Februarii 1930, *AAS,* XXII (1930), 196.

[193] Cf. *supra,* p. 94.

[194] *AAS,* XXXI (1939), 131; Bouscaren, *Canon Law Digest,* II, 547.

[195] Cf. Instr. *Provida,* Art. 41, § 3.

[196] Cf. Triebs, "De Promotore Iustitiae in Causis Nullitatis Matrimonii," *Apollinaris,* X (1937), 398.

[197] Cf. Canon 87.

tion from the Holy Office is conditionally recognized by the response of the Holy Office of March 22, 1939.[198] The condition that must be present is that the nullity of the marriage affects the public good in the judgment of the Ordinary. The significance of this condition becomes more apparent if it is remembered that no denunciation, whether it is made by a Catholic or a non-Catholic, can be acted upon by the institution of the process unless the Ordinary determines that the public good requires it.[199] Moreover, the denunciation by a non-Catholic becomes juridically effective not simply when there is verified the demand of the public good, but also when there is present the additional conditions outlined in Articles 38 and 39 of the *Provida.*[200]

Section IV. The Right of Recourse by the Promoter of Justice against the Judgment of the Ordinary Relative to Articles 38 and 39

Two unlikely but possible situations may arise involving a conflict of minds between the Ordinary and the promoter of justice. It may happen that the conscience of a particular promoter of justice may be disturbed by a decision of the Ordinary that the conditions of Articles 38 and 39 are fulfilled and that a public accusation of the validity of a marriage should be made.[201] Conversely, it may happen that a promoter of justice may be absolutely convinced that the decision of the Ordinary, which forbids a public accusation, is not in accord with the provisions of Articles 38 and 39.[202]

In the first supposition, the most practical solution is the appointment by the Ordinary of a new promoter of justice for

[198] "Utrum Promotor Iustitiae, vi canonis 1971, nulla praehibita facultate a S. Officio, matrimonium accusare possit si nullitas matrimonii fuerit denuntiata a coniuge acatholico." "R. Negative, nisi publicum bonum, Ordinarii iudicio, id postulet."—S.C.S. Officii, 22 Martii, 1939, *AAS,* XXXI (1939), 131; Bouscaren, *Canon Law Digest,* II, 547.

[199] Cf. Canon 1586; Instr. *Provida,* Art. 35, § 1, 2°.

[200] Cf. *supra,* p. 222.

[201] Cf. Instr. *Provida,* Art. 16, § 1.

[202] *Loc. cit.*

this particular case.[203] If this means is impossible, the Ordinary may decree that the promoter of justice accuse the marriage.[204] If the conscience of the promoter of justice will not allow him to abide by the decree of the Ordinary, the promoter of justice has the right of recourse to the competent S. Congregation of the Holy See.[205]

In the second supposition, that is, if the promoter of justice is convinced that an accusation is warranted, but the Ordinary fails to agree and determines that an accusation should not be made, the promoter of justice again has the right of recourse to the competent Sacred Congregation.[206]

In this regard, attention is called to the reply of the Code Commission of July 8, 1940 which stated that the Sacred Congregation of the Sacraments cannot intervene in the steps which precede the accusation of the nullity of a marriage, in a case of the denunciation of the nullity of a marriage mentioned in Canon 1971, § 2, without prejudice to recourse against a judgment of the Ordinary, *re adhuc integra.*[207]

The reply of the Code Commission of July 8, 1940 establishes three pertinent facts. First, the law recognizes the right of recourse by the promoter of justice against the judgment of the Ordinary in the steps which precede the accusation by the promoter of justice. Second, recourse is made in this case to the Sacred Congregation for the Discipline of the Sacraments or to the Congregation that is competent to handle the question.[208] Third, no recourse is to be made to the Sacred Congregation of

[203] Canons 1586, 1589, § 1; Instr. *Provida,* Art. 19, § 1; Cappello, *De Matrimonio,* 5. ed., p. 887.

[204] Cf. S.R.R. *Decisiones,* XXIX (1937), 721, n. 8.

[205] Cf. Canon 1601; Instr. *Provida,* Art. 2, § 4; Canons 249, § 2; 247, § 3; 252, § 4; 257; *supra,* p. 189, note 371; " . . . contra vero decretum Ordinarii recursus via patebit ad ipsam S. Congregationem."—S.R.R. *Decisiones,* XXXIII (1941), 464, n. 3.

[206] *Loc. cit.*

[207] "An et quomodo eadem Sacra Congregatio in casu denuntiationis nullitatis matrimonii, de qua in canone 1971, § 2, sese ingerere possit in iis quae praecedunt accusationem nullitatis matrimonii? R. Negative, salvo, re adhuc integra, recursu adversus Ordinarii iudicium."—*AAS,* XXXII (1940), 317-318; cf. Bouscaren, *Canon Law Digest,* II, 106-107.

[208] Cf. *supra,* note 205.

the Sacraments or to any other Sacred Congregation, except the Congregation of the Holy Office,[209] against a decree of the Ordinary, once the promoter of justice has accused the marriage, and the defendant has been legitimately cited or has spontaneously appeared in court according to Canon 1725, 1°.[210] The manner in which the promoter of justice may proceed in this latter case is treated in the following section.

Section V. The Right of the Promoter of Justice to Withdraw from an Accusation

The promoter of justice has the right to withdraw from an accusation that he has placed before the tribunal if he discovers that the accusation cannot be sustained either in law or in fact.[211] In practise, the withdrawal of the promoter of justice from an accusation should occur rarely, inasmuch as it is presumed that the accusation was made only after it was determined that

[209] Cf. Canon 1555, § 1.

[210] "Cum citatio legitime peracta fuerit aut partes sponte in iudicium venerint: Res desinit esse integra." Cf. Instr. *Provida,* Art. 75. Doheny visualizes the case in which the promoter of justice, without consulting the Ordinary, refuses to accept a denunciation which fulfills the conditions of Article 38 and 39 of the *Provida.* Doheny advises that, in this instance, the norms of Article 67 of the *Provida* should be followed. According to the employment of Article 67, after the expiration of a month, the denouncer could again request the intervention of the promoter of justice. If no action was taken within five days, a recourse could then be made by the denouncer to the local Ordinary or to a tribunal of second instance. Doheny holds that if these means fail, the denouncer could lodge his case with the Sacred Congregation of the Sacraments, the Rota, or the Apostolic Signatura. Moreover, if the refusal of the promoter of justice was "unjustifiable and culpable" and if it caused harm to the parties, Doheny would extend Canon 1625, § 1 to permit that the promoter of justice be punished by the Bishop. Canon 1625, § 1 states that judges whose competency is certain and evident or who do an injustice or otherwise cause damage to the contending parties, are liable for damages and can be punished by the local Ordinary. *Ex similibus,* Canon 1625, § 3 lends support to the opinion of Doheny. In any case, Canon 1590, § 2 allows the bishop to remove the promoter of justice for a just cause. Cf. *Canonical Procedure,* I, 150-151.

[211] Promotoris iustitiae est ab accusatione recedere si postea sibi constiterit, factam accusationem sustineri non posse vel in iure vel in facto. —Instr. *Provida,* Art. 41, § 4; cf. Canon 1740, § 1; S.R.R. *Decisiones,* XXVIII (1936), 77, n. 9.

the arguments favoring the nullity of marriage were certain and valid.[212] In general, the reasons that will prompt the promoter of justice to withdraw from an accusation will be based on insufficient or uncertain evidence or the fact that the public good is not involved.

If the reason for the withdrawal is based on insufficient or uncertain evidence, Cappello holds that Canon 1740, § 2 applies.[213] Thus, the promoter of justice must make a written and signed attestation of the renunciation of the cause. Cappello feels that "omnibus perpensis," the tribunal cannot interfere with the decision of the promoter of justice to withdraw from the cause because the evidence is considered by the promoter of justice to be uncertain or invalid.[214] In this regard, both Torre [215] and Bartoccetti [216] suggest that the decision of the promoter of justice to withdraw from an accusation because of the lack of evidence is not to be made by him alone, but is subject to the scrutiny and approval of the judges of the tribunal. They hold that it is the office of the judge, not of the promoter of justice, to weigh and evaluate evidence. In a dispute between the denouncers and the promoter of justice as to the sufficiency of evidence, it would seem that the same judges who accepted the *libellus* should pass judgment on the value of the evidence presented in the later stage of the trial. If the evidence is not sufficient, the judge will most certainly agree with the promoter of justice to withdraw from the case.[217] Roberti asserts that according to Canon 1740, § 2, a renunciation of the cause by the promoter of justice must be made known to the parties and to the judge.[218] According to Roberti, though the parties are not able to oppose the renunciation, they can denounce to the Ordinary any arbitrary withdrawal by the promoter of justice from

212 Cf. Instr. *Provida*, Art. 38, § 2; 39; Bartoccetti, "De iure et officio promotoris iustitiae accusandi matrimonium," *Apollinaris*, X (1937), 571.

213 *De Matrimonio*, 5. ed., p. 887.

214 *Loc. cit.*

215 *Processus Matrimonialis*, 3. ed., pp. 125-126.

216 Lega (ed. Bart.), *Iudicia Ecclesiastica*, III, 106 *-107 *.

217 Torre, *loc. cit.*; Lega (ed. Bart.), *loc. cit.*

218 "De recessu ab accusatione matrimonii per promotorem iustitiae," *Apollinaris*, XII (1939), 528.

his accusation.[219] Moreover, Roberti holds that the judge may admit or reject the renunciation, and that his decision is binding on the promoter of justice.[220] If the tribunal decides to reject the renunciation of the cause by the promoter of justice, the promoter of justice may appeal the decision to a superior court,[221] and, if necessary, to the Sacred Roman Rota.[222]

To be asked here is whether the promoter of justice enjoys a right of recourse to the Sacred Congregation for the Discipline of the Sacraments, if he feels aggrieved by the decision of the Ordinary to withdraw from an accusation before or after the litigation is pending.[223] According to the reply of the Code Commission of July 8, 1940, which stated that recourse to the Sacred Congregation of the Sacraments against the judgment of the Ordinary is permitted, provided the case is still *res integra,*[224] a distinction must be made.

If the accusation has been made by the promoter of justice, but the parties have not yet been cited,[225] the promoter of justice has the right of recourse to the competent Sacred Congregation against the decree of the Ordinary to withdraw from the accusation.[226] But if the accusation has been made and the parties have been summoned, so that the case ceases to be *res integra* according to Canon 1725, 1°, the Sacred Congregation of the Sacraments can no longer intervene in the case, and hence any recourse to this Sacred Congregation by the promoter of justice against the decree of the Ordinary would be completely useless.[227]

If the withdrawal of the promoter of justice from an accusa-

219 "De condicione processuali . . . ," *Apollinaris,* XI (1938), 579.

220 *Loc. cit.*

221 Cf. Canon 1879, 1709, § 3.

222 Cf. Canon 1598.

223 Cf. Canon 1598.

224 *AAS,* XXXII (1940), 317-318; cf. Bouscaren, *Canon Law Digest,* II, 106-107.

225 Cf. Canon 1725, 1°.

226 Cf. Canons 249, § 3; 247, § 3; 257, § 1; 252, § 1.

227 Cf. Bidagor, "Ad responsa de competentia annotationes," *Periodica,* XXX (1941), 58.

tion is motivated not by the lack of evidence, but rather because of the fact that the public good does not demand it, it would seem that Canon 1586 and Articles 38, § 2 and 39 of the *Provida* apply. The exercise of the right of the promoter of justice to desist from accusing a marriage, because the common good does not require it, is subject always to the judgment of the Ordinary. On November 27, 1937, the Rota asserted that in a case in which a marriage has been legitimately accused by the promoter of justice, the Ordinary does not forfeit his office of caring for the public good, and neither does he lose the power of deciding whether the promoter of justice must recede or pursue the accusation, without prejudice to recourse against the decree of the Ordinary to the competent Sacred Congregation.[228] In this regard, attention is called to the private response of the Code Commission of July 24, 1939 which was approved and confirmed by Pope Pius XII on July 27, 1939.[229] In this response, the Code Commission declared that after a marriage has been accused by the promoter of justice, and an action has thereupon been instituted, the Sacred Congregation of the Sacraments does not have the right to intervene on the ground that there is no reason to urge the removal of scandal which is the only reason for which the promoter of justice can introduce a case *ex officio*.[230]

Two observations may be made concerning this reply of the Code Commission. First, contrary to the assertion made by the

[228] "Vero si de ratione, qua promotor justitiae cessat ab accusando, nascitur quaestio, an id expediat bono publico, huius quaestionis solutio pertinet ad Ordinarium, qui matrimonio legitime accusato a promotore iustitiae, non amittit officium suum invigilandi in bonum publicum, ideo nec amittit potestatem decernendi, utrum promotor justitiae, recedere ab accusatione an eam prosequi debeat, salvo recursu adversus decretum Ordinarii ad SC competentem."—S.R.R. *Decisiones*, XXIX (1937), 721, n. 8.

[229] Cf. Bouscaren, *Canon Law Digest*, II, 547.

[230] An, accusata per Promotorem iustitiae matrimonii nullitate et inde instructo iudicio, S. Congregationi de Sacramentis competat ius interveniendi, eo quod non constet urgere remotionem scandali, ob quam solummodo Promotor iustitiae causam ex officio introducere potest. Resp. Negative." Cf. Toso, "De Potestate S.C. De Sacramentis Quod Attinet Ad Matrimonia Per Promotorem Justitiae Accusanda," *Jus Pontificium*, XIX (1939), 120.

Rota in its decision of November 27, 1937, no allowance is made by this response for recourse by the promoter of justice to the Sacred Congregation of the Sacraments against the decree of the Ordinary to withdraw from an accusation on the ground that there is no reason to urge the removal of scandal, provided that the promoter of justice has already accused the marriage and an action has been thereupon instituted. Second, the response seems to infer, in the mind of the writer, that once the Ordinary has decided that the invalidity of a marriage causes the public good to be in jeopardy, and the promoter of justice has thereupon instituted an action against the invalidity of a marriage, any contrary determination on the part of the Ordinary in respect to the necessity of the accusation to preserve the common good is subject to the adjudication and decision of the diocesan tribunal. Relative to this opinion, let it first be observed that the writer is well aware that the promotion of the public good or the removal of a public evil in a diocese pertains to the ordinary power of the bishop by divine institution.[231] According to Canon 1618, however, the judge, *ex officio,* also possesses rights and duties relative to the public good and the salvation of souls.[232] Moreover, according to Canon 1601, the Congregation of the Sacraments is most certainly competent to entertain recourses against the administrative decrees of the Ordinary. Thus, as long as a case is still *res integra,* recourse is permitted to the Sacred Congregation of the Sacraments against the judgment of the Ordinary in matters which precede the accusation of marriage by the promoter of justice.[233] Yet, the Code Commission has declared that the Congregation of the Sacraments does not have the right to intervene on the ground that there is no reason to urge the removal of scandal once the marriage has been accused by the promoter of justice and the action has thereupon been instituted. In the mind of the writer, there are two sufficient juridic reasons for forbidding the promoter of justice recourse to

231 Cf. Canons 329, § 1; 336, § 2.

232 ". . . iudex procedere potest . . . in iis quae publicum Ecclesiae bonum aut animarum salutem respiciunt, etiam ex officio."

233 *AAS,* XXXII (1940), 317-318; Bouscaren, *Canon Law Digest,* II, 106-107.

the Sacred Congregation of the Sacraments in a case in which a trial has already been instituted. The first is that as an administrative body, the Sacred Congregation of the Sacraments can claim no faculty to intervene in particular matrimonial causes judicially instituted.[234] Thus, Canon 1569, § 2 states that (even) recourse to the Holy See does not suspend, except in a case of appeal, the exercise of jurisdiction by the judge who has already begun the trial of the case. He may continue the case and pronounce final sentence until it is known that the Holy See has reserved the case to itself. Secondly, the renunciation of a cause begun by the promoter of justice (which is prompted in this case by a reversal of an administrative decision of the Ordinary in respect to the necessity of an accusation in behalf of the common good) is subject to the admission or rejection by the tribunal according to Canon 1740, § 2. Clearly, it is to be expected that in the normal course of affairs the decision of the tribunal to admit the renunciation of the promoter of justice will be in accord with the judgment of the Ordinary that the public welfare no longer requires a public accusation. But if, in a most exceptional case, the tribunal rejects the petition of the promoter of justice to renounce the cause, the promoter of justice may have recourse to a superior court.[235] The decision of the superior court, in turn, is definitive according to Canons 1709, § 3 and 1880, 7°.[236] If, on the other hand, the petition of the promoter of justice is accepted by the court of first instance, the ruling of this court is final and no further judicial appeal is permitted according to Article 190, § 1 of the *Provida.*[237]

Section VI. The Recourse Available to Spouses against the Abandonment of an Accusation by the Promoter of Justice

In cases in which the accusation has been abandoned by the promoter of justice in first instance, the remedies available to the spouses seem to be governed by the provisions of the re-

[234] Cf. Toso, "art. cit.," *Jus Pontificium,* XIX (1939), 120-121.

[235] Cf. Canons 1709, § 3; 1838; Instr. *Provida,* Art. 66, § 1.

[236] Cf. Instr. *Provida,* Art. 66, § 1.

[237] Cf. Canon 1840, § 1.

sponses of the Code Commission of July 24, 1939 and July 8, 1940 which have been considered in the preceding section.

Thus, if the case is still *res integra,* that is, if the parties have not yet been cited according to Canon 1725, 1°, they have the right of recourse against the judgment of the Ordinary to the Sacred Congregation of the Sacraments or to the Sacred Congregation that is competent in this particular case.[238] If, however, the parties have already been cited, and upon the instance of the promoter of justice the Ordinary determines that the case should be abandoned, either because of insufficient evidence or because the public good does not demand an accusation, the Congregation of the Sacraments is not competent to intervene in behalf of the culpable spouses. On the other hand, the decision of the Ordinary to abandon the cause is not, in itself, sufficient to effect a valid renunciation of the cause by the promoter of justice. According to Canon 1740, § 2, the renunciation of the cause[239] must be admitted by the judge.[240] As indicated in the previous section, if the judge refuses to accept the petition of the promoter of justice to renounce the cause, the latter may have recourse to a superior court.[241] The appellate court will either sustain the decision of the inferior court or reject it. If the appellate court upholds the decision of the inferior court, the judicial procedure is terminated.[242] The parties have no further ordinary procedural recourse. They cannot appeal the decision of the superior court because the law does not permit such.[243] But it would seem that since the judicial process is terminated, the restriction contained in the response of the Code Commission of July 24, 1939 no longer applies.[244] Therefore, it would appear that the means of redress available to the parties in these circumstances would be recourse to the competent Sacred Congregation

[238] Cf. Canons 249, § 3; 247, § 3; 257, § 1; 252, § 1.

[239] Cf. Canons 1709; 1838-1840.

[240] Cf. Canon 1732.

[241] Cf. Canons 1709, § 3; 1838; Instr. *Provida,* Art. 66, § 1.

[242] Cf. Canons 1732; 1740, § 2; 1709, § 3; 1880, 7°.

[243] Cf. Canons 1709, § 3; 1880, 7°.

[244] Cf. *supra,* p. 246.

of the Holy See,[245] not excluding the Supreme Sacred Congregation of the Holy Office. The latter remedy would be juridically available because of two considerations. First, the matter at hand ultimately concerns the practise of faith and morals of the culpable spouses.[246] Second, the Congregation of the Holy Office proceeds according to its own rules and customs.[247]

On the other hand, if the superior court determines that the petition of the promoter of justice should be accepted, the case must be remanded to the collegiate tribunal of the court of first instance which must rule on the substantive character of the petition. If the court of first instance decides in favor of the renunciation of the cause by the promoter of justice, the judicial procedure is terminated according to Article 190, § 1 of the *Provida*. The parties in this case would have no further judicial remedy. It would seem that the parties could, nevertheless, have recourse to the competent Congregation of the Holy See since the restriction contained in the response of the Code Commission of July 24, 1939 does not appear to be applicable except in cases in which the action is actually in the process of being adjudicated.[248]

Section VII. The Right of the Promoter of Justice to Refuse to Appeal an Unfavorable Sentence

In Article 1 of Section V of the preceding Chapter, it was determined that in a case in which the promoter of justice accuses a marriage previously denounced by a spouse who has been deprived of the right to accuse a marriage, the latter does not have the right to appeal a sentence which upholds the validity of the matrimonial bond. The only remedy permitted to the spouse in this case is extrajudicial recourse.[249] The extrajudicial means available to the spouses who are penalized under Canon 1971, § 1, 1° take the form either of a papal dispensation from the penalty or of the institution of an appeal by the promoter of jus-

[245] Cf. Canons 7; 1569, § 1.

[246] Cf. Canon 247, § 1.

[247] Cf. Canons 1555, § 1; 243, § 1.

[248] Cf. *supra*, p. 248.

[249] Comm. Pont., May 3, 1945, *AAS*, XXXVII (1945), 149; *supra*, p. 188.

tice who introduced the action into the court of first instance.[250] The right of the promoter of justice to appeal a decision of the court which upholds the validity of a marriage is founded in Canon 1897, which states that a party who feels aggrieved over a sentence, and also the promoter of justice or the defender of the bond in a trial in which either took part, have a right to appeal from a sentence unless it is a case in which the law does not admit an appeal.[251]

The question to be considered here is whether the promoter of justice has the right to refuse to appeal a sentence upholding the validity of a marriage which he himself has accused subsequent to a previous denunciation by a spouse who was the culpable cause of the impediment or of the nullity of the marriage. This question has been answered by the Rota on several occasions and in the same manner. For example, on November 27, 1937 the Rota (*coram* Jullien) observed that in matrimonial causes there is no law by which the promoter of justice is always held to pursue a cause to the ultimate instance possible; he is even less obliged to appeal a sentence which is contrary to himself, notwithstanding the fact that he introduced the case at the judgment of the Ordinary.[252] The Rota continued that it is not unusual that the spouses themselves abandon a cause following an initial sentence declaring the invalidity of a marriage and a second sentence upholding the validity of the same marriage, because they recognize that the evidence for the nullity of the marriage is insufficient. Similarly, a promoter of justice is able to withdraw from appealing or prosecuting a cause, because of his moral certainty, based on reasons revealed in the sentence, or because of new circumstances, that the public good no longer demands that the cause be prosecuted further.[253] If, on the other

[250] *Supra*, p. 188.

[251] Cf. Instr. *Provida*, Art. 212, § 1.

[252] "Siquidem de causis matrimonialibus nulla lata est lex, qua promotor iustitiae semper teneatur ad causam prosequendam usque ad ultimam possibilem instantiam, sin minus ad appellandum a quavis sententia sibi contraria, etiam si causam judicio Ordinarii introduxerit . . ."—*Decisiones*, XXIX (1937), 721, n. 9.

[253] Similiter promotor iustitiae potest recedere a causa appellanda vel

hand, the public good is in question, the promoter of justice, by reason of his office, has the duty to appeal the sentence favoring the validity of the matrimonial bond against which he has brought the accusation.[254]

SCHOLION 1. THE JURIDIC CONSEQUENCES OF AN ACCUSATION BY THE PROMOTER OF JUSTICE "DEFICIENTIBUS CONDITIONIBUS"

What is to be said of the juridic consequences of an accusation by the promoter of justice who fails to observe the conditions outlined in Articles 38 and 39 of the *Provida?* On the one hand, it may be answered that the conditions concerning the repentance of the consort, the publicity of the nullity of the marriage, the valid and certain evidence of the invalidity of the marriage, and the exhortation of the consorts to convalidate the marriage are not required for the validity of an accusation by the promoter of justice because the law neither expressly nor equivalently demands that these conditions be verified before a valid accusation can be made.[255] On the other hand, the right of the promoter of justice to accuse a marriage is recognized by law only insofar as the public good is endangered. It would seem, however, that if the tribunal, because of an oversight, erroneously accepted a *libellus* of a promoter of justice who was incapable of accusing marriage because the public good was not in question, the sentence would not labor under irremediable nullity according to Canon 1892, 2°. The reason for this opinion is based, *ex analogia*, on the response of the Code Commission of

---

prosequenda, quia moraliter certus est propter motiva in sententia exposita aut propter adjuncta nova non amplius expedire bono publico, ut causam prosequatur."—*Loc. cit.;* cf. *Decisiones,* XLI (1949), 465, n. 11. See also the reply of the Sacred Congregation for the Discipline of the Sacraments to the Cardinal Archbishop of Milan on January 18, 1938 in Bouscaren, *Canon Law Digest,* II, 546, n. 7; Triebs, "De Promotore Iustitiae in Causis Nullitatis Matrimonii," *Apollinaris,* X (1937), 406.

[254] Cf. Regatillo, *Interpretatio et Iurisprudentia CIC,* p. 539; Cappello, *De Matrimonio,* 5. ed., p. 887.

[255] Cf. Canon 11.

January 4, 1946.[256] This response stated that the incapacity of the spouses to accuse a marriage according to Canon 1971, § 1, 1° does not imply the incapacity to stand in judgment so that the sentence labors under irremediable nullity according to Canon 1892, 2°. This conclusion is, at least, in partial conformity with the opinion of Doheny who asserts that if the promoter of justice accused the validity of a marriage that falls under the category of Article 39 (no reference is made to Article 38), without observing all the norms stipulated for such causes, he would be acting validly but illicitly.[257]

Against this opinion it may be held that no foundation exists on which to base an analogy between accusations made by culpable spouses and accusations made by the promoter of justice. In the first case, the spouses exercise a right which they are forbidden to exercise by force of Canon 1971, § 1, 1°. In the second case, the promoter of justice exercises no right because he has no right to begin with. The latter case may be better understood if it is remembered that if the condition of the public good is not verified in a particular case, the right of the promoter of justice to accuse a marriage it totally devoid of juridic foundation since he can claim no rights other than those which are within the scope of his office. Since the promoter of justice has no right, *vi muneris sui,* to exercise a public action against the validity of a matrimonial bond under such circumstances, it would seem that a sentence consequent to the exercise of an action by a promoter of justice who introduced a cause which has no relation to the public good, labors under irremediable nullity according to Canon 1892, 2°. Moreover, since the demands of the public good pertain to the substance of the execution of the rights of the promoter of justice, a public action exercised by the promoter of justice in a cause in which the public good is not in jeopardy is null and void according to Canon 1680, § 1. It would appear that the sentence would also be invalid according to Canon 1892, 2°.[258]

[256] *AAS,* XXXVIII (1946), 162.

[257] *Canonical Procedure,* 2. ed., I, 144; cf. De Guise, *Le Promoteur de la Justice dans les Causes Matrimoniales,* p. 209.

[258] Cf. Canon 1680, § 2.

SCHOLION 2. THE RIGHT OF THE ORDINARY TO ACCUSE A MARRIAGE PREVIOUSLY DENOUNCED

According to Canon 1572, the local Ordinary is the judge of first instance in every diocese and for all causes that are not expressly excepted by law.[259] The local Ordinary can exercise this judicial power in person or through others according to the prescriptions of the Code.[260] The bishop may always preside in person over the tribunal except in those cases which are reserved to the Holy See,[261] or which relate to the rights or temporal goods of the bishop, or of the *mensa episcopalis* or of the diocesan Curia.[262] Canon 1578 must be viewed in the light of Article 14, § 3 of the *Provida,* which states that although the bishop may preside over his tribunal in marriage trials it is highly expedient that he refrain from doing so, unless special reasons demand otherwise.

It is also the mind of the legislator that the Ordinary should never accuse a marriage.[263] This holds true even though a denunciation of the nullity of the marriage has been made to him according to Canon 1971, § 2.[264] In these cases, the Ordinary is directed to refer the denunciation to the promoter of justice who, in turn, is to proceed according to the prescriptions of Articles 38 and 39 of the *Provida.*[265] This determination of law undoubtedly has many practical advantages. The juridic reason for cautioning the Ordinary against accusing a marriage seems to be found in Article 14, § 3 of the *Provida.* Thus, according to Article 14, § 3, the bishop is warned not to preside over a matrimonial court. But there could be visualized a case in which his presidency is demanded.[266] In this event, if the bishop was al-

[259] Cf. Canons 1557, 1572, § 2.

[260] Canon 1578.

[261] Canon 1557.

[262] Canon 1572, § 2.

[263] Instr. *Provida,* Art. 40.

[264] Cf. Canon 1578; Instr. *Provida,* Art. 14, § 3; 35, § 2; 40.

[265] Instr. *Provida,* Art. 40.

[266] De Guise, *op. cit.,* pp. 200-201.

ready the accuser in the case, there would exist the juridically impossible situation of the accuser acting in the capacity of judge. Needless to say, such a circumstance the law will not tolerate.[267] Doheny [268] observes that if the bishop ignored the prescription of Article 40 of the *Provida* and proceeded personally to accuse a marriage previously denounced to himself, he would act validly [269] but reprehensibly. Moreover, it would be within the office of the promoter of justice to indicate to the bishop the ruling of the law in this matter according to Article 16, § 1 of the *Provida*.

SCHOLION 3. THE JURIDIC STATUS OF THE PROMOTER OF JUSTICE, THE SPOUSES INCAPABLE OF ACCUSING MARRIAGE, AND THE DEFENDER OF THE BOND

To be considered here is the question which concerns the juridic relations that exist among the promoter of justice, the spouses who are incapable of accusing marriage, and the defender of the bond when the invalidity of marriage has been publicly accused by the promoter of justice.

It may be safely stated that all authors are agreed that the promoter of justice is, at least, the principal *actor* in matrimonial causes which he introduces by virtue of his office to protect the common good.[270] Thus, the *Provida* directs that when the promoter of justice accuses a marriage he is to propose to the defender of the bond questions to be asked of the parties, witnesses and experts.[271] Moreover, the promoter of justice may call wit-

[267] Cf. Torre, *Processus Matrimonialis,* 3. ed., p. 124; De Guise, *op. cit.*, pp. 199-200.

[268] *Canonical Procedure,* 2. ed., I, 144-145.

[269] Cf. Canon 11.

[270] Cf. Roberti, "De condicione processuali . . . ," *Apollinaris,* XI (1938), 578, 581; Cappello, *De Matrimonio,* 5. ed., p. 887; Toso, "De Munere Promotoris Justitiae Matrimonium Accusantis," *Jus Pontificium,* XVIII (1938), 4; Torre, *Processus Matrimonialis,* 3. ed., p. 77; Triebs, "De Promotoris Justitiae in Causis Nullitatis Matrimonii," *Apollinaris,* X (1937), 406.

[271] Instr. *Provida,* Art. 71, § 2.

nesses,[272] propose incidental questions,[273] present his defense,[274] and appeal from the sentence of the tribunal.[275]

As regards the juridic figure of the spouses, there are three basically different opinions held by authors. The first opinion is that of Triebs who holds that when a promoter of justice accuses a marriage following the denunciation of the invalidity of the marriage by the culpable spouses, there is no doubt that the party who has an interest in the declaration of the nullity of the marriage may participate in the judicial process.[276] Triebs notes that Article 46 of the Instruction *Provida* itself permits the spouse incapable of accusing marriage to appoint an advocate. Triebs asserts that the same spouse is able to place other procedural acts which the parties themselves are capable of placing, for example, the presentation of evidence to prove the nullity of the marriage.[277]

The second opinion is that of Roberti who holds that in cases in which the promoter of justice accuses the validity of marriage denounced by spouses who have been deprived of the right to accuse their marriage, the spouses themselves are necessary third parties to the cause called *ex officio*.[278] According to Roberti, the spouses cannot be considered as remaining *extra processum* in a cause in which the validity of their own marriage is being adjudicated, and in which a substantial relation exists between themselves and the tribunal of judges by whose decision the

[272] Instr. *Provida*, Art. 123, § 1; cf. Canon 1759.

[273] Instr. *Provida*, Art. 187; Canon 1837.

[274] Instr. *Provida*, Art. 179, § 1; cf. Canon 1862.

[275] Instr. *Provida*, Art. 212, § 1; cf. Canons 1879, 1986.

[276] "De Promotoris Justitiae in Causis Nullitatis Matrimonii," *Apollinaris*, X (1937), 406.

[277] "Ex quo eruitur, eundem coniugem posse etiam alios processus actus, qui partibus congruunt, ponere ut est comparatio argumentorum . . ."—*Loc. cit.*

[278] Can. 1853.—Si tertii interventus appareat necessarius, iudex ad instantiam partis vel etiam ex officio debet interventum in causa iubere. Cf. Roberti, "De condicione processuali . . . ," *Apollinaris*, XI (1938), 581; De Guise, *Le Promoteur de La Justice dans Les Causis Matrimoniales*, pp. 205-206; Graziani, "De Iure Accusandi Matrimonium," *Ephemerides Iuris Canonici*, II (1946), 129; Haring, "De Promotore Justitiae in Processu Matrimoniali Controversiae," *Jus Pontificium*, XX (1940), 147.

spouses are bound. The spouses, therefore, whose marriage is publicly accused by the promoter of justice, should be afforded the possibility of defending themselves. And since, in cases instituted by the promoter of justice, the defender of the bond is to be considered as the *reus conventus*, an accusation brought formally against the defender of the bond extends also to the spouses as accessory respondents (*rei conventi necessarii una cum vinculi defensore*). Moreover, the spouses are also able to assist the promoter of justice, for example, in the adducing of evidence, and they are to be considered third parties called *ex officio* according to Canon 1853.[279]

Roberti calls attention to the fact that in cases in which the promoter of justice accuses marriage, the spouses are referred to not as mere witnesses but as parties,[280] that is, parties who, though they are deprived of *legitimatio activa*, or the right to exercise an action as plaintiff, enjoy nevertheless *legitimatio passiva*, or the right to respond after having been legitimately cited. The latter suffices for the spouses to act as necessary third party respondents called *ex officio*. Wherefore, Roberti concludes that the following dispositions of the Instruction *Provida* are to be understood as pertaining to the spouses. The spouses are subject to interrogation by the tribunal.[281] They are to submit to the examination of experts.[282] They have the right of presenting witnesses.[283] They have the right to reply to the animadversions of the defender of the bond within a period of ten days.[284] And, finally, they have a right to appoint their own advocate.[285]

The third opinion, held principally by Cappello, is that the

[279] Roberti, "De condicione processuali . . . ," *Apollinaris*, XI (1938), 581-582.

[280] Quando promotor iustitiae matrimonium accusat, ipse quoque proponere debet vinculi defensori articulos pro interrogatoriis deferendis partibus, testibus, ac peritis.—Instr. *Provida,* Art. 71, § 2; Roberti also cites Articles 179, § 1 and 227, § 1; *loc. cit.*

[281] Cf. Canon 1742, Instr. *Provida,* Art. 110-117.

[282] Cf. Canons 1976, 1983; Instr. *Provida,* Art. 150-151.

[283] Canon 1759, §§ 1, 2; Instr. *Provida,* Art. 123, § 1.

[284] Canon 1862, § 1; Instr. *Provida,* Art. 180, § 2.

[285] Instr. *Provida,* Art. 46; cf. Roberti, "De condicione processuali . . . ," *Apollinaris,* XI (1938), 582.

spouses who are deprived of the right to accuse marriage are unable to act as *verae partes in causa* whether through themselves or through another. They are deprived of all the rights that accrue to parties to a cause and therefore cannot, for example, propose an exception of incompetence of a tribunal, or of suspicion against the judge or ministers of the tribunal, or appeal a sentence. Cappello appears to challenge the juridic value of the provision of Article 46 of the *Provida* which explicitly grants to the spouses the right to appoint an advocate. Cappello states that granting the hypothesis that the spouses are not true parties to the trial, it is patently obvious that they cannot select either an advocate or a procurator.[286] Cappello reasons that the faculty of appointing an advocate or procurator belongs to the parties only, that is, either to the plaintiff or to the respondent.[287] He notes that this provision of law is clearly contained in the common law of the Code and the prescriptions of the Instruction *Provida*.[288] Cappello then adds: *"Non obstat art. 46, qui facultatem tribuit advocatum constituendi."* According to Cappello, then, the spouses in the case under consideration are called to trial and interrogated but only in order that the truth of the matter may be determined. The only role played by the spouses is that of providing the promoter of justice with assistance in proving the nullity of the marriage in the same manner in which a denouncer proceeds in a criminal case.

In rebuttal of the opinion of those who hold that the spouses are to be considered as third parties called *ex officio,* Cappello makes the following observations. When a person enters a cause by means of accessory intervention, he is not constituted a true party, that is, he does not act in his own right but by virtue of the right of another inasmuch as he joins himself to the plaintiff or to the defendant and assists one or the other in the action or in the defense. The spouse who is deprived of the right to accuse marriage cannot be considered as joining himself to the promoter of justice or to the defender of the bond either by way of volun-

[286] ". . . liquido patet eosdem summo iure sibi eligere non posse procuratorem et advocatum . . ."—*De Matrimonio,* 5. ed., p. 889.

[287] *Loc. cit.*

[288] Cf. Canons 1655-1666; Instr. *Provida,* Art. 43-54.

tary accessory intervention or necessary accessory intervention. This is true first because in this case the spouse acts in the cause in his own behalf and not in behalf of the principal to which he is attached; and secondly because, by virtue of Canon 1852, § 2, the spouse under consideration may be admitted to enter the cause only insofar as he indicates that he has the right to intervene, which right is completely excluded by Canon 1971, § 1, 1° itself.[289]

Relative to the solution of this question are observations made by the Sacred Roman Rota. On January 30, 1936, the Rota (*coram* Wynen) [290] considered the question whether the promoter of justice, after he has accused a marriage of invalidity, is bound to all the prescriptions of law which oblige him in his capacity of promoter of justice and which, if neglected, cause the procedural acts and the sentence to be invalid.[291] In answer to this question the Rota distinguished between causes in which the promoter of justice, *reduplicative* or *qua talis*, has intervened in the trial, and causes in which the promoter of justice *vestem actoris induens matrimonium accusavit.* In the latter the case, after the accusation has been made and the cause has been thereby legitimately introduced, the promoter of justice has performed his duty and all other procedural acts are to be carried out as in other causes.[292] The Rota adds, however, that the promoter of justice is not denied the right of withdrawing from his accusation during the construction of the case and thus making an end to a cause which he knows to be futile. But the obligation to intervene in every act under the penalty of nullity is not to be imposed upon him.[293]

To support its position the Rota presented three arguments. First, the incapacity to accuse a marriage incurred by the parties

[289] *De Matrimonio,* 5. ed., p. 888.

[290] *Decisiones,* XXVIII (1936), 77, n. 9.

[291] Cf. Canon 1587.

[292] "Facta autem accusatione matrimonii et sic causa legitime introducta, Promotor iustitiae munere suo functus est, atque alii actus processuales sicuti in ceteris causis absolvendi sunt."—*Decisiones,* XXVIII (1936), 77, n. 9.

[293] *Loc. cit.*

in punishment of their crime is restricted to the act of accusation itself and is not to be extended to include the other acts of the process.[294] Hence, the parties, though incapable of accusing marriage, are not to be deprived the right of appointing an advocate who may propose witnesses to be questioned, inspect the acts, and present a defense, etc.[295] Second, if the promoter of justice acts in the course of the process as the *actor*, then the culpable spouse, whom the promoter of justice represents, reaps a great advantage thereby and is constituted in a privileged position.[296] The culpable spouse in this case would be represented by a qualified public person acting with all his authority and skill, and not by a mere private person as in other cases. The third argument of the Rota is based on the practice of tribunals, especially of the tribunal of the Sacred Roman Rota itself. In this regard the Rota stated that many marriage cases are introduced by the promoter of justice into the tribunal of the Rota, but it has never been observed that the promoter of justice acted the part of the advocate of him who has denounced the nullity of marriage, or that the promoter of justice intervened in the construction of the cause as if he then acted as the promoter of justice as such and not as a simple accuser of marriage in place of him whose interest it is that the marriage be declared null.[297] The Rota then concludes with the rather force-

[294] "Ergo inhabilitas, qua illi coniuges in poenam delicti commissi plectuntur, restringenda est ad ipsum actum accusationis, non autem extendi potest ad alios actus processuales . . ."—*Ibid.*, n. 10.

[295] Cf. Instr. *Provida,* Art. 46. It is to be noted that this decision was handed down approximately six months before the publication of the Instruction *Provida.*

[296] ". . . tunc coniux culpabilis, quem Promotor iustitiae representat, magnum lucrum reportaret et constitueretur in condicione privilegiata." —*Op. cit.,* n. 10.

[297] "In Nostro enim Auditorio, pariter in multis tribunalibus dioecesanis, interea non paucae causae introductae sunt accusante matrimonium Promotore iustitiae, sed numquam observatum est eundem Promotorem in se suscepisse etiam munus patroni illius, qui matrimonii nullitatem denuntiavit, aut in instruenda causa intervenisse, veluti si ageret tamquam Promotor iustitiae qua talis, non uti simplex accusator matrimonii loco illius, cuius interest ut matrimonium declaretur nullum."—*Loc. cit.*

ful admonition that unless the Holy See decrees otherwise in the future, there is to be no receding from the practice as explained in this decision.[298]

Certain general observations may be made concerning the foregoing opinions. The opinion of Triebs that a culpable spouse, who has an interest in the declaration of the nullity of his marriage, has a right to pursue this interest in a judicial process once the promoter of justice has accused the marriage, seems to lack juridic foundation. The reason is that an action introduced into court by the promoter of justice is a public action, not a private action. An accusation by the promoter of justice of the invalidity of the marriage of the culpable spouse is made solely in behalf of the common good. It follows that any act performed by the culpable spouse in such a cause must tend toward and must be determined by one consideration, the common good. The culpable spouse is present in a trial instituted by the promoter of justice not on his own behalf, but solely to assist the promoter of justice in the fulfillment of his duty to protect the public good.

The opinion of Roberti is not only opposed by the above-mentioned decision of the Rota and the criticism of Cappello, but also seems to labor under an aura of unreality. Roberti fails to make clear how spouses, who have denounced their marriage to the Ordinary or to the promoter of justice as being invalid, become in the process accessories to the defender of the bond, so that all of the efforts of the spouses are supposedly directed toward the defense of the matrimonial bond which they themselves have denounced as invalid. Moreover, Roberti does not explain precisely how the spouses are to assist the defender of the bond in presenting evidence that points to the validity of their marriage and, at the same time, are to provide the promoter of justice with assistance that will lead to the proving of the nullity of the marriage. In law and in fact, the opinion of Roberti seems to be untenable.

It will be observed that not once does Cappello refer to the

298 ". . . a qua praxi non est recedendum, nisi S. Sedes pro futuro aliud statuerit."—*Loc. cit.; contra* Graziani, "De Iure Accusandi Matrimonium," *Ephemerides Iuris Canonici,* II (1946), 130.

culpable spouses as mere witnesses. He describes the juridic status of the culpable spouses only in a negative manner, namely, "*non . . . partes propriae dictae.*"[299] Cappello's apparent disregard for Article 46 of the *Provida* may be rooted in the truth that the canons of the Code are in no manner changed by the provisions of the Instruction *Provida.*[300]

In the light of the principles of law presented in this dissertation and mindful of the opinions of the authors and the observations of the Sacred Roman Rota, the writer submits the following remarks. In discussing the juridic status of the promoter of justice, the spouses, and the defender of the bond, a distinction must be made between cases in which the promoter of justice, *ex officio*, places an accusation against a marriage, which accusation, *de facto*, is opposed by the spouses to the marriage; and cases in which the accusation of the promoter of justice is in accord with the intentions and desires of the culpable spouses. In the first supposition, the promoter of justice is most certainly the plaintiff,[301] and the spouses appear to be party respondents.[302] In the second case, it would seem that the promoter of justice is, once again, the only true *actor* in the cause and the defender of of the bond is the formal *pars conventa.*[303] The spouses, on the other hand, appear to be *partes sui generis* to the extent that once the accusation has been made by the promoter of justice, for the sake of the common good, the spouses can aggregate them-

[299] *De Matrimonio,* 5. ed., p. 889.

[300] "... quo plenius ipsis iidem Codicis canones, quibus derogatum non est . . ."—*Decretum,* Instr. *Provida.*

[301] Cf. Instr. *Provida,* Art. 71, § 2.

[302] Cf. Instr. *Provida,* Art. 75. This opinion is akin to that of Torre who holds that if the promoter of justice accuses marriage without a previous denunciation in cases in which the impediment is public of its nature, the promoter of justice is the actor, and the spouses are the *partes conventae;* cf. *Processus Matrimonialis,* 3. ed., p. 77; Triebs, "De Promotoris Justitiae in Causis Nullitatis Matrimonii," *Apollinaris,* X (1937), 406.

[303] Cf. Cappello, *De Matrimonio,* 5. ed., p. 887; Roberti, "De condicione processuali . . . ," *Apollinaris,* XI (1938), 580; De Guise, *Le Promoteur de La Justice dans Les Causes Matrimoniales,* p. 203.

selves to the promoter of justice as accessories to a principal on whom they are totally dependent,[304] to whom they can offer assistance,[305] and without whom their judicial rights cease to exist.[306]

304 Cf. S.R.R. *Decisiones,* XXIX (1937), 719; "Accessorium naturam sequi congruit principalis."—R.J. in VI°, 42.

305 Cf. Cappello, *De Matrimonio,* 5. ed., pp. 888-889; Roberti, "De condicione processuali . . . ," *Apollinaris,* XI (1938), 581.

306 Cf. Instr. *Provida,* Art. 46.

CONCLUSIONS

Chapter I

The norms governing the right of a party to introduce a matrimonial cause before a competent ecclesiastical tribunal did not begin to crystallize until the later eleventh and the twelfth centuries of the Christian era. (p. 9)

Chapter II

1. The distinction drawn in Canon 1971 between the right of the spouses to accuse the validity of marriage and the right of all others to denounce a marriage has its origin in the jurisprudence that followed the Decretals of Gregory IX. (p. 17)

2. The right of the promoter of justice to accuse a marriage the invalidity of which is publicly known and detrimental to the common good has its origin in the Decretals of Gregory IX. (p. 24)

3. The penalty of the juridic withdrawal of the right to accuse marriage which is incurred by a spouse who is the *causa dolosa* of the invalidity of his or her marriage has its origin in the Decretals of Gregory IX. (p. 25)

Chapter III

The distinction between impediments of public right and impediments of private right, introduced by German canonists in the nineteenth century, did not represent an entirely new canonical institute, but rather a new manner of expressing a division of impediments *ratione iuris accusandi matrimonium*, made by seventeenth and eighteenth century canonists. (p. 50)

Chapter IV

1. The expressions "regular accusation" and "legal petition" employed in Canon 1970 should be interpreted in the light of Canon 1552, § 1, 2°, which delineates the formal object of contentious causes. The object of a regular accusation is the pros-

ecution or vindication of a right. The object of a legal petition is the declaration of a juridic fact by the tribunal. (p. 63)

2. An accusation against the validity of marriage is not an extrajudicial act; that is, an act which is preliminary to the exercise of an action in court. Rather, this accusation of marriage is a judicial procedural act by means of which a person who has the right to stand in judgment institutes an action to obtain a declaration of the nullity of his marriage. (p. 76)

3. The right to accuse the validity of a marriage is precisely the right to place the first procedural act (the act of accusation) in the exercise of an action to obtain a declaration of the nullity of a marriage. (p. 85)

4. In the response of January 4, 1946, the Commission for the Authentic Interpretation of the Code did not imply that the spouse who is juridically incapable of accusing the validity of marriage according to Canon 1971, § 1, 1° can legally proffer a demand, based on the right of action, that his matrimonial cause be heard and adjudicated, and that a declaration of nullity be granted. The Code Commission did assert in this response that the juridic inability of a spouse to accuse the validity of a marriage does not imply the incapacity to stand in judgment to place all other procedural acts which follow upon the act of accusation and which culminate in a valid judicial sentence. (p. 87)

Chapter V

1. The most notable difference between the old law and the new law in respect to the right to accuse the validity of marriage is that the new law of the Code withdrew this right from all Catholics other than the spouses themselves and the promoter of justice, acting *vi muneris sui.* (p. 92)

2. The prohibition of non-Catholics to accuse a marriage without authorization from the S. Congregation of the Holy Office does not extend to cases envisioned under Canon 1990. (p. 100)

3. The juridic incapacity to accuse marriage is a *latae sententiae* vindicative penalty. (p. 109)

4. A party is to be considered the direct cause of the impediment or of the nullity of marriage if the impediment proceeds

from the will of the party as an effect from a cause, inasmuch as the will has exercised a positive influence in the producing of the impediment or in effecting the nullity of the marriage. (p. 142)

5. A party is to be considered the dolose cause of the impediment or of the nullity of marriage only insofar as he or she knowingly and willingly violates the law by intending to contract an invalidating impediment or by intending to effect the nullity of marriage. (p. 170)

6. The penalty of the juridic withdrawal of the right to accuse marriage is not to be extended in its application to causes adjudicated according to the rules of summary judicial procedure prescribed in Canon 1990. (p. 181)

7. The response of the Commission for the Authentic Interpretation of the Code of January 4, 1946 cannot be cited as the juridic foundation of the right of a spouse, incapable of accusing marriage according to Canon 1971, § 1, 1°, to appeal judicially a sentence upholding the validity of marriage. (p. 187)

CHAPTER VI

1. The exercise of the right of the promoter of justice to accuse a marriage of invalidity is subject to and not independent of the judgment of the Ordinary, regardless of the nature of the impediment involved. (p. 192)

2. Every accusation of the validity of marriage by the promoter of justice must have as its end the safeguarding of the public good, regardless of the nature of the impediment involved. (p. 195)

3. The promoter of justice, without a previous denunciation, has the right to accuse a marriage invalid because of an impediment which is not public of its nature if, in the judgment of the Ordinary, the public good requires it. (p. 207)

4. The promoter of justice, without a previous denunciation, does not have the right to accuse a marriage invalid because of an impediment public of its nature, if, in the judgment of the Ordinary, the public good is not in jeopardy. (p. 209)

5. The promoter of justice may accuse a marriage between

two baptized non-Catholics which has been denounced by a Catholic party, provided the conditions of Articles 38 or 39 of the *Provida* are duly fulfilled. (p. 219)

6. Every accusation of the validity of marriage by the promoter of justice is made *vi muneris sui,* regardless of the nature of the impediment involved. (p. 221)

7. The right of the promoter of justice to withdraw from an accusation because of insufficient evidence is subject to the decision of the ecclesiastical tribunal provided the case has ceased to be *res integra.* (p. 245)

8. The right of the promoter of justice to withdraw from an accusation, because the public good does not require it, is subject initially to the judgment of the Ordinary, and finally to the decision of the ecclesiastical tribunal, provided the judicial action has already been instituted. (p. 247)

9. The right of the promoter of justice to refuse to appeal an unfavorable sentence is not absolute, but is conditioned on the premise that, in the judgment of the Ordinary, the common good is not thereby jeopardized. (p. 250)

10. The sentence of the ecclesiastical tribunal consequent to an accusation made by the promoter of justice who introduces a cause which has no relation to the common good is irremediably invalid. (p. 253)

11. In cases in which the accusation by the promoter of justice against the validity of a marriage is opposed by the spouses, the promoter of justice is the *actor* and the spouses are the *partes conventae.* In cases in which the accusation by the promoter of justice against the validity of a marriage is in accord with the intentions and desires of the spouses, the spouses may be considered *"partes sui generis,"* insofar as they may aggregate themselves in an accessory capacity to the promoter of justice and assist him in proving the nullity of the marriage. (p. 262)

BIBLIOGRAPHY

Sources

Acta Apostolicae Sedis, Commentarium Officiale, Romae, 1909-1929; Civitate Vaticana, 1929-

Acta et Decreta Concilii Plenarii Baltimorensis Tertii, A.D. MDCCCLXXXIV, Baltimore: John Murphy, 1886.

Acta et Decreta Sacrorum Conciliorum Recentiorum, Collectio Lacensis, 7 vols., Friburgi Brisgoviae: Herder, 1870-1892.

Analecta Iuris Pontificii, 28 vols., Romae, 1855-1869; Parisiis, 1872-1891.

Bouscaren, T. Lincoln, *The Canon Law Digest,* 4 vols. and Supplements through 1958-1859, Milwaukee: Bruce and Company, 1934-1959.

Bruns, H., *Canones Apostolorum et Conciliorum Saeculorum* IV-VII, 2 vols., Berolini, 1839.

Civil Law, The, a translation by S. P. Scott, 11 vols., Cincinnati, 1932.

Codex Iuris Canonici, Pii X Pontificis Maximi iussu digestus, Benedicti Papae XV auctoritate promulgatus, Romae: Typis polyglottis Vaticanis, 1917; reimpressio, 1952.

Codex Theodosianus, ed. P. Krueger, Berolini: Apud Weidmannos, 1926.

Collectanea S. Congregationis de Propaganda Fide, Romae: Typographia Polyglotta, 1893.

Concilium Tridentinum, Diariorum, Actorum, Epistularum, Tractatuum Nova Collectio, 13 vols., Friburgi Brisgoviae, Herder: 1901-1938.

Corpus Iuris Canonici, editio Lipensis secunda, post Aemilii Ludovici Richteri curas ad librorum manu scriptorum et editionis Romanae fidem recognovit et adnotatione critica instruxit Aemilius Friedburg, 2 vols., Vol. I, *Decretum Magistri Gratiani,* Vol. II, *Decretalium Collectiones Gregorii* IX, Lipsiae: Tauchnitz, 1928.

Corpus Iuris Civilis, 3 vols., Vol. I, *Institutiones,* quas recognovit P. Kreuger; *Digesta,* quae recognovit T. Mommsen et retractavit P. Kreuger, ed. stereotypa 15.; Vol. II, *Codex Justinianus,* quem recognovit et rectractavit P. Kreuger, ed. stereotypa 10.; Vol. III, *Novellae Constitutiones,* ed., stereotypa 5., a R. Schoell; opus Schoelli morte interceptum absolvit G. Kroll, Berolini: Apud Weidmannos, 1928-1929.

Decretales Gregorii Papae IX, suae integritati una cum glossis restitutae, 2 vols., Romae, 1852.

Decretum Gratiani, emendatum et notationibus illustratum una cum glossis, 2 vols., Romae, 1852.

Hardouin, J., *Acta Conciliorum et Epistolae Decretales ac Constitutiones Summorum Pontificum,* 12 vols., Parisiis, 1714-1715.

Jaffé, Phillipus, *Regesta Pontificum Romanorum ab condita ecclesia ad annum post Christum natum* MCXCVIII, 2. ed., curaverunt F. Kaltenbrunner, P. Ewald, S. Loewenfeld, 2 vols., Lipsiae, 1855-1888.

Liber Sextus Decretalium D. Bonifacii Papae VIII, suae integritati una cum Clementinis et Extravagantibus, earumque Glossis restitutus, Romae, 1582.

Mansi, Joannes, *Sacrorum Conciliorum Nova et Amplissima Collectio,* 53 vols. in 60, Parisiis, 1901-1907.

Monumenta Germaniae Historica, 188 vols., incomplete, Hannoverae, 1826-; Leges in 4, Sectio III (Concilia), Tom. II, ed. A. Werminghoff, 1904-1908.

Potthast, Augustus, *Regesta Pontificum Romanorum, inde ab anno post Christum natum* MCXCVIII ad annum MCCCIV, 2 vols., Berolini, 1274-1275.

Richter, Aemilius–Schulte, Joannes von, *Canones et Decreta Concilii Tridentini . . . accedunt S. Congr. Conc. Trid. Interpretum Declarationes ac Resolutiones . . . et Constitiones Pontificiae Recentiores,* Lipsiae, 1853.

S. Romanae Rotae Decisiones seu Sententiae ab anno 1909, Romae: Typis Polyglottis Vaticanis, 1912-

Schroeder, H. J., *Canons and Decrees of the Council of Trent,* St. Louis: Herder, 1941.

Thomae De Aquino, St., *Summa Theologiae* cura et studio Instituti Studiorum Medievalium Ottaviensis ad textum Pii V iussu confectum recognita, 5 vols., Ottawa, Canada: Garden City Press, 1941.

Reference Works

Abbo, John A.–Hannan, Jerome D., *The Sacred Canons,* 2. ed., 2 vols., St. Louis: Herder, 1957.

Aertnys, Joseph–Damen, C. A., *Theologia Moralis,* 14. ed., 2 vols., Taurinorum Augustae: Marietti, 1944.

Aichner, Simon, *Compendium Iuris Ecclesiastici,* 6. ed., Brixinae, 1887.

Alphonsus Liquori, St., *Theologia Moralis,* ed. L. Gaudé, 4 vols., Romae: Typis Polyglottis Vaticanis, 1905-1912.

Ayrinhac, H. A., *Marriage Legislation in the New Code of Canon Law,* revised and enlarged by P. J. Lydon, New York: Benziger, 1952.

Baiiso, Guido a, *Rosarium, seu in Decretorum Volumen Commentaria,* Venetiis, 1577.

Bandinelli, Rolandus, *Summa,* ed. by Friedrich Thaner, Innsbruck, 1874.

Berger, Adolph, "Encyclopedic Dictionary of Roman Law," *Transactions of the American Philosophical Society,* New Series, n. XLIII, Philadelphia; The American Philosophical Society, 1953.

Berutti, Christoforo, *Institutiones Iuris Canonici,* 6 vols., Taurinae-Romae: Marietti, 1938.

Beste, Udalricus, *Introductio in Codicem,* 4. ed., Collegeville, Minnesota: St. John's Abbey Press, 1956.

Blat, A., *Commentarium Textus Codicis Iuris Canonici,* 5 vols., Romae, 1921-1927.

Boich, Henricus, *In Quinque Libros Commentaria,* Venetiis, 1576.

Bouix, Dominicus, *Tractatus de Judiciis Ecclesiasticis,* 2 vols. in 1, Parisiis, 1855.

Bucceroni, Gennaro, *Institutiones Theologiae Moralis,* 6. ed., Romae: Ex Typographia in Instituto Pii X, 1914-1915.

Buckland, William W., *A Textbook of Roman Law from Augustus to Justinian,* 2. ed., Cambridge: University Press, 1932.

Cappello, Felix M., *Summa Iuris Canonici,* 3 vols., Romae: Apud Aedes Universitatis Gregorianae, 1940.

———, *Tractatus Canonico-Moralis de Sacramentis,* 5 vols., Vol. V, *De Matrimonio,* 5. ed., Romae: Marietti, 1947.

Chelodi, J., *Jus Poenale,* Tridenti, 1925.

Cicognani, A., *Canon Law,* 2. ed. authorized English version by M. O'Hara and Francis J. Brennan, Westminster: Newman, 1934.

Claeys Bouuaert, F.–Simenon, G., *Manuale Iuris Canonici,* 5. ed., 3 vols., Grandae et Leodii: H. Dessain, 1943.

Cocchi, Guidus, *Commentarium in Codicem Iuris Canonici,* Taurinarum Augustae, 1925.

Conte a Coronata, Matthaeus, *Institutiones Iuris Canonici,* 4 vols., Vols. I-III, 4. ed., Vol. IV, 3. ed., Taurini: Marietti, 1950-1956.

Corbett, Percy E., *The Roman Law of Marriage,* Oxford: Clarendon Press, 1930.

Daoyz, Stephen, *Iuris Pontificii,* 4 toms. in 2, Burdigalae, 1624.

De Becker, *De Matrimonio,* ed. nova, Louvain, 1931.

———, *De Sponsalibus et Matrimonio,* 2. ed., Lovanii, 1903-1913.

De Guise, Leo, *Le Promoteur de la Justice dans les Causes Matrimoniales,* Universitas Catholica Ottaviensis, Series Canonica, n. 8, Ottawa, Ontario: Les Editions de l'Université d'Ottawa, 1944.

De Smet, Aloisius, *De Sponsalibus et Matrimonio,* 4. ed., Brugis: Carolus Beyaert, 1927.

Doheny, William J., *Canonical Procedure in Matrimonial Cases,* 2 vols, Vol. I, *Formal Judicial Procedure,* 2. ed., 1948; Vol. II, *Informal Procedure,* 2. printing, 1948; Milwaukee: Bruce Publishing Company.

Durandus, *Speculum Iuris,* Venetiis, 1577.

Engel, Ludovicus, *Collegium Universi Juris Canonici,* 9. ed. a Gaspare Barthel, Beneventi, 1760.

Esmein, Adhemar, *Le Mariage en Droit Canonique,* 2. ed., 2 vols., Paris: Recueil Sirez, 1929-1935.

Feije, Henricus, *De Impedimentis et Dispensationibus Matrimonialibus,* 3. ed., New York: Benziger, 1885.

Gaius, *Institutiones,* 7. ed., by P. Krueger, Berolini: Apud Weidmannos, 1923.

Gasparri, Pietro, *Tractatus Canonicus de Matrimonio,* 2 vols., Paris, 1891.

———, *Tractatus Canonicus de Matrimonio,* ed. nova, 2 vols., Romae: Typis Polyglottis Vaticanis, 1932.

Glynn, John C., *The Promoter of Justice,* The Catholic University of America Canon Law Studies, n. 101, Washington, D. C. : The Catholic University of America, 1936.

Gonzales-Tellez, Emanuel, *Commentaria Perpetua in Singulos Textus Quinque Librorum Decretalium Gregorii* IX, 5 vols., Lugduni, 1673.

Graesse, Johann, *Orbis Latinus,* Berlin: R. C. Schmidt, 1909.

Hackett, John Henry, *The Concept of Public Order,* The Catholic University of America Canon Law Studies, n. 399, Washington, D. C.: The Catholic University of America Press, 1959.

Holböck, Carolus, *Tractatus de Iurisprudentia Sacrae Romanae Rotae,* Graetiae, Austria: Universitats-Buchdruckerei Styria, 1952.

Hostiensis, Cardinalis (Henricus de Segusia), *Commentaria in Quinque Decretalium Libros,* 6 vols. in 4, Venetiis, 1581.

———, *Summa Aurea,* Lugduni, 1568.

Jemolo, A., *Il Matrimonio nel Diritto Canonico,* Milano: Vallardi, 1949.

Johnson, Josephus, *De Processibus Matrimonialibus Exceptis,* Romae: Apud Custodiam Librariam Pont. Instituti Utriusque Iuris, 1937.

Jolowicz, Herbert, *Historical Introduction to the Study of Roman Law,* 2. ed., Cambridge: University Press, 1952.

Joyce, George H., *Christian Marriage,* London: Sheed and Ward, 1933.

Kehr, Paulus, *Regesta Pontificium Romanorum,* 3 vols., Berolini: Apud Weidmannos, 1906.

King, James P., *The Canonical Procedure in Separation Cases,* The Catholic University of America Canon Law Studies, n. 325, Washington, D. C.: The Catholic University of America Press, 1952.

Kurtscheid, B.-Wilches, F., *Historia Iuris Canonici,* 2 vols., Romae: Officium Libri Catholici, 1943.

Leage, R. N., *Roman Private Law,* 2. ed. by C. H. Ziegler, London: Macmillan, 1948.

Lega, M., *De Iudiciis Ecclesiasticis,* 4 vols., Romae: Typis Vaticanis, 1896-1901.

———, *Commentarius in Iudicia Ecclesiastica iuxta Codicem Iuris Canonici,* 3 vols., ed. a V. Bartoccetti, Romae: Azienda Libraria Cattolica Italiana, 1950.

McCloskey, Joseph A., *The Subject of Ecclesiastical Law According to Canon 12,* The Catholic University of America Canon Law Studies, n. 165, Washington, D. C.: The Catholic University of America Press, 1943.

McCoy, Alan E., *Force and Fear in Relation to Delictual Imputability and Penal Responsibility,* The Catholic University of America Canon Law Studies, n. 200, Washington, D. C.: The Catholic University of America Press, 1944.

Marquardt, J. J., *The Loss of Right to Accuse a Marriage,* Rome: Catholic Book Agency, 1951.

Merkelbach, Benedictus Henricus, *Summa Theologiae Moralis,* 10. ed., 3 vols., Brugis, Belgica: Desclée de Brouwer, 1954.

Michiels, Gommarus, *De Delictis et Poenis,* Lublin: Universitas Catholica, 1934.

———, *Normae Generales Iuris Canonici,* ed. altera, 2 vols., Parisiis-Tornaci-Romae: Desclée, 1949.

Muirhead, James, *Historical Introduction to the Private Law of Rome,* 3. ed., London, 1916.

Naz, Raoul, *La Procédure des Actions en Nullité de Mariage,* Paris: Librarie Letouzey et Ané, 1938.

Noldin, H., *Summa Theologiae Moralis,* recognovit A. Schmitt, Vol. I-II, 31. ed., Vol. III, 30. ed. paravit G. Heinzel, Oeniponte: Typis et Sumptibus Feliciani Rauch, 1950-1956.

Noone, John J., *Nullity in Judicial Acts,* The Catholic University of America Canon Law Studies, n. 297, Washington, D. C.: The Catholic University of America Press, 1950.

Noval, J., *Commentarium Codicis Iuris Canonici,* Liber IV, *De Processibus,* Pars I, *De Judiciis,* Augustae Taurinarum-Romae: Marietti, 1920.

Ottaviani, Alaphridus, *Institutiones Iuris Publici Ecclesiastici,* 2. ed., 2 vols., Romae: Typis Polyglottis Vaticanis, 1935-1936.

Panormitanus, Abbas (Nicholas de Tudeschis), *Commentaria in Quinque Libros Decretalium,* 5 vols. in 7, Venetiis, 1588.

Pirhing, E., *Ius Canonicum,* 5 vols., Dilingae, 1674-1678.

Raymundus de Pennafort, *Summa,* ed. nova, Veronae, 1744.

Regatillo, Eduardus, *Institutiones Iuris Canonici,* 2 vols., Santander: Sal Terrae, 1941-1942.

———, *Interpretatio et Iurisprudentia Codicis Iuris Canonici,* Santander: Sal Terrae, 1949.

Regatillo, E. F.–Zalba, M., *Theologiae Moralis Summa,* 3 vols., Matriti: Biblioteca de Autores Cristianos, 1952-1954.

Reiffenstuel, Anacletus, *Jus Canonicum Universum,* 5 vols. in 6, Romae, 1831-1834.

Roberti, Franciscus, *De Delictis Poenis,* Romae: Libraria Pontificii Instituti Utriusque Iuris, 1938.

———, *De Processibus,* vol. I, 4. ed., Romae: Apud Custodiam Librariam Pontificii Instituti Utriusque Iuris, 1956.

Romani, Sylvius, *Summa Juris Canonici Lineamenta,* Romae: Apud Auctorem, 1939.

Rufinus, *Die Summa Decretorum,* herausgeben von H. Singer, Paderborn, 1902.

Sanchez, Thomas, *De Sancto Matrimonii Sacramento Disputationum,* posterior et accuratior editio, 2 toms. in 1, Venetiis: Apud Nicolaum Pezzana, 1726.

Schmalzgrueber, Franciscus, *Jus Ecclesiasticum Universum*, 5 vols. in 12, Romae, 1843-1845.

Sherman, Charles P., *Roman Law in the Modern World*, 2. ed., 3 vols., New York: Baker, Voorhis, 1924.

Sipos, Istvan, *Enchiridion Iuris Canonici*, 6. ed., Romae: Herder, 1954.

Smith, S. B., *Elements of Ecclesiastical Law*, 3 vols., New York, 1882.

———, *The Marriage Process in the United States*, New York, 1893.

Stitt, Archibald M., *De Promotore Justitiae*, Romae: Ed. Scientifica Internazionale, 1939.

Streit, Carolus, *Atlas Hierarchicus*, Freiburg im Breisgau: Herder, 1913.

Swoboda, Innocent R., *Ignorance in Relation to the Imputability of Delicts*, The Catholic University of America Canon Law Studies, n. 143, Washington, D. C.: The Catholic University of America Press, 1941.

Torre, Joannes, *Processus Matrimonialis*, 3. ed., Neapoli: M. D'Auria, Pontificius Editor, 1956.

Van Hove, Alphonsus, *Commentarium Lovaniense in Codicem Iuris Canonici*, 1 vol. in 5 toms., Tom. I, *Prolegomena*, 2. ed., 1945; Tom. II, *De Legibus Ecclesiasticis*, 1930, Romae: Dessain.

Vermeersch, A., *Theologiae Moralis, Principia, Responsa, Consilia*, 4 vols., 2. ed., Romae: Universita Gregoriana, 1926-1928.

Vermeersch, A.-Creusen, J., *Epitome Iuris Canonici*, 3 vols., Vol. II, 6. ed., Romae: H. Dessain, 1940.

Vitale, S., *De Accusandi Matrimonium*, Romae: Anonima Libraria Cattolica Italiana, 1937.

Vlaming, Theodorus M., *Praelectiones Iuris Matrimonii*, 4. ed., Bussum, Holland: Paulus Brand, 1950.

Wernz, F. X., *Jus Decretalium*, 4 vols., Romae, 1899-1905.

Wernz, F. X.-Vidal, Petrus, *Ius Canonicum*, 7 vols. in 8, Vol. V, 3. ed., 1946; Vol. VI, 2. ed., 1949; Romae: Apud Aedes Universitatis Gregorianae.

Woywod, Stanislaus, *A Practical Commentary on the Code of Canon Law*, revised and enlarged edition by C. Smith, 2 vols. in 1, New York: Joseph Wagner, Inc., 1957.

Articles

Anon., "Non-Catholics in Matrimonial Courts," *Theological Studies*, I (1940), 438-439.

Aguirre, Ph., "Annotationes," *Periodica*, XXXIII (1944), 286-289.

———, "Annotationes," *Periodica*, XXXIV (1945), 285-287.

Bartoccetti, Victorius, "De iure et officio Promotoris iustitiae accusandi matrimonium," *Apollinaris*, X (1937), 570-588.

———, "Circa inhabilitatem conjugum accusandi matrimonium," *Apollinaris*, XI (1938), 201-214.

Bertola, Arnaldo, "Ius Accusandi Matrimonium," *Miscellanea Vermeersch*, I (1935), 437-451.

Bevilacqua, Anthony J., "Competence of the Ordinary in the Documentary Process of Canons 1990-1992," *The Jurist,* XXII (1961), 236-262.

Bidagor, Raymundus, "Ad Responsa de competentia annotationes," *Periodica,* XXX (1941), 51-58.

Caron, Arthur, "Moral Certitude in Canonical Decisions," *The Jurist,* XIX (1959), 12-28.

Cappello, Felix M., "De Iure Accusandi Matrimonium," *Periodica,* XVI (1927), 228-237.

———, "De Acatholicorum Incapacitate Agendi in Foro Ecclesiastico," *Miscellanea Vermeersch,* I (1935), 392-402.

———, "Annotationes," *Periodica,* XXXV (1946), 195-198.

Ciprotti, Pius, "De coniuge dubie habili ad matrimonium accusandum," *Apollinaris,* XII (1939), 265-267.

Conway, W., "Right of Instituting Nullity Proceedings," *The Irish Ecclesiastical Record,* LXVII (1946), 53.

———, "Matrimonial Processes: Culpable Spouse," *The Irish Ecclesiastical Record,* LXIX (1947), 54-56.

———, "Invalidity of Marriage Unsuspected by Parties," *The Irish Ecclesiastical Record,* LXXVII (1952), 377-378.

———, "Right to Bring an Action of Nullity of Marriage," *The Irish Ecclesiastical Record,* LXXXIV (1955), 421-422.

Creusen, J., "De Iure Accusandi Matrimonium," *Nouvelle Revue Théologique,* LXVIII (1946), 344-345.

Doheny, William J., "Procedure in Summary Cases," *The Jurist,* IV (1944), 1-53.

Donnelly, Francis B., "Fraud and the Estoppel of Canon 1971, § 1, 1°," *The Jurist,* VI (1946), 378-400.

Ellis, Adam C., "Notes on Canon Law," *Theological Studies,* VIII (1947), 123-126.

Fair, Bartholomew F., "The Promoter of Justice and His Duty to Impugn the Validity of a Marriage," *The Jurist,* VII (1947), 378-395.

Fallen, M. J., "Competence in Non-Catholic Matrimonial Causes," *The Ecclesiastical Record,* LVII (1941), 568-571.

Fallon, M. J., "Meaning of Public Impediment in the Code," *The Irish Ecclesiastical Record,* LIX (1942), 270-273.

———, "Meaning of Dolus in Canon Law," *The Irish Ecclesiastical Record,* LX (1942), 303-304.

Graziani, Ermanno, "Limitazioni al Diritto del Coniuge di Accusare la Nullità del Matrimonio," *Il Diritto Ecclesiastico,* XLVI (1935), 114-126.

———, "De Iure Accusandi Matrimonium," *Ephemerides Iures Canonici,* II (1946), 128-131.

———, "De Iure Accusandi Matrimonium," *Ephemerides Iures Canonici,* II (1946), 145-148.

———, "De Canone 1971, § 1, n. 1 eiusque interpretatione," *Ephemerides Iuris Canonici,* II (1946), 166-181.

———, "De Causa Dolosa Impedimenti," *Ephemerides Iuris Canonici,* III (1947), 174-180.

Hannan, Jerome D., "Non-Catholic Petitioners and Plaintiffs," *The Jurist,* IV (1944), 623-626.

Hassen, Antonius, "De sanctione nullitatis in processu canonico," *Apollinaris,* XI (1938), 215-263.

Haring, J., "De Promotore Justitiae in Processu Matrimoniali Controversiae," *Jus Pontificium,* XX (1940), 145-147.

———, "De Iure Matrimonium Accusandi," *Apollinaris,* VI (1933), 243-244.

Kuttner, Stephan, "Ecclesia De Occultis Non Judicat," *Jus Pontificium,* XVII (1937), 13-28.

———, "The Father of the Science of Canon Law," *The Jurist,* I (1941), 2-19.

Le Picard, René, "Le Notion d'Ordre Public en Droit Canonique," *Nouvelle Revue Theologique,* LV (1928), 352-372.

———, "Bien Public, Bien Privé," *Dictionnaire de Droit Canonique,* II (1937), col. 826-835.

Mahoney, Edward, "Non-Catholic's Marriage Petition," *The Clergy Review,* XXV (1945), 124-125.

———, "De Iure Accusandi Matrimonium," *The Clergy Review,* XXVI (1946), 660-664.

———, "Marriage Nullity: The Guilty Party," *The Clergy Review,* XXIV (1950), 118-120.

———, "Non-Catholics and Marriage Nullity," *The Clergy Review,* XXXIV (1950), 403-404.

———, "Remedial Nullity of Marriage Sentence," *The Clergy Review,* XXXV (1951), 323-324.

———, "Marriage Causes of Non-Catholics," *The Clergy Review,* XXXVIII (1953), 748-749.

McReavy, L. L., Matrimonial Nullity—Plea of Good Faith in Regard to the Cause," *The Clergy Review,* XL (1955), 46-48.

Park, Charles, "Competence of the Ordinary in a Case under Canon 1990," *The American Ecclesiastical Review,* LXXXVI (1932), 68-73.

Pendola, Joannes, "De Iure Accusandi Matrimonium," *Periodica,* XXXVIII (1949), 140-165; 235-251.

Reh, Francis F., "Guilt of the Plaintiff in a Marriage Case," *The Jurist,* III (1943), 404-415.

Restrepo, I. M., "Annotationes," *Periodica,* XXXII (1943), 114-117.

Roberti, Franciscus, "Animadversiones ad responsiones S. Officii, 27 ian. 1928," *Apollinaris,* I (1928), 215-219.

———, "De Iure Accusandi Matrimonium," *Apollinaris,* III (1930), 52-59.

———, "De Iure Denuntiandi Nullitatem Matrimonii," *Apollinaris,* III (1930), 248-250.

———, "De Matrimonii Accusatione," *Apollinaris,* VI (1933), 442-444.

———, "De obligatione promotoris iustitiae accusandi nullitatem matrimonii," *Apollinaris,* X (1937), 113-116.

———, "De officio promotoris justitiae accusandi matrimonia acatholicorum," *Apollinaris,* X (1937), 595-597.

———, "De actione promotoris justitiae et conjugum in causis matrimonialibus," *Apollinaris,* XI (1938), 571-575.

———, "De condicione processuali promotoris justitiae, defensoris vinculi, et conjugum in causis matrimonialibus," *Apollinaris,* XI (1938), 575-584.

———, "Annotationes ad decretum S. Officii, 22 mar. 1939," *Apollinaris,* XII (1939), 158-161.

———, "Quando coniux dicendus sit dubie habilis ad accusandum matrimonium," *Apollinaris,* XII (1939), 267-270.

———, "De nullitate sententiae ob defectum habilitatis ad accusandum matrimonium," *Apollinaris,* XII (1939), 414-417.

———, "De recessu ab accusatione matrimonii per promotorem justitiae," *Apollinaris,* XII (1939), 527-530.

Roelker, Edward, "The Concept of Invalidating Laws," *The Jurist,* III (1943), 32-63.

Schaaf, Valentine, "Diocesan Tribunal Lacks Competence over Marriages between Non-Catholics," *The American Ecclesiastical Review,* XCI (1934), 75-82.

Toso, A., "De Iure Accusandi Matrimonium," *Jus Pontificium,* IX (1929), 107-108.

———, "De Matrimonii Accusatione," *Jus Pontificium,* XIII (1933), 187-188.

———, "Consultationes," *Jus Pontificium,* VI (1936), 159-161.

———, "De Matrimonio Accusando vel Denuntiando," *Jus Pontificium,* XVII (1937), 5-12.

———, "De Munere Promotoris Justitiae Matrimonium Accusantis," *Jus Pontificium,* XVIII (1938), 3-9.

———, "De Potestate S. C. De Sacramentis Quod Attinet Ad Matrimonia per Promotorem Justitiae Accusanda," *Jus Pontificium,* XIX (1939), 120-122.

Triebs, Franciscus, "De Promotore Justitiae in Causis Nullitatis Matrimonii ac Praesertim de Eius Iure Accusandi," *Apollinaris,* X (1937), 395-407.

Vermeersch, Arturus, "De Iure Denuntiandi Matrimonia," *Periodica,* XIX (1930), 269.

Wolter, Joseph L., "The Promoter of Justice and the Common Good in Matrimonial Causes," *The Jurist,* XI (1951), 206-225.

Dictionaries

Dictionnaire de Droit Canonique, ed. by A. Villien, E. Magnin, A. Amanieu, R. Naz, Paris: Letouzey et Ané, 1924-

Webster's New International Dictionary of the English Language, 5 vols., 2. ed. by W. A. Neilson, T. Knott, P. Carhart, Springfield, Mass.: G. and C. Merriam, 1957.

Periodicals

American Ecclesiastical Review, The, Vols. I-XXXII, Philadelphia, 1889-1905; *The Ecclesiastical Review*, Vols. XXXIII-CIX, Philadelphia, 1905-1943; *The American Ecclesiastical Review*, Washington, D. C., from Vol. CX, 1944-

Apollinaris, Romae, 1928-

Clergy Review, The, London, 1931-

Ephemerides Iuris Canonici, Romae, 1945-

Ephemerides Theologicae Lovanienses, Brugis, 1924-

Irish Ecclesiastical Record, The, Dublin, 1864-

Ius Pontificium, Romae, 1921-1940.

Jurist, The, Washington, D. C., 1941-

Miscellanea-Vermeersch, 2 vols., Romae, 1935.

Monitor Ecclesiasticus, Romae, 1876-

Nouvelle Revue Théologique, Paris, 1869-

Periodica de Re Canonica et Morali, Brugis, 1920-1927; *Periodica de Re Morali, Canonica, Liturgica*, Brugis, 1927-1936, et Romae, 1937-

Theological Studies, New York, 1940-

ABBREVIATIONS

AAS	*Acta Apostolicae Sedis*
art.	article
C.	*Codex Justiniani, canon, caput, causa*
col.	column
Comm. Pont.	*Commissio Pontificia ad Codicis Canones Authentice Interpretendo*
Conc. Trid.	*Concilium Tridentinum*
D.	*Digesta Justiniani*
fol.	folio
Fontes	*Codicis Iuris Canonici Fontes*
Instr. Austr.	*Instructio Austriaca*
Instr. *Provida*	*S. Congregatio de Disciplina Sacramentorum, Instructio servanda a tribunalibus dioecesanis in pertractandis causis de nullitate matrimoniorum,* Aug. 15, 1936.
JE	*Regesta Pontificum Romanorum* ed. by P. Ewald (592-882)
JK	*Regesta Pontificum Romanorum* ed. by F. Kaltenbrunner (—— to 590)
JL	*Regesta Pontificum Romanorum* ed. by S. Lowenfeld (882-1198)
Lib.	*Liber*
litt. encyc.	*littera encyclica*
Mansi	*Sacrorum Conciliorum Nova et Amplissima Collectio*
Nov.	*Novellae Constitutiones*
Potthast	*Regesta Pontificum Romanorum* inde ab anno . . . MCXCVIII ad annum MCCCIV
q.	*quaestio*
S.C.C.	*Sacra Congregatio Concilii*
S.C. de Prop. Fide	*Sacra Congregatio de Propaganda Fide*
S.C. de Sacr.	*Sacra Congregatio de Disciplina Sacramentorum*
S.C.S. Off.	*Sacra Congregatio Sancti Officii*
sess.	*sessio*
S.R.R.	*Sacra Romana Rota*
s. v.	*sub verbo*
tit.	*titulus*
X	*Decretales* Gregorii IX

ALPHABETICAL INDEX

BIOGRAPHICAL NOTE

Arthur J. Nace was born on October 16, 1927, in Philadelphia, Pennsylvania. He received his elementary education in that city at Incarnation of Our Lord Parochial School. He graduated from Saint Joseph's College Preparatory School in 1945 and received the degree of Bachelor of Arts from Saint Joseph's College in 1949. He taught in the Public School System of Philadelphia from 1949 until 1952 and received the degree of Master of Arts in English Literature from Temple University in 1951.

In September, 1952, he entered Saint Charles Seminary, Overbrook, Pennsylvania and was ordained to the priesthood by His Excellency John F. O'Hara in May, 1957. After ordination, he served as an assistant in the parish of Saint Jerome, Tamaqua, Pennsylvania and as a professor in Cardinal Dougherty High School, Philadelphia, Pennsylvania. In September, 1958, he was enrolled in the School of Canon Law of the Catholic University of America. He received the degree of the Baccalureate in Canon Law in June, 1959, and the degree of Licentiate in Canon Law in June, 1960.

www.ingramcontent.com/pod-product-compliance
Lightning Source LLC
LaVergne TN
LVHW050256080826
844660LV00012B/645

* 9 7 8 0 8 1 3 2 2 5 7 5 3 *